Dissertations and Project Reports

A step by step guide

Palgrave Study Skills

Titles in this series by Stella Cottrell
Critical Thinking Skills (2nd edn)
Dissertations and Project Reports
The Exam Skills Handbook (2nd edn)
The Palgrave Student Planner
Skills for Success (2nd edn)
Study Skills Connected
The Study Skills Handbook (4th edn)
Teaching Study Skills and Supporting
   Learning
You2Uni: Decide. Prepare. Apply

Business Degree Success
Career Skills
Cite Them Right (9th edn)
e-Learning Skills (2nd edn)
The Graduate Career Guidebook
Great Ways to Learn Anatomy and Physiology
How to Begin Studying English Literature (3rd edn)
How to Study Foreign Languages
How to Study Linguistics (2nd edn)
How to Use Your Reading in Your Essays (2nd edn)
How to Write Better Essays (3rd edn)
How to Write Your Undergraduate Dissertation
Improve Your Grammar

Information Skills
The International Student Handbook
The Mature Student's Guide to Writing (3rd edn)
The Mature Student's Handbook
Practical Criticism
Presentation Skills for Students (2nd edn)
The Principles of Writing in Psychology
Professional Writing (3rd edn)
Researching Online
The Student's Guide to Writing (3rd edn)
The Student Phrase Book
Study Skills for International Postgraduates
Study Skills for Speakers of English as a Second Language
Studying History (3rd edn)
Studying Law (3rd edn)
Studying Modern Drama (2nd edn)
Studying Psychology (2nd edn)
Success in Academic Writing
The Undergraduate Research Handbook
The Work-Based Learning Student Handbook
Work Placements – A Survival Guide for Students
Write it Right (2nd edn)
Writing for Engineers (3rd edn)
Writing for Law
Writing for Nursing and Midwifery Students (2nd edn)

Pocket Study Skills

14 Days to Exam Success
Blogs, Wikis, Podcasts and More
Brilliant Writing Tips for Students
Completing Your PhD
Doing Research
Getting Critical
Planning Your Dissertation
Planning Your Essay
Planning Your PhD

Reading and Making Notes
Referencing and Understanding Plagiarism
Reflective Writing
Report Writing
Science Study Skills
Studying with Dyslexia
Success in Groupwork
Time Management
Writing for University

Palgrave Research Skills

Authoring a PhD
The Foundations of Research (2nd edn)
Getting to Grips with Doctoral Research
The Good Supervisor (2nd edn)

The Postgraduate Research Handbook (2nd edn)
The Professional Doctorate
Structuring Your Research Thesis

For a complete listing of all our titles in this area please visit **www.palgrave.com/studyskills**

Dissertations and Project Reports

A step by step guide

Stella Cottrell

palgrave
macmillan

First published 2014 by
PALGRAVE MACMILLAN

Palgrave Macmillan in the UK is an imprint of Macmillan Publishers Limited, registered in England, company number 785998, of Houndmills, Basingstoke, Hampshire RG21 6XS.

Palgrave Macmillan in the US is a division of St Martin's Press LLC, 175 Fifth Avenue, New York, NY 10010.

Palgrave Macmillan is the global academic imprint of the above companies and has companies and representatives throughout the world.

Palgrave® and Macmillan® are registered trademarks in the United States, the United Kingdom, Europe and other countries

ISBN: 978-1-137-36426-5

This book is printed on paper suitable for recycling and made from fully managed and sustained forest sources. Logging, pulping and manufacturing processes are expected to conform to the environmental regulations of the country of origin.

A catalogue record for this book is available from the British Library.

A catalog record for this book is available from the Library of Congress.
Self-evaluations, checklists, planners and record sheets may be photocopied by individual students for their personal use only.

Printed in China

Contents

Introduction   1

Preparation and planning   7

1   'Where do I start?'   9
2   What makes a good dissertation or research project?   19
3   Project manage your dissertation   31
4   Managing yourself for the task   43
5   Using time effectively   51
6   Working with your supervisor   57

Developing your proposal   61

7   Understanding the assignment brief   63
8   Choosing your topic and title   67
9   Literature search and review   77
10   Principles of good research   89
11   Methodological approaches   97
12   Ethical considerations   107
13   Writing the research proposal   113

Conducting your research   119

14   The evidence base   121
15   Working with participants   129
16   Experiments   137
17   Observations   143
18   Surveys and questionnaires   151
19   Interviews   157
20   Case studies   163
21   Interpreting your findings   169

Writing it up   177

22   Your writing strategy   179
23   Getting the structure right   185
24   Fine-tuning your writing   197
25   Viva exams   203

Final considerations   209
References   210
Index   212

Introduction

> The dissertation was the best part of my whole course …

> I was terrified of doing the dissertation. I can't believe I ever got through it and made such a good job of it!

> Not at all what I expected! So much harder! So much work! So much more rewarding than I could ever have imagined. And I learnt so much about myself.

> Doing a research project of my own – I loved it …

An enjoyable experience …

Joel's philosophy was always to mix business with pleasure

An opportunity …

Almost all degree, Masters and doctoral level courses require you to complete a larger-scale, research-based, assignment. This might be a final year project, an in-depth case study, long essay or dissertation. Although, at the start, students may have mixed feelings about the prospect, by the end, they are usually glad to have had the chance to research a topic in depth. They tend to be very proud of their achievement – to have completed such a major task and created a piece of original work with their name on it.

A daunting challenge …?

Students often approach such projects with some trepidation – not least because they contribute so many marks to the final grade or degree classification. If you are feeling anxious, you won't be alone. At such times, it can be reassuring to have a step by step guide to the process.

On balance, long assignments are often the most enjoyable part of the course. Students' reasons for thinking this do vary, but include such factors as:

- creating something of their own
- the high level of challenge, and feeling stretched intellectually – that they are really using their brains
- having choice over what they study
- the chance to focus on a favourite topic
- more choice in the way they can go about their studies
- doing something completely different, such as working in a new context, linking study and employment or engaging with new resources
- applying skills gained through earlier study – seeing how much they have learnt already that they hadn't realised
- the feeling of expertise that it brings.

Is this book for me?

Are any of these statements true of you?

- I am undertaking a large-scale assignment (dissertation, long essay, research project) for a higher level qualification.
- It will involve a lot of independent study.
- I am rather daunted by the scale of the task.
- I am not sure where to start.
- I need further guidance on how to go about it.
- I want reassurance that I am going about it the right way.
- I want to approach the assignment in an organised and systematic way, as a managed process.
- I would find it helpful to use a step-by-step approach.
- I would find it useful to work with detailed checklists to help me to keep track of where I am in the process.
- I would find it useful to have tools provided to help me to structure my thinking about the assignment and what I need to do.
- I would find it valuable to gain a sense of the experiences of other students who have undertaken similar kinds of assignment, and how they coped.

You may not have agreed with every statement – it is unlikely that every single one will apply to you. However, your responses should serve as a useful guide as to whether this book is right for you. If you agreed with one or more statements, this book is likely to be relevant to you. Look also at the aims of the book, opposite.

Aims of the book

If the aims of the book, listed below, appeal to you, then this is the book for you.

Indicate those that apply ✓

The aims are:

- ☐ to help you to manage your research project or dissertation in as organised and stress-free a manner as possible
- ☐ to help you conceptualise the process of producing larger-scale, complex assignments, from start to finish
- ☐ to help you through the process by providing a step by step, project management approach
- ☐ to help you to clarify what would make a good dissertation or research project in your field
- ☐ to provide insights into where students go wrong, so you can consider how to avoid this yourself
- ☐ to provide prompts to help you to structure your thinking about your assignment
- ☐ to provide checklists to help you to track your progress, so that you are clear what you have to do, what has been completed, and what still remains to be done
- ☐ to provide guidance and tools that help you to manage effectively the myriad of small questions and actions that are likely to arise
- ☐ to help you to manage deadlines and complete your assignment on time
- ☐ to help you to manage effectively your relationship with your supervisor
- ☐ to help you to manage peaks and troughs in your motivation
- ☐ to help you to feel confident that you can manage such large-scale assignments successfully.

Where do the challenges really lie?

Students can sometimes be anxious about whether their academic skills will be good enough for such a large assignment. However, in practice, by this stage of the course, you should be reasonably prepared for the academic level of the work; your course is likely to provide classes in specialist skills. Typically, the following issues are much more of a challenge than the academic work.

1 **Managing the scale and complexity** – keeping the overall structure of the task in mind, as well as all the details, and fitting it all together.

2 **The 'project nature' of the assignment** – especially if you are not used to managing such scale and complexity from start to finish and as a systematic process.

3 **Getting the early stages right and choosing the right project** – it is easy to underestimate the importance of detailed early preparation work and finding a feasible project that is original and will keep you motivated.

4 **Keeping track of where you are** – there are so many different aspects to consider and so many little things to check out or remember to do, over such a long time scale.

5 **The depth of thought and reflection** – and that this needs to be given to all aspects of managing the task.

6 **Independent learning – and being able to find ways of learning from others** – You work on your own much of the time so it can be difficult to know whether your own experiences are typical of those of other people or how other people have managed similar issues. Coping with the solitude can also be an issue.

7 **Being in charge and having to manage yourself** – it can come as a shock to realise how much is usually worked out or arranged in advance for you, which you now have to do for yourself. It can be especially challenging to keep yourself motivated, self-disciplined and on task, with a sense of 'urgency' whilst also maintaining a balanced perspective.

Reflection: Challenges

Which of these challenges do you consider will be ones that are relevant to you for your dissertation or project?

What are your initial ideas for how you will manage these?

Key features designed to help your project

This book was designed in such a way as to best help students address the kinds of challenges described on page 3. Its key features reflect that aim and are outlined below.

1 Managing the scale and complexity

Structure

The book is structured to help you to conceptualise and manage a complex task in as straightforward a way as possible. It is divided into four main parts, each of which represents a key stage in the task, or assignment:

1 Preparation and planning
2 Developing your proposal
3 Conducting the research
4 Writing it up.

This helps to clarify what is involved and to emphasise the importance of essential aspects that are often overlooked. The footer of each page identifies where you are in relation to these four parts.

All four parts, or stages, are important. Despite that, it is natural to want to leap to the third stage and start gathering information straightaway – and some students find it easiest to stay immersed in such activity for almost all of the time available for the entire assignment. Indeed, some have to be dragged 'kicking and screaming' to consider any of the other stages.

It can be especially tempting to whizz through the preparation, planning and proposal stages, hoping that these will take care of themselves. However, all four parts merit careful attention. More details about them all can be found in Part 1.

Explanations

Each of the four parts is preceded by a short introduction to provide you with an overview of that stage of your project. Explanations of purpose or rationales for specific steps are provided at relevant points in the text.

'Bite size' pieces, step by step

Each part of your assignment is broken down into workable stages and steps. This helps to focus your thinking and to make the project feel more manageable.

2 Project management

For large-scale tasks of any kind, including assignments, it is useful to take a 'project-management approach'. The 'process' is a significant aspect of completing the assignment and a task to be managed in its own right.

As most students have little experience of this, guidance is provided to take you through the key steps in project management as a process, from start to finish. This covers such activities as working out steps in the process and identifying component tasks, through to tracking progress, scheduling, identifying risks and managing resources.

Key features continued

3 Getting the early stages right

With longer assignments, it is especially important to consider the early stages of planning and preparing. This is because, the larger the task, the more difficult it is to:

- conceptualise it as a whole
- hold in mind diverse activities and information
- see the best way to fit the pieces together
- remember what you need to do and when
- start again if you proceed too far in a direction that might prove problematic.

Miranda was oblivious to impending project disaster

Conversely, if the early stages are well managed, you lay good foundations for completing your assignment. For those reasons, a key feature of the book is that it lays great emphasis on:

- elaborating in depth the exact nature of the task – what you need to do, why, and how
- choosing the best possible topic: most problems stem from a poor proposal
- considering and trialling various options before you settle on a proposal
- working up your proposal in depth before you get going, so as to reduce the chance of unpleasant surprises as you go along.

4 Keeping track: checklists

As there are so many things to decide, juggle simultaneously, plan for and remember, it is essential to develop an excellent system for keeping track of what has been completed and what you still need to do. Detailed checklists and other tools are provided to help you with this at each stage of the assignment.

5 Structured reflection

One unique feature of the book is that it provides checklists and prompts to structure and encourage active reflection about essential aspects of the assignment. These cover such areas as what constitutes good research and assignments, analysing research articles, and time management.

In addition, at many points, the information that you need to consider is provided in the form of checklists, prompts or other organisational tools, rather than as a paragraph of text. This serves to assist the thought process. It also encourages you to make decisions about whether you have addressed all aspects fully.

6 Learning from others

There are many short-cuts that can be learnt from the experiences of others, both students and teaching staff. In the book, you will find insights gathered from others to help address typical challenges in completing large assignments.

7 Managing yourself for the task

Larger-scale assignments call for significant skills of self-management, from time management and organisation through to maintaining contact with others, managing the relationship with your supervisor, and creating the right mindset to get the job done. Skills in self-management are not usually addressed explicitly as part of a course of study, but can make all the difference to how well you succeed. This is addressed in Part 1, to set you off on the right track.

Using this book

Sequence

As the book takes a step by step approach, it makes sense to start with Chapter 1 and work through early chapters in order. Once you have a sense of the process, decide which of the later chapters are relevant and in which order. Return to earlier steps to refocus as your project progresses.

Terminology

To prevent the repetition of lists of different kinds of assignment throughout the book, terms such as 'research project', 'assignment' or 'your work' are used to apply to all kinds of long assignment. Most of the material will be relevant to most research assignments, irrespective of what they are called.

Maintaining a project log

It is useful to keep a project log to record your thoughts and keep them in one place. You can then locate them easily, check that you have addressed all the points as you wished, and look back over how far you have travelled over the course of your project.

It can take any form that suits you, unless a specific requirement has been set for your course. It could be, for example:

- your responses to questions and reflections presented in the following chapters, or that you set for yourself, kept on a computer, camera or digital recorder
- a 'To do list' that you keep on a mobile device
- a plain notebook for thoughts, lists and ideas
- a more reflective journal or blog to elaborate your thinking; be wary of making this public before your assignment is submitted.

It is up to you to decide how much detail is useful for you in recording your thoughts.

Selecting what to use

Many such tools are provided in the book, to help you to think, reflect and organise your assignment effectively.

You won't need all of these, so select those that you find the most relevant. Cross out any items on the checklists that do not apply to your project. If a checklist doesn't quite fit, you can use it as the basis for designing one of your own.

Identifying your skills requirements

Academic skills you have already …

It is likely that you already bring a good range of relevant skills, acquired through previous study. However, you may find it useful to use the self-evaluation *Do I have the right skills?* (page 15). This is especially important if:

- you struggled at previous levels of study, *or*
- you have had a gap in your formal education immediately prior to starting this level of study.

This can help clarify if you would benefit from refreshing your underlying skills before launching into your research. You could do this using a standard study skills book; see Cottrell (2013).

Higher level skills for dissertations/projects

Use the skills audit on pages 17–18 to consider the skills needed for this new level of study. Identify:

- where you have strengths already; this may increase your confidence in completing the assignment
- specific aspects to follow up, using this book and other resources
- priorities for your immediate attention.

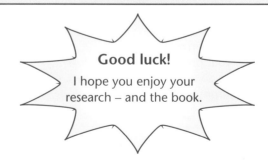

Good luck!
I hope you enjoy your research – and the book.

Part 1
Preparation and planning

The secret to successful research

The secret to a successful research project is in the preparation. This means:

- checking whether you share the same assumptions as your supervisor and examiners about what you are setting out to do, and why
- developing a solid understanding of what is expected and what to deliver
- detailed planning and decision-making.

It can be tempting to rush the early preparation, assuming that it is either self-evident or, conversely, so mysterious and inaccessible that there is no point wasting time on it. This is the path taken by many research students. It can work, but usually it doesn't work very well. The time spent on sound preparation is invaluable for:

- building your confidence
- avoiding problems and stress
- using your time most effectively
- creating time to think
- fitting other things into your life
- being able to enjoy the process.

A personal endeavour

An extended research project, even if undertaken for a client, is a highly personal enterprise. Unlike previous assignments, you are, to a large extent, your own teacher, counsellor, support and guide. You are in charge of much of your time and you have

to develop a good sense of what will work for you – and what will not. You can draw on the experience of others but, ultimately, it will be up to you to chart your own way through the experience.

Contents of Part 1

Part 1 introduces the broader planning context. It addresses many of the fundamental issues facing students on their first large-scale assignment.

1 'Where do I start?'
2 What makes a good dissertation or research project?
3 Project manage your dissertation
4 Managing yourself for the task
5 Using time effectively
6 Working with your supervisor.

What students say ...

I thought I could spend as little time as possible on this phase. All I needed to do was choose a title, read things, and everything else would fall into place. It was a bad, bad plan!

I didn't want to see my supervisor. I didn't want her to poke holes in my ideas or tell me what might not work. I could see where some problems might lie and didn't want her to tell me to stop. I thought if I kept going, it would prove it could be done.

I was terrified about letting myself down, and embarrassed in case anyone found out. I didn't want to ask questions as that felt I wasn't doing the research myself. I didn't realise asking questions at the right time was part of what was expected.

Naturally enough, I kept thinking writing a dissertation was about 'writing'. I seemed to zone out when my supervisor asked about anything else. I couldn't really focus on the idea that it might be helpful to think a bit about how I was going to get everything done.

I was determined to research this subject. I didn't want to concentrate on how I was going to get hold of some of the more obscure material I needed – or even whether my supervisor might be able to help.

I must have written about 55 versions of the first chapter! Maybe one or two, with some serious redrafting of these, would have been enough. Eventually, I realised my ideas were not clearly formulated – my thinking was all over the place. I wasn't really sure what I was doing – just that I enjoyed reading about the subject.

My supervisor was an international expert in the field. When I look back, I can't believe I made such appalling use of the opportunity. When I first met him, I wanted to impress him by how great my ideas were. Then when my dissertation started to crumble, I felt too embarrassed to go back and see him or to ask for advice.

I looked at some dissertations but I wasn't sure if they were good, bad or indifferent. I imagined everyone else would know automatically. I didn't want to let anyone know that I didn't.

It started to feel like a very lonely and isolating experience. I began to worry that I wasn't up to it. I had a fantasy that 'a real researcher' would know everything and be satisfied just doing the research. I didn't see any other students so didn't know if they were feeling the same way.

There wasn't much organised for us and I couldn't make the one seminar that was arranged. I lost touch with people. It was like working in a vacuum. I got fed up and wanted to stop.

I didn't know where to begin – so I didn't!

Reflection: Learning from others

- What, if anything, can you learn from these students' reflections on their research experiences?
- What actions do their reflections prompt you to consider now, at the start of your project?

Chapter 1
'Where do I start?'

'Where do I start?' This tends to be first question students ask.

Is it better to find a topic before starting any reading?

Or do all the reading and then settle on a topic?

Or see the supervisor first for guidance?

Or find a topic and then consult the supervisor?

Or jot down ideas and see what emerges?

Or do some reading and see if ideas emerge?

Or do something else?

search?

Notes

The answer depends, to some extent, on whether you have decided yet what you want to research.

Know what you want to research?

If you do, then it can be tempting to launch straight in to collecting the evidence. However, before doing so, it is worth pausing to consider:

● a range of topic options, just to be sure you have made the right choice
● the distinct skills and demands of larger-scale projects and how to manage these.

(See *Laying good foundations*, next page.)

Not yet decided on a topic?

If you do not yet know what you want to research, then don't be too concerned; it is not unusual. Start by gaining a sense of the process. Chapter 9 provides steps to help you select a topic.

The 3 basics

Research is sometimes summarised as three basic components:

1 **A question**
2 **Methods of arriving at an answer**
3 **The answer.**

Although this summary of the basics conceals the complexities of research, it can be helpful to return to these building blocks to help clarify the task and refocus your thinking if you start to lose direction.

Plus 2 more ...

In addition to the 3 basics above, it is useful to add two more.

4 **Bringing out significance.** Why does it matter? What is the relevance? So what?
5 **Writing it up.** Communicating your research to others and opening it up to scrutiny.

Laying good foundations

It is generally better to lay solid foundations upon which to build your research project, rather than jumping in without thinking it through. Below, are some key aspects to consider.

Gain a sense of the 'end product'

Before starting, develop a feel for what is expected as the 'end product'. You are then more likely to produce it. (See Chapters 2 and 7.)

Gain a sense of the overall process

Getting from A to B to C

This has many advantages.

- You'll know what to expect.
- It helps you to take charge of the process and make it more coherent for yourself.
- It will help you to see where specific tasks fit into the whole.
- It helps you schedule tasks in the best order.

(See pages 35–6.)

Build your understanding in stages

The overall process can seem complicated, as there are many aspects to consider. Build your sense of the process in stages, working from the basic building blocks to a deeper understanding of a multi-layered process.

- Start with the 3 + 2 basics (page 9).
- Gain an overview of the tasks (page 11).
- Develop a more detailed overview.
- Start to consider the complexities associated with the basic processes (page 13).
- Achieve a more detailed sense of what each of these tasks entails (page 12).
- Gain a grasp of the project planning process (Chapter 3).

Sort out the steps

Tasks do not necessarily fall into sequence. As you can see from the overview of the task on page 11, you will be starting some new tasks before you finish others.

This means it is important to:
- clarify what the steps are
- work out the best order for your project
- use checklists and charts to keep yourself organised.

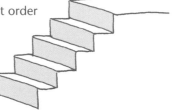

Plan your time – as soon as possible

- Start work on the assignment now: don't wait till near the deadline as this always comes around much faster than people expect.
- Schedule the whole process in detail. (See Chapter 3.)

Consider the self-management aspects

You will be studying largely on your own, so knowing how to get yourself through the process is an essential consideration – and one that is often underestimated. Give thought to how you will manage such aspects as solitude, motivation, maintaining momentum, gaining inspiration and keeping in touch with others. (See pages 43–50.)

Overview of the task

Chapter 3 looks at managing your assignment as a research project. It details the process as a set of steps to manage. At this point, it is useful to gain a sense of the four main parts of the task and when you would undertake each in relation to the others.

On the left, below, are the four main parts of the project task, from planning to writing up. The numbers in brackets indicate how these relate to the '3 + 2 basics' described on page 9.

On the right is a broad outline of how each of the four overarching parts relates to the others in terms of scale and timing. Each is also mapped against a start-to-finish line to indicate when, across the timeline of your research project or dissertation, you would be working on that part.

Part   Start .... Finish

Preparation

Get yourself organised to do a good job and to manage the practical realities.

Preparation and planning

Developing the proposal

Work out the question and how to answer it (1, 2, 4, 5).

Developing the proposal

Conducting the research

Follow your proposal to arrive at an answer (2 and 3).

Pilot

Conducting the research

Writing it up

Report to others the answer to your question, how you found out, and its significance (1–5).

Writing it up

Overview of the task

Below is an overview of what is involved in a typical research-based assignment. Tasks are organised broadly according to the four 'parts' into which this book is divided. It is likely that, as you work, you will move back and forwards between the various tasks, rather than following them in a simple sequence.

Prepare and plan ↓	Develop the proposal ↓	Conduct research ↓	Write up/Present ↓
Don't dive straight in: orientate yourself to the task from start to finish	Conduct your literature search; focus your reading and thinking towards potential topics	Fine-tune your thinking, research question and methods; raise major changes with your supervisor	Write your introduction – what questions did your research set out to answer and why?
Get a feel for the end product and process: read examples from your field	Consider the practicalities of each potential topic	Set up the conditions needed for gathering your data	Finalise your literature review, indicating how your research builds on what has gone before
Get to grips with the project management aspect of the assignment	Narrow your focus to select a specific topic; formulate research questions or hypotheses	Collect your raw materials, such as documents, texts, data	Write up your methods – what exactly did you do to arrive at your results?
Know your assignment brief inside out	Design your research: how will you answer the question or test your hypotheses?	Keep accurate records of what you do	Set out your results: summarise findings in words and in tables or diagrams if appropriate
Survey the field; find an area that interests you; generate options so that you have choices	Review the literature, writing this up. Read broadly, keeping details for citations and references	Keep accurate records of what happens/what you find out; compare these with previous research or theory	Discuss what you found, analysing it critically; draw out its significance and any emerging issues
Build your relationship with your supervisor	Refine your question and decide on your approach and methods; ensure the project is feasible, ethical and meets the brief	Organise your material or data so that you can see what you have found out	Draw conclusions, synthesising your findings with your understanding of previous research
Self-management: give serious consideration to how you will keep yourself on track	Prepare materials and record forms; pilot your methods and materials, if relevant	Refer back to previous research to make sense of your findings	Write the wrap-around sections such as the abstract, references, and appendices
Organise support: for ideas, social contact, and motivation	Discuss a draft of your proposal with your supervisor	Select the most salient findings and examples	Fine tune your drafts until your assignment flows well
Start to schedule everything	Finalise your proposal; submit for formal approval if required	Set out your findings so that the salient points stand out clearly	Prepare for a viva or presentation, if required

The basics v. The complexities

In practice, the experience of completing a large-scale assignment is more complex than suggested by the '3 + 2 basics' outlined on page 9. Below are some of the practical realities associated with each of the 'basics', as experienced by students.

The basics 3 + 2 – the heart of the matter	The complexities – the practical realities as experienced by students
1 A question: what do you want to find out?	'There seem to be a lot of other things that you have to sort out before you get to the point of deciding on a "question".' 'I don't have anything in particular that I want to find out.' 'I have lots of questions: how do I decide between them?' 'I have a brilliant question, but my supervisor says it isn't feasible.' 'How can I choose a topic if I don't know what is known already?' 'How do you start to find a "question" if you haven't got one?' 'How big a question does it need to be for me to have to spend so long researching it?'
2 A way of finding out the answer: the methods	'The lectures did cover methods, but I was only paying attention to *what* people found out rather than *how* …' 'They gave us an outline to follow for previous projects/experiments, but for this assignment, I have to plan it all out myself …' 'I don't understand why I can't just ask friends, family and people what they think about the subject – they'd be happy to help. I don't like to ask strangers to be participants.' 'I have great ideas of my own: why have I got to include other people's theories?' 'How much reading is enough anyway?' 'Methodology? Methods? What is the difference?'
3 An answer	'"The answer" sounded so short, but seems to need a lot of analysis and discussion …' 'What kind of answer takes 1000s of words to write?' 'What if I don't get the right answer?' 'I am investigating an issue – so what would a "question" and "answer" be like?'
4 The significance: 'So what?'	'I have shown what happened, but what does it mean?' 'I have found out why this occurs, but that opens up even more questions.' 'Does this have any relevance to other researchers in my field?' 'I made this amazing discovery, but is there any practical application?' 'How does this change anything? It is so little compared to what is published already …'
5 Writing	'I have a mass of information, but how do I organise it into something coherent?' 'I know the answer, but getting it down in words seems harder than the research.' 'I am only half way through and am already nearly at the word limit …'

Do I have the right skills?

How prepared am I already?

In considering some of the 'complexities' raised on page 13, you may wonder whether you have the necessary skills. It is likely that you do have a great deal of relevant experience and skill to draw upon: courses are usually carefully designed to ensure that previous assignments and current coursework provide a good foundation for this level of challenge.

If you can check off ☑ most of the items on the list below and the skills on page 15, then you are in a strong position for this kind of assignment.

Previous academic experience

Typically, by now, you would have:

- ☐ completed many smaller-scale assignments
- ☐ developed a range of study skills (see page 15)
- ☐ developed skills in independent study
- ☐ built your knowledge base in the subject
- ☐ become familiar with broad theoretical frameworks in your subject
- ☐ been introduced to specialist journals or texts
- ☐ seen how evidence is collected and put under scrutiny within your subject discipline
- ☐ been introduced to specialist research methods within your subject.

Building on existing study skills

At every new level of study, there is a greater level of difficulty and/or complexity. This means that you are expected to build on pre-existing study skills, fine-tuning and adapting them to suit new contexts.

At earlier stages of study, many of the skills you need are common to most types of study. As you move to higher levels of study, the skills relevant to your academic work tend to become less generic and increasingly specialist.

Nonetheless, there are strategies and approaches common to most large-scale assignments. These are not usually covered in detail as part of a course of study at this level as it is assumed that the skills would have evolved through previous study. However, many people find that they have gaps in these skills, or anxieties about what is required, or want a road map to help navigate the demands of the assignment.

Specialist research skills

Every academic discipline focuses on a specific branch of knowledge and investigates particular kinds of issues. Each draws on different types of original source material or raw data as its evidence base and uses distinct methodologies and techniques to find, analyse and make use of the evidence.

Training in these discipline-specific ways of thinking and working will form part of your course. You are likely to receive guidance on:

- ethical issues relevant to your subject
- recognising good quality sources, materials or data
- gathering your own data in ways that are recognised as sound within the subject
- interpreting source materials and data
- relevant statistical methods
- using statistical software packages
- using specialist equipment
- reporting your findings or writing about your material in ways that fit the culture of the subject discipline.

These may be introduced to you at the same time that your dissertation or project is set. If not, you may need a specialist text that looks in detail at methods used within your subject.

Do I have the right skills?

Typically, by the time you are set larger-scale assignments, you would have developed a good base of skills and self-knowledge through earlier, shorter assignments. If you can check off ☑ most of the following list with well-grounded confidence, then you are starting with good foundations.

1 Self-management skills

☐ Knowing how and when you learn best, and organising your study accordingly

☐ Personalising your learning in order to play to your learning strengths and preferences

☐ Keeping yourself motivated

☐ Setting priorities

☐ Keeping yourself organised

☐ Resilience and good coping strategies

☐ Asking for support and help when needed.

2 Academic skills

☐ Understanding academic conventions that apply within your subject

☐ Conducting online searches

☐ Reading at a reasonable speed with good reading strategies and comprehension

☐ Analysing reading material and data using critical thinking skills

☐ Interpreting and presenting numerical data

☐ Recognising quality evidence for your subject

☐ Making relevant notes as you read

☐ Synthesising information from many sources

☐ Developing a good line of reasoning within your own work, supported by evidence

☐ Structuring your thinking, organising concepts

☐ Organising your ideas when writing

☐ Writing clearly and precisely in academic style

☐ Citing and referencing sources correctly.

3 People skills

☐ Offering support to others without sharing your work in ways that are not permitted for the course

☐ Contributing to group seminars and classes

☐ Presenting information to a given audience, typically your tutor or other students

☐ Answering questions about your work.

4 Task management

☐ Understanding the role of the assignment title

☐ Being able to identify the question implicit within the title, as well as the key issues it raises

☐ Producing pieces of work that are closely focused on the assignment title or question

☐ Identifying component parts of assignments

☐ Managing your time to meet deadlines

☐ Presenting numbers and charts as required

☐ Structuring your writing to designated formats

☐ Writing up work in the required style and format

☐ Fine-tuning drafts and editing your work, checking for errors and correcting them.

What if I need to develop these skills?

You will develop and fine-tune these skills over time as you work on your research project. However, it is preferable to have a good foundation in these skills before you start such a large assignment.

If these study skills are new to you, or if you have a gap in your recent studies and feel that these skills might be rusty, see Cottrell (2013), *The Study Skills Handbook,* to help you get started.

What kinds of skills will I need to develop?

What kind of skills will I need?

Long assignments are demanding in terms of word length, scale of operation, breadth of reading, depth of thought and quality of research. That requires you not only to fine-tune existing skills, such as those outlined on page 15, but also to learn new skills, from academic skills through to project management.

As with any increase in challenge, you will probably find that research projects test your personal skills and qualities to the limit. This means that preparing well for the task ahead, and keeping yourself going, over the longer term, are just as essential as academic ability.

1   Self-management skills

Managing yourself well is usually the key to completing a larger assignment well. This skill tends to be the one that is least understood or valued and, consequently, it is most easily overlooked. It is where the greatest risks often lie. 'Self-management' involves a range of skills, all addressed in Part 1, and related to:

(a) Developing the right mindset
(b) Maintaining high levels of motivation
(c) Nurturing your intellectual curiosity
(d) Managing time effectively.

2   Academic skills

For research assignments, the generic skills typical of these assignments include:

(a) being able to read widely and wisely, to help develop an expert knowledge base
(b) knowing when you have found the right topic
(c) working intelligently with existing theory, research methods and knowledge in the subject domain
(d) being able to synthesise ideas effectively
(e) being systematic in your approach
(f) thinking critically about your own work
(g) transforming 'information' into 'knowledge'
(h) communicating your work in writing, using appropriate conventions
(i) discussing your work and answering questions, such as through a viva exam.

3   People skills

Although your assignment will involve a great deal of independent working, it also calls for good 'people' skills. In the first instance, this means developing a working relationship with your supervisor or tutor. Maintaining contact with peers can be harder but can be invaluable. Your project may also mean working directly with a range of participants or clients.

4   Task management skills

In the case of dissertations and extended research assignments, this means skills related to project management. That includes such skills as:

(a) understanding the brief and elaborating the task requirements
(b) project managing the assignment, forward planning so as to manage time, deadlines, resources and risks
(c) understanding the project both as a whole and in terms of its component parts.

Skills for research-based assignments

What skills do you bring already?

- Conduct an audit of your skills for research-based assignments, using the checklist below.
- Rate your current skills on a scale of 0–5, where 0 = 'none yet' and 5 is 'excellent'.
- Identify ✓ whether you need to develop further. If so, follow up the relevant chapter or pages.

Self-management skills	Current skill level 0 – 5	Develop further? ✓	Pages
1 Developing the right mindset			45, 49
2 Nurturing my own intellectual curiosity			46; 49
3 Envisaging myself as a researcher			47; 130
4 Maintaining high levels of motivation			45; 46; 48; 50; 55
5 Managing time effectively			51–6; 180–2
Academic skills	Current skill level 0 – 5	Develop further? ✓	Pages
6 Understanding what is meant by 'research'			19–30; 88–96
7 Awareness of different approaches to research			97–106
8 Reading background literature to develop my knowledge			77–86
9 Writing up a literature review			86–88
10 Selecting an appropriate topic as the subject of research			46; 67–76
11 Formulating a suitable question title and/or hypothesis			75–6; 115–16
12 Drawing upon relevant theoretical frameworks			82–3; 86
13 Selecting a research methodology			97–106
14 Choosing research methods			119–68
15 Gathering, selecting and organising material/data			119–68
16 Thinking critically about material and findings			169–70
17 Synthesising material and ideas			86; 169–74
18 Structuring my material appropriately in writing			185–96
19 Communicating my work well in writing			200–1
20 Discussing my work verbally such as in a viva exam			203–8

Skills for research-based assignments

People skills			Current skill level 0 – 5	Develop further? ✓	Pages
21	Working effectively with my supervisor or tutor				57–60
22	Giving and receiving support from peers				49–50; 55
23	Working with participants				129–36
24	Working with children/vulnerable groups as participants				134
25	Gathering data from surveys				151–6
26	Conducting interviews				157–62
27	Understanding the ethical issues				107–12
Task management skills			Current skill level 0 – 5	Develop further? ✓	Pages
28	Being able to pause and reflect constructively				46; 71–2
29	Clarifying the assignment brief				63–6
30	Project management skills				31–42
31	Understanding the overall process of such assignments				10–13
32	Maintaining a sense of the project as a whole				10–13; 21–3; 31–3
33	Understanding the component parts of the process				32
34	Managing resources				37–8
35	Managing risks				39–42; 111
36	Forward planning and scheduling tasks to meet deadlines				33–6
37	Preparing a proposal				113–18
38	Organising myself for writing				179–84
39	Preparing for a viva exam				203–6
Other skills relevant to my project			Current skill level 0 – 5	Develop further? ✓	

Chapter 2
What makes a good dissertation or research project?

If you have been looking forward to working on your own research project, it can be tempting to immerse yourself in a favourite topic and rush to gather books to read on that subject or to start gathering source material and data.

Before launching into your own research, it is well worth pausing first to consider the nature of the academic task before you and form a sense of what your finished work would look like. This is useful for a number of reasons:

- you will have a better idea of the quality of the work expected, so you can orientate your thinking and planning accordingly
- you will start to identify where particular methodological challenges may lie for you, and start to think how you would address these

- you gain a sense of some of the difficulties that others have grappled with and the kinds of solutions they found that may be of use to you
- you may be able to avoid some of the difficulties that others encountered by knowing where some of the methodological issues lie
- you will develop an ambient knowledge of work already being undertaken in your field.

Key considerations

Your thinking about the nature of the task should be informed by questions about what constitutes good research, in general terms, and what that means in your particular context.

What is meant by research?

In the everyday sense of the word

We research things as part of our daily lives – every time we hunt out information. In everyday usage, research means simply:

- wanting to know more about something
- looking for information about it
- making sense of the information available.

In effect, this involves:

- a question: what do you want to know?
- an investigation: a search for information
- a result: this might be information that provides an answer – or you may find that the information just isn't available.

Research in higher education

Research in higher education starts from the same principles as those above, which means that you can draw on your everyday research skills. However, the term 'research' is used in higher education to indicate something more specific than just 'finding out'. It generally has the following characteristics. It is:

1 Significant

- an investigation into topics that are relevant and of interest to those working and studying in your field

2 Systematic

- using a process that is more sustained and systematic than that typical in everyday life

3 Informed

- involving reading around the subject to find out what is known already
- knowing who the experts are in the field and what their perspective is on the issue
- building on what is already known rather than launching into the unknown

4 Contributory

- the findings or results of the research should add to knowledge and understanding within the field in some way

5 Evidence-based

- involving the collection of information (data, documents, interviews, etc.) to provide evidence for the position you take, any arguments you make and conclusions that you draw

6 Positioned

- providing a position on the issues covered, presented as a reasoned argument based on the evidence

7 Objective

- you gather, evaluate, use and present information in a fair, balanced way, rather than favouring that which supports your own purposes or point of view

8 Communicated

- it is written and/or presented in an appropriate style and format for others to read
- it communicates messages about research in the field as well as about the specific topic being researched

9 Has academic integrity

- it is your own work; see page 28
- you acknowledge whose work you have drawn upon for information, ideas, theories and methods
- you conduct the research and present findings in a manner that is honest, truthful, trustworthy and reliable.

What is a dissertation?

A dissertation is an extended piece of work that takes the form of a research project. Depending on your subject, you may be asked to write this in the form of an extended essay or report. If you have written good essays or reports before, then you already have a solid basis for producing your extended assignment.

Depth

The key feature of a dissertation is that you study a single topic in greater depth. This means specialising in a narrow area, and developing your expertise in the background research, theory, methods and issues relevant to the topic.

Contribution to knowledge

In a dissertation, as for a research project, you are making a contribution to existing knowledge. Your work will need to demonstrate the following.

Awareness of the relevant knowledge base

This might include the theoretical base; the positions on the key issue taken by different schools of thought; seminal works in the field; the more minor works that contributed to new understandings or which are taking research in the area into new directions.

How your research builds on existing research

You will need to:

- select writings and findings that indicate the chain of research upon which you draw
- show how that chain leads directly to the point where your own research commences
- be clear how you drew on previous work to inform your own thinking and methods.

See Chapter 9 about the importance of the literature search and review.

Choice and decision-making

Normally, you can choose your own topic and title for your dissertation. This is both an opportunity and a risk to be managed. You have more control over the nature and scope of your assignment. This can feel very liberating and people tend to become highly engaged in investigating their chosen topic. However, you have to make wise decisions, and many of them, to ensure that you are well positioned to complete your work on time, to the right level and to meet the brief.

Length

Dissertations tend to be much longer than previous assignments. Typically, they are of 10,000 to 20,000 words, but length does vary depending on the subject, level and course. A doctoral thesis would be closer to 100,000 words.

Managed pieces of work

The length of the assignment, the time you are given to complete it and the number of 'credits' it is awarded by your course are all reflective of the amount of work required. That applies to each stage, from understanding the context of your research and identifying the right focus, through to managing the amount of material you collect so that you write a compelling piece of writing of the correct length and quality.

In total, this amounts to a significant effort that cannot usually be handled through last minute or ad hoc strategies that may have worked for shorter assignments. You need a managed approach.

A different way of working

This assignment may be the sole focus of your study over a considerable period of time. All of your time may become dedicated to managing, researching and writing up your project. That calls for a different way of working. It is likely that you will have:

- few, or no, taught sessions
- nobody else to work with on the same topic
- individual but infrequent time with a supervisor
- much greater reliance on yourself.

What is a research project?

Scale

It carries a greater workload at each stage, with more thinking and input by you as a student, and is of sufficient magnitude to require systematic planning.

Unique

Your project will be an original piece of work. O*riginality*, here, does not mean that you initiate a major new line of enquiry or devise a new theory from scratch. Instead, it usually means:

- doing your own work, rather than working and writing collaboratively with other students
- new work rather than that already submitted for a qualification, or previously published
- bringing a new angle or focus to an issue
- making your own particular selection of raw materials, participants or data, or your interpretation of existing data.

It would still be 'original' if you chose to:

- replicate previous research to test its findings
- test out previous findings with a different population or new set of variables
- re-examine the interpretations of previous source materials, bringing a fresh angle.

Informed

Your own research must be informed by previous research methods, findings and theory. Draw on the most relevant and up-to-date sources. Make it clear, in your work, how you drew upon these in devising your own project and/or interpreting your findings.

Focused

Your selected topic must be narrowly focused so as to be manageable within time and word constraints. The content of your report should be closely focused on the title and/or hypotheses you formulate. Avoid interesting tangents. See page 71.

Distinct

As each project is unique, you work largely on your own, to your own plan. It won't fit easily into more routine forms of course or class delivery.

Time-bound

Research projects tend to run to a given deadline. For larger pieces of work, this may be months or years, which can seem a long time. However, the workload is significant. Each aspect can take much longer than you might be used to, especially thinking it through, reading more complicated texts, and writing it up. It can be easy to run out of time if it is not managed well.

Managed

Projects require close attention to detail and excellent forward planning. Give thought, from the beginning, to how you will manage the work overall, rather than aiming to manage each aspect as you go along. Identify the advance preparation required to ensure each step is completed on time. Management tasks are not difficult, but are essential. See Chapter 3 for project managing your work.

Purpose and challenge

Dissertations and other research assignments serve several purposes. Understanding these helps you to ascertain what is expected of you.

What is their purpose?

A chance to shine

They provide an opportunity for you to draw together the expertise you acquired throughout your course, to demonstrate your abilities and put your personal stamp on a piece of work.

Choice and independence

You have a chance to focus on an area of special interest or expertise. If you choose your topic well, this can help further your research or work career.

Understanding your discipline

You work with raw materials typical of the discipline, generating your own data and findings. Doing this, and relating your findings to previous research, gives you a better appreciation of how knowledge is constructed and advanced within your field. It gives you insights into the difficulties that can arise, the uncertainties and setbacks that have to be addressed, and the kinds of issues that need to be considered.

A research 'apprenticeship'

You gain a sense of what an academic life or research-based occupation would be like and the chance to decide whether these would suit you.

Extending your skills and employability

They provide excellent opportunities to develop skills transferable to employment, such as

- project management
- advanced organisational skills
- time management and scheduling
- self-management – keeping yourself on task for extended periods.

Comparison with earlier assignments

The basic requirements of larger-scale assignments (page 9) are likely to be familiar to you from previous assignments. However, larger-scale assignments bring a new challenge, as detailed below. In reading the characteristics of that challenge, it's worth identifying which of these are most significant in your case.

The nature of the challenge

Which aspects matter most to you? ☑

- ☐ They carry many more marks, so contribute significantly to my overall grade.
- ☐ They involve greater word limits.
- ☐ They take longer to complete.
- ☐ They are more complicated to plan/manage.
- ☐ They call for more independent study.
- ☐ They involve working more in isolation.
- ☐ They require greater originality.
- ☐ They require more personal decision-making.
- ☐ They require excellent organisational skills.
- ☐ They require strong self-motivation.
- ☐ I have to identify the topic and title for myself.
- ☐ I have to read a lot more material.
- ☐ I have to find the material for myself.
- ☐ I have to generate my own evidence base.
- ☐ They require more in-depth thought, analysis and synthesis.
- ☐ I have to produce work that uses the same methods and conventions as experts in my field.

Reflection: Coping with challenge

- How will you manage these challenges?
- Where can you find help for them in this book?
- What other help is available to you?

The challenge: what students say

Motivation

The difficulties weren't at all what I expected. I thought I would find the work demanding, but the really hard thing was driving myself to do it at all. I was interested in the subject and did want to do the work, but I kept finding excuses not to actually sit down and just do it. It takes a lot of will power, but it was worth it when I held the finished item and realised that I had done it all by myself.

Independent study

You do so much of an extended essay on your own that you can get a bit lost and lonely and start to wonder what it is all for. That can go on for weeks if you let it. On my course, a group of us decided to meet up twice a week to talk through how we were managing our research and share ideas about getting it written up. That made all the difference to me and kept me going.

Length

My dissertation was for 10,000 words. The longest essay I had written before that was about 2000. The idea of producing so many words just overwhelmed me. I couldn't pull back from it to think where to begin. If I was doing it again, I would be less scared at the word count – you just scale up the amount of everything you would normally do for an essay – but I would put more time and thought into planning at the beginning.

Pacing

The thing I hadn't expected was that you can't sit down and do all the reading one day and then write it up the next, which is what I did for my essays. You have to do it in more sections. This can mean that you forget what you have already read if you don't keep a good record. I work full time so I had to write it up in sections over many, many weekends – more than I like to think. I hadn't thought that stopping and starting could make it sound disjointed. My style of writing changed each time I sat down to write. My supervisor advised me to go back over it so that it sounded as if it was written by one person. If I was doing it again, I would take a week or two of my annual leave to write up the final draft to make it easier to maintain the same style and flow throughout. It would have held together better as a whole.

'Mulling over'

The biggest challenge for me was that it wasn't just that there was more reading and writing to do. It was that I needed a lot more thinking time than I had assumed anyone could need just to weigh up the relative importance of everything, how it all fitted together and what material I was actually going to use. My advice to others would be to be aware that you need time to let your ideas mature – and that you might change your mind a lot.

Reflection: The challenge

- What insights can you gain from these students' experiences?
- How would you need to plan your assignment to make sure you took those insights on board?

What supervisors say: good and bad

The best work

… captures what the subject discipline is about, what research means for academics working in that area. It may not be as polished as professional research but it shows a dedication to getting to grips with the issues and to understanding how these would be approached within the discipline. You can see the developmental path, and where the students' next research would take them.

We value most those dissertations that leave us wanting to know more. Often, this is because they are so good at pointing out where future research could take their research further. It leaves us wanting to see where that next piece of research would take us. If that is combined with proper analysis of the material, and a good critique of its limitations, it can be magic – a delight to read.

You can tell when a student has a real passion for the subject. It's not that they state this – you can tell they have read an enormous amount, their work suggests they are hungry to know everything about the subject, and have clearly thought about what they have read in a considered way.

With some research projects, you get the impression that there is an elegant simplicity. This isn't easy to achieve. The student has found a way of gathering data in ways that are clear and straightforward, even though it might not have been apparent at the start how that might be achieved.

What you are looking for, as a supervisor, is someone who brings ideas to their work. It isn't a case of 'collect the material, put it into charts, and say what it means'. That may get a pass mark. What I love is to see the thinking process shining through the work. It may be manifest in all kinds of ways – from some ingenious angle in their methods, or evident grappling with the methodological framework. Or it might be that they are fired up by some aspect of theory and really want to see for themselves whether it can be substantiated if they test it from a particular angle.

The worst work

… looks as if it was rushed at the last minute.

The worst ones … are rambling and wordy, as if the author hasn't a lot to say, so stretches everything out in a repetitious or pompous way.

… is when the students are disorganised in their thinking. They hop back and forth, and it is hard to gain a sense of the direction of their argument.

… is when students are evidently taking every short cut, including 'borrowing' ideas and bibliographies from elsewhere.

… either lacks imagination or tries to be so innovative that it ends up confused and unmanageable.

I don't like projects that adopt a basic formula … such as replicating previous research almost exactly as previously undertaken, without bringing any kind of interesting twist or new kind of participant group. It makes me wonder what the student gets from doing such research.

 Reflection: The challenge

- What insights can you gain from these comments?
- How would you plan your assignment so as take these on board?

Good research assignments: a summary

A strong dissertation, long essay, research project or thesis demonstrates the following features.

Meets the brief
It meets all criteria well.

Solid understanding of the discipline
It shows knowledge of the subject discipline such as topical issues and how these are researched; the theoretical base that informs the discipline; the contributions of experts in the field; historic and current debates; differences of approach and perspective within the discipline; good understanding of ethical issues.

Breadth of reading
It shows awareness of a wide range of relevant work by the leading experts in the field; the best work tends to draw on some lesser known, specialist texts or research papers.

A well chosen topic
It is of the right scale and level of difficulty, brings a different angle, and is relevant to the discipline.

A systematic approach
It uses carefully designed research methods; shows due care and attention to detail; the right methods are selected for the topic chosen; it shows strong organisation, with materials or data carefully gathered and closely analysed; it has carefully formulated hypotheses or research proposals.

Use of evidence
It shows accurate, reliable, selective and critical use of data and source materials.

Comprehensive
There is good coverage of key issues and sources, whilst it is selective in their use. Although the work can't cover every angle, it covers all essentials.

Good overall structure
The writing flows well. Material is presented in a logical order, is well linked, and the argument is clear to the reader.

Builds well on previous research
It shows awareness of how to make best use of existing research to inform its own direction and focus and reinforce or challenge its own argument.

A good understanding of the material
It shows a sophisticated grasp of all sources, whether background reading, data or other material. It interprets and draws on these correctly, recognising relevance and significance, explaining them correctly and using them appropriately.

Strong critical awareness
It identifies potential gaps, weaknesses and flaws in arguments or in the evidence base used to draw conclusions, whether in the dissertation itself or in the work of others.

Awareness of ambiguity and nuance
It demonstrates an understanding of the complexities of the issues, such as why apparently obvious explanations might not tell the full story, or how slight variations in theories or interpretations of evidence might lead to different conclusions.

Clear and appropriate use of language
It is written in a formal style appropriate to the discipline, with proper use of specialist vocabulary and technical terms, clarity of expression, and a style that is easy to read without being simplistic.

Excellent synthesis
It draws together key information and perspectives to provide interesting insights and conclusions.

Check this for yourself
Use the checklist on page 30 to evaluate one or more dissertations in your own field.

Things to avoid in dissertations and reports

Poor choice of subject

Getting this wrong at the outset, as this is one of the hardest things to put right later on. See Chapter 8.

Poor use of evidence

- **Long quotations**. These eat up the word limit without gaining you any marks. Use of short, well chosen quotations can be helpful in indicating the breadth of your research and your recognition of particularly good summaries or phrasing.

- **Use of anecdote**. These may be interesting but represent a narrow database and generally are distractions from the flow of your argument. You would normally be expected to use a sound and objective database rather than anecdotes.

- **Use of personal experience**, unless you are on a counselling or similar course, or for reflective aspects of certain assignments where you are explicitly asked to use personal experience.

- **References to personal beliefs and opinions** (unless specifically required).

- **Treating unusual examples and exceptions as if they were the norm**.

- **Use of Wikipedia** or other encyclopaedias as source materials. You may find these helpful to commence your trail in hunting for good sources, but look up their references for yourself and then cite these. At this level, you would be expected to use sources that are more specialist than those generally found in an encyclopaedia.

Poor writing

- **'Waffle' or excessive wordiness**: long-winded sentences; using a paragraph when a well worded phrase would suffice; repetition of the same point using different phrasing; making broad, unsubstantiated generalisations; making sweeping statements, especially in introductory and concluding sections, such as 'history has shown time and time again …' or 'all research has its flaws …'.

- **Careless expression** and use of language. Avoid using:
  - abbreviations
  - 'texting', slang and idiom
  - lists
  - terminology you don't really understand
  - flowery or pompous language.

Disorganisation and poor structure

With so much material to cover, and with the need to research and write over a long time frame, it is a challenge to remember what you have already read, material to which you already referred, which points you were making or how these connect to your main arguments. If your material is disorganised and your work does not have a strong and suitable structure, your reader may not be able to keep track of your argument. See Chapter 13 and Part 4.

Ignoring the formal requirements

However excellent your ideas and research, you need to adhere to the brief. If you find the brief is constraining your work, speak to your supervisors before deviating from it; follow their advice. See Chapter 3.

Reflection: The challenge

- To which of these aspects will you need to pay most attention?
- Which is likely to be your weakest point if not managed well?

Academic Integrity

'All my own work' …

When you submit your work, you sign a form to say that it is your own work. That is a declaration of its integrity. If it is found that you received more help than is permitted, or did not write it all yourself, this is taken seriously. It will mean one of the following, depending on the level of study and gravity of the offence.

- Your grade is likely to be severely affected, and you may be awarded a 'fail'.
- It may be recorded on your transcript that you received a zero mark, which would raise questions if you needed to submit the transcript when applying for jobs.
- Your work may not be accepted and you may not be allowed to resubmit. If so, it is probable that you will not be allowed to start again with a new qualification.
- For Masters and doctorates, you would not gain the qualification.

'Dissertations for sale'

There are many websites that offer services to students for assignments at all levels, including dissertations and theses. Avoid these. If you need help, go through the official channels for help and support at your college or university. These would be such sources as:

- your supervisor or another tutor
- subject specialist librarians
- Student Support offices
- a Skills Centre/Learning Resource Centre
- the International Office (if relevant)
- disability or dyslexia staff (if relevant).

Never …

- Never pay for someone else to write some or all of your dissertation, thesis or any other assignment, unless you have the formal agreement of your university (such as for certain disabilities).
- Never pay for someone to check through your work. If there is a good reason to do so, such as a disability, use only the official channels at your university or college: they will be aware of what is permissible – and what is not.
- Never submit the work of another student as if it were your own – either in its entirety or sharing sections, data or tables.
- Never buy a pre-written piece of work, such as from previous students or websites selling assignments – even if these advertise that they are 'original', 'not plagiarised' or can avoid detection software. It is too great a risk – and does not demonstrate academic integrity.
- Never submit any of your dissertation or thesis for discussion through websites offering feedback, advice, guidance, other students' views, or which purport to be expert advice.
- Never give students electronic copy or other access to your work: they could reproduce it in their work, with or without your permission, and it may be assumed you copied from them.

Attributing your sources

You would be expected to draw on the work of experts within your field. Whenever you do so, even if this is just a passing reference:

- acknowledge the source by citing it in your writing, usually by giving the author's surname and date of publication as in: (Jones, 2103)
- provide full details of the reference at the end of your work
- use the referencing system required by your institution: they will provide details.

Referencing software

You can use referencing software such as Mendeley or Zotero to help you draw down, store and list your references.

Use existing models for guidance

What are dissertations or research reports really like?

Every subject discipline and institution will look for different things in a student assignment. The requirements will be outlined in the course documentation, typically as a project brief and/or marking criteria. Chapter 7 looks at these aspects in more detail.

Draw on real examples

However, it is much easier to gain a sense of what those criteria mean in practice if you look at some examples. Your college library or departmental office is likely to have copies of previous dissertations that you can read. Some provide digitised versions. If your own university or college does not do this, the librarian should be able to direct you to examples that are available elsewhere.

Make use of previous research

It can feel daunting looking at the finished product and wondering how the authors managed to achieve it. You may feel you are a long way from producing similar work.

Before you have undertaken your own research, the most relevant questions may not immediately jump to mind when looking at other dissertations. The following activities can help to structure your thinking. Identify which might be useful to you, and then plan time to complete these as part of your project schedule.

Using previous research as models

☐ Rapid browse

- Call up at least 10 dissertations or research reports relevant to your level of study, of broadly the same length.
- Browse these at speed. Develop a feel for what a dissertation/report of that word limit is like as a whole.
- Notice the kind of topics that are covered in your field. Are they mainly theoretical? Experimental? Based on source materials? Based on data that students collect?
- What kind of 'originality' or contribution to knowledge do these make? What would be considered acceptable for a student dissertation?
- Notice how the different sections are laid out. Do they use headings? If so, what kinds of section headings are used in the best reports?
- What use, if any, is made of diagrams, tables, illustrations etc.? Where do these appear in the work? How do writers make reference to them within the text?

☐ Detailed study

Select 3 or 4 dissertations and read these in more detail.
- What are they like to read?
- What kinds of titles have been used in previous years?
- What kinds of data do students use?

☐ Checklist and project log (next page)

Use the checklist overleaf; jot down your observations in a project log or notebook.

Adapted versions of this checklist are provided in later chapters to focus your thinking in more detail on particular features relevant to that stage of your research.

Reflection: Using existing models

- Once you have completed your consideration of previous work using the checklist on page 30, jot down your observations about what is required in order to complete such an assignment well.

Browse existing work

Aspect
Use this checklist to help your browsing and reading of dissertations or reports available through your library or department. Check off ☑ each aspect once you have considered it.

☐ **Choice of topic**
- When you were choosing items to read, which topics and titles attracted your interest, and why? Which ones were off-putting and why?
- What initial thoughts does that give you about selecting your own topic?

☐ **Choice of title**
- What kinds of titles have been used in previous years?
- How are the titles structured?
- What initial thoughts does that give you about selecting your own title?

☐ **Scale and scope**
- How did the authors design their research so as to keep it manageable in size and length?
- What initial thoughts does this give you about setting the right scale for your assignment?

☐ **Methods**
- What tips did you pick up on techniques and strategies that you could replicate or adapt?

☐ **Ethical considerations**
- What kinds of ethical issues were addressed, or might have arisen, in the works you read?
- Which of these might be relevant to your own dissertation?

☐ **Structure**
- What did you notice about the way works were structured?
- How did these vary from each other and from the requirements in your assignment brief?

☐ **Style**
- What are these works like to read? How well do they flow?
- From reading sections of different works, what did you observe about the writing styles used?
- What thoughts were inspired in you for the writing style for your own work?

☐ **Citations and references**
- How are citations and references used? How would that use apply to your own work?

☐ **Presentation**
- Were any works more inviting or off-putting because of the way they were presented and laid out?
- What ideas did you gain for presenting your own dissertation?

☐ **Abstract**
- From the abstracts that you read, what features would be useful for your own work?

☐ **Any other observations**
- What other observations did you make from your browsing and reading of these works that could help you in completing your own?

Chapter 3
Project manage your dissertation

With larger scale research assignments, you are, in effect, managing a project. It makes sense to take a project planning approach. In practice, this requires you to draw a distinction between:

- meeting the assignment brief (outputs)
- managing the project (process).

Many students focus only on the assignment brief without taking on board the implications of managing the production of a large-scale piece of work. The difference is set out below.

Fear not everyone, for I have completed a dissertation – I can handle this.

Amina was a dab hand at seeing practical applications arising from her academic study

Managing two tasks in one ...

Meeting the brief

The assignment brief is set by your course and specifies the requirements you must meet, such as the type of report, word limits, deadlines, methods, format, referencing style, and any regulations that apply. It may also specify the permitted topics or content.

Project managing the process

'Project management' refers to the process that enables you to deliver on the brief. It covers all practical aspects of organisation, planning and coordination that enable you to meet deadlines and the requirements of the brief. It doesn't refer to the content of your dissertation or such things as writing style or structure.

Although your course may provide substantial help in getting to grips with specialist research skills, equipment and software, generally little help is provided with the project management aspects of such assignments. It is assumed that you could address this by yourself. That is where a large part of the challenge lies, and where many students run into difficulties.

As with many other tasks, it is often only after you have completed such an assignment for the first time that you are in a good position to judge the best way for you to do things – and to work out how you would approach a similar task in future. However, for larger-scale assignments, there isn't usually a second run, so good project planning is essential.

What is project management?

In this context, project management means standing back from the academic aspects of the task and considering how you will coordinate the process of producing your assignment from start to finish.

Key features of project management

1 **Form an overview**: develop a global sense of the context and rationale.

2 **Elaborate the task**: work out the details of what is required as outputs and process.

3 **Plan**: take a systematic approach to working out how you will complete all components' tasks.

4 **Manage resources**: attend to the details of resources that you need.

5 **Identify and manage risks**: work out what might prevent you from achieving your objectives; put strategies into place to reduce those risks.

6 **Implement self-management strategies**: work out how you will keep yourself on task. See Chapter 4.

7 **Implement time management strategies**: use time effectively, meeting deadlines. See Chapter 5.

8 **Use people skills**: work effectively with your supervisor (Chapter 6), peers (Chapter 4) and participants (Chapter 15).

1 Form an overview

Before launching into your project, formulate as clear an impression as possible of the 'big picture'. Ultimately, this makes it easier to complete your project.

Understand your field: find out about the nature of research in your subject; use the checklist on page 30 to get a sense of how research is conducted and written up.

Understand the rationale: consider the logic for setting such assignments within the context of your course: what skills or abilities are you meant to develop? What do they want you to demonstrate?

2 Elaborate the task

You elaborate the requirements of the task in several stages, building up the details.

(a) Clarify the outputs
At the outset, clarify exactly what you have to produce. You started this in Chapter 2. Find out the level and quality of work required. If you haven't done so already, use the checklist on page 30 to identify what is expected. This will be picked up in Part 2.

(b) Clarify the overall process
Work out the process you will use in order to produce the outputs. It can be challenging to hold on to a sense of the 'big picture' and the myriad of details to be addressed.

(c) Simplify
Start by simplifying the process, identifying its core parts, as in the diagram below.

> **Before ⇒ Start ⇒ Middle ⇒ End**
> a **Before**: Preparation and planning
> b **Start**: Developing a proposal
> c **Middle**: Conducting the research
> d **End**: Writing it up

(d) Build up the detail of the process
- Once you have a clear mental structure for your process, work out the tasks associated with each part (see page 12).
- Gradually, detail the process, adding in more steps; consider how these relate to each other (pages 34–5).
- Then, list and schedule component tasks for each stage in the process (pages 33 and 36).

Plan

Close and flexible planning

Close planning

Set out with the intention of planning each step closely, in order to minimise unwanted surprises and delays later on.

Flexibility

Leave room for some flexibility as not everything goes to plan. Be flexible at the start of the project to help ensure a feasible project and workable plans. It becomes increasingly difficult to implement changes the further you progress into the project. Be prepared to:

- consider the whole process in detail more than once, thinking through how it will all fit together
- go over the details several times early on, so as to reduce the need to do so later
- fine-tune your plans as a result of your reading, research, and guidance from your supervisor
- be ready to rethink everything in detail as the project unfolds.

a – b – c sequence of steps?

It is important to identify the stages and steps as if they will follow on naturally from a to b to c. This helps you keep track of where you are. However, it is also important to be realistic in recognising that the outline model of your project may not work exactly like that in practice. It is likely that you will move back and forth between steps.

An iterative process

The process is 'iterative' rather than just sequential. The more you find out, the more you discover new things to follow up and to plan for. You will come across new material to read, different perspectives to consider, recently published research that makes you think again about your own proposal, or new software that makes possible new kinds of analysis.

Forward planning

As your project is time-bound, many tasks may need to be undertaken concurrently or out of sequence. For example, you may need to:

- book times to see your supervisor when they are available, not to suit your project schedule
- start to look for potential participants early on
- book facilities or order materials in advance
- arrange a time for your dissertation to be bound.

Forward planning helps you to do this well.

- Make as complete a list as possible of everything you will need to do, so nothing is forgotten.
- Work out whether you have the time to do all the things you are planning to do.
- Identify things you need to address at once.
- Work out which tasks you are likely to return to more than once. Plan these into the schedule.

Develop a system

Design a system that enables you to keep track of where you are in the process.

- Develop a detailed schedule: see page 36.
- Write detailed checklists as reminders, using or adapting those provided in the book.
- Write daily 'To do' lists, based on your checklists.
- Check off ☑ items once completed.
- Plan time into your diary to do everything on your lists.
- Plan in time to take stock of whether everything is going to plan and for updating your schedule.

Make detailed 'To do' lists: example

Step: conduct the pilot. Tasks are:
(a) Set dates and times for the pilot
(b) Book rooms for the pilot
(c) Write an advert for participants
(d) Check suitability of participants
(e) Write instructions for participants
(f) ... etc.

Detailing the process

Preparation and planning

> ### 1   Organisation and planning
> Using your project brief and this list as a guide:
> - Analyse the brief in detail
> - Break down stages to steps and tasks
> - List everything you need to do and the best order to complete tasks
> - Draw up an action plan
> - Schedule each task in your diary
> - Agree meetings with your supervisor
> - Plan in support from peers
> - Book facilities, participants, binding, etc.
>
> Chapters 4–7.

Developing a proposal

> ### 2   Prepare the groundwork
> - Literature search: survey the field for inspiration and background reading
> - Brainstorm potential topics
> - Read more about these topics
> - Narrow down your choices, reading more about the ones you select
> - Check potential topics for feasibility
> - Consider methodology and methods Consider ethical implications of each.
>
> Chapters 8 and 12.

> ### 3   Decide on topic, title and strategy
> - Decide on a topic
> - Clarify exactly what you are setting out to investigate and demonstrate
> - Specify your research question or title
> - Write a project hypothesis/thesis statement as required
> - Devise a research strategy/method of investigating the topic.
>
> Chapters 8–11.

Conducting the research

> ### 6   Implement your research design
> - Fine-tune your methods, scaling the project to the brief
> - Identify participants and/or equipment
> - Design materials (if needed)
> - Develop forms or databases to gather and record data
> - Collect data or analyse source materials, keeping accurate records of findings
> - Write up your methods.
>
> Chapters 14–20.

> ### 5   Draw up and agree your proposal
> - Draw up a specific proposal or outline
> - Identify potential risks and how you will manage these
> - Check with your tutor/supervisor that the project is suitable
> - Gain Ethics Committee approval, if needed
> - Pilot the project methods if required
> - Submit for approval
> - Revise the proposal as advised.
>
> Chapters 3, 6, 12 and 13.

> ### 4   Undertake a literature review
> - Undertake focused reading of the best published literature relevant to your topic
> - Keep details for your references
> - Identify the most relevant material/points
> - Write up a focused review of selected literature, demonstrating its relevance to your work
> - Synthesise what has been achieved through previous research and the significance of this for where you are taking up the research.
>
> Chapters 9, 22 and 23.

Detailing the process

7 Present and discuss results
- Collate data, drawing up tables and graphs if relevant
- Summarise your results and their significance
- Identify whether they support the research hypothesis.

Chapters 14–21.

8 Discuss your findings, drawing conclusions
- Write the discussion section, bringing critical analysis to your methods and findings
- Identify the significance of your research and ways that the topic could be further researched
- Draw conclusions and/or make recommendations based on your findings and analysis.

Chapters 21–3.

Writing it up

9 Complete your outline report
- Write up any remaining sections
- Complete any tables and appendices.

Chapters 22–3.

Other steps

List any other key steps relevant to your project.

12 Prepare for handing in
- Check you meet presentation requirements in the brief
- Check heading levels and page numbering
- Add appendices, numbering these as you did in the report
- Fine-tune your phrasing to improve the style
- Edit and proof – several times.

Chapter 24.

11 Write the abstract and references
- Write your abstract or summary (if required)
- List all references and citations carefully.

Chapters 9 and 23.

10 Re-work your drafts
- Go back over each section, checking that the argument and the details are consistent and that you meet the brief
- Make sure everything is in the right section and material is presented in the best order
- Make sure that your argument comes across clearly from start to finish
- If anything sounds muddled, rewrite it
- If you have too much information, rewrite wordier sections more succinctly
- Check that you have built in reference to any relevant new material published since you started your research
- Check whether earlier sections need rewriting in the light of what you have written in later sections.

Chapters 23–4.

PLANNING TOOL

Thinking through your schedule

Once you have a sense of the process and tasks associated with each stage, you are ready to start scheduling. You will need to consider the following questions.

- Is my list of tasks complete?
- Do any things need to be booked or organised straightaway, or out of sequence?
- What is the best order for doing things?
- How much time should I allocate for each broad stage of the process?
- How much time do I think I *need* for each task?
- How much time do I *have*, actually, for each?
- If I need more time than I seem to have, where will I save time so that I complete to deadline?

On the chart, dark shading represents when the bulk of the task will be undertaken, and lighter shading when only aspects or finishing off will take place.

Scheduling activity

From the chart below, you can see that several aspects of the assignment may overlap or be spread across the year. This is one reason why it is useful to create a good chart, to map out everything you need to do and also to put specific times for each task into your diary.

Scheduling

List: jot down everything you will need to do.

Measure: work out how long each task will take.

Chart: create a plan for completing each task on your list.

Diarise: enter exact times for starting, undertaking and completing these into your diary or planner.

Scheduling checklist

Check off each item once done.

- ☐ I have a complete list of all necessary tasks.
- ☐ I am clear which tasks to do straightaway.
- ☐ I have worked out the best order to complete tasks.
- ☐ I have worked out how much time I have for each task.
- ☐ I have charted when I will work on each key task.
- ☐ I have put task start and end times into my diary/planner.
- ☐ I have built in time to deal with any unexpected delays.

Chart activity: example

	Oct	Nov	Dec	Jan	Feb	Mar	Apr	May
Book rooms	■							
Organise binding								■
Literature search	■							
Reading	■	■	■	■	▨			
Select topic		■						
Submit proposal		■						
Review topic		■						
Finalise the title			■					
Write Lit. review			■					
Develop methods			■					
Write up method			■	■			■	
Find participants				■				
Gather info.				■	■	▨		
Analyse findings					■	■		
Write report		■	■	■	■	■	■	
Fine-tune report							■	
Submit								▨

Managing resources

Work out the resources you need to organise and for which dates. Consider ☑ whether each of the following are likely to apply to you.

People

- ☐ Booking meetings with supervisor/ tutor
- ☐ Finding participants and making arrangements for their involvement
- ☐ Support from other students
- ☐ Support from employers
- ☐ Support from others

See Chapter 15.

Equipment and software

- ☐ Skype or conferencing tools
- ☐ Survey tools
- ☐ Statistics software
- ☐ Camera/recorder
- ☐ Reference management tools (page 28)
- ☐ Other equipment

Permissions

- ☐ Permission from employers to use work premises, data, work time or resources
- ☐ Permission from participants
- ☐ Permission from parents for children's participation
- ☐ Permission to use facilities or resources
- ☐ Permission to use or reproduce materials
- ☐ Criminal records checks (DBS) if working unsupervised with children and/or vulnerable adults

Sources and materials

- ☐ Journal articles or texts on inter-library loan
- ☐ Documents, film, photographs or other materials that need to be ordered (see page 124)
- ☐ Information or materials to be prepared for use by participants
- ☐ Sheets for participants to sign to give permission for use of their data, photograph, video, etc.
- ☐ Tools to track progress
- ☐ Tools to record your findings and results
- ☐ Tools to analyse findings and results
- ☐ Other materials

Rooms and facilities

- ☐ Labs or other space for experiments
- ☐ Places to meet other students
- ☐ Interview spaces
- ☐ Other facilities

Finances

- ☐ Are there substantial financial costs involved?
- ☐ Will you need to find further finance to support this research project?
- ☐ Are sources available – through your college, university, union, student union or employer?
- ☐ Is it likely that you would find a financial sponsor?
- ☐ Can you afford to research the topic as currently designed?

See page 38 below.

Finances

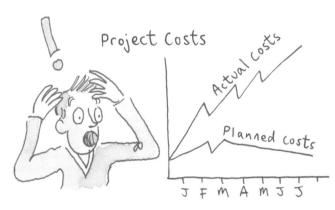

Most student projects are run with very low costs, making use of the resources available. If your research is more ambitious, involves fieldwork, extensive travel, specialist equipment, access to special collections, or has many participants, then the costs can mount up.

Before launching into your project, think through all potentially hidden costs. If these are higher than you can afford, your supervisor or your student union may be able to advise you on sources of finance.

Work out whether you can afford your project before starting. If not, give careful thought to how you might fine-tune your proposal to make it manageable financially. This is, again, an area where your supervisor should offer sound advice on how to retain as much as possible of your original idea.

Kurt realised he would be living on baked beans for a long time …

Item	Likely cost
Inter-library loans: journals, books, documents, sources	
Access to specialist collections, libraries, galleries, etc.	
Purchase of books	
Photocopying materials for myself or participants	
Travel costs for myself	
Travel costs for participants	
Cost of criminal records checks (DBS checks)	
Room hire	
Specialist software/equipment hire or purchase	
Fieldwork costs	
Binding the dissertation or report (if required)	
Other costs:	
Total	

Sources of funding open to me	Likely amount
Through my department or college	
Through the student union	
Through my employer	
Earnings from a part-time job	
Through a sponsor, charity or professional body	
Other sources:	
Total	

Identify and manage potential risks

Dealing with unforeseen difficulties eats into time and resources, such as the time it takes to change direction or find a solution, the loss of the goodwill of participants that you might have lined up for surveys, case studies or experiments, and the cost of hiring venues, equipment, sources or creating materials. For any project, it is a good management strategy to consider what, realistically, might go wrong and how you would deal with such occurrences.

Key risks to consider

1 **Not meeting the criteria**, so the work can't achieve a pass or the marks you want
2 **Not meeting the deadline**: often work is capped at the minimum pass mark if late, or not accepted at all
3 **Wrong level of challenge**: the assignment chosen was too advanced or too basic for the level of study
4 **Lack of academic integrity**: the work is not considered to be all your own
5 **Not thinking through the challenges**: setbacks come as a greater shock and are harder to manage.

Mitigating against the risks

Identify the risks likely to apply to you

Read through the following reasons why these risks arise. Decide ☑ which are likely to be relevant to you.

Identify how you will manage those risks

Then consider how you will manage the risks that you identify.

Risk 1: Not meeting the criteria

☑ *Likely to be true of me?*

☐ Not reading the criteria at all
☐ Not really understanding the criteria but not asking for clarification right at the start
☐ Deciding the project is so good or interesting that it won't really matter if the criteria aren't met
☐ Not using the criteria in a rigorous way
☐ Not planning sufficiently how to meet the criteria
☐ Lacking underlying skills so I can't deliver well against the criteria
☐ Not checking the criteria at regular intervals to make sure the assignment is on target to meet them.

I'll manage this potential risk by ...

☐ Ensuring I understand the brief and the criteria. See pages 63–6.
☐ Putting time aside early on, to think through exactly what is meant by the brief, clarifying any uncertain areas with my tutor/supervisor
☐ Planning specific times into my diary for checking that I am sticking to the brief and marking criteria
☐ Checking whether there are underlying skills that I need to develop (see pages 17–18 above) and putting time aside to do so.

Reflection: Meeting the criteria

How else might you manage this risk?

Identify and manage potential risks

Risk 2: Not meeting deadlines

☑ *Likely to be true of me?*

- [ ] Putting off getting started, as the deadline seems a long way off
- [ ] Choosing too large-scale a topic
- [ ] Poor planning: under-estimating the time it will take to complete all tasks
- [ ] Writing a poor proposal: if a revised proposal had to be submitted, I would have less time to complete later stages of the assignment
- [ ] Failing to factor in delays such as waiting for supervisor or interviewee availability, or for documents and texts to arrive on inter-library loan. I may be unable to proceed until these delaying factors are resolved.
- [ ] Perfectionism: constantly reworking the assignment; considering it unworthy to submit.

I'll manage this potential risk by ...

- [ ] Identifying a few specific tasks that I can start and complete straight away
- [ ] Careful, detailed scheduling (pages 33–6)
- [ ] Good time management (pages 51–6)
- [ ] Putting sufficient time into choosing a feasible topic (see pages 67–76)
- [ ] Building in time for things to go wrong – so that I don't fall too far behind schedule
- [ ] Taking on board my supervisors' advice if they advise against my proposal
- [ ] Being realistic about when the proposal is good enough.

Risk 3: Choosing the wrong level of challenge

☑ *Likely to be true of me?*

- [ ] Being swept away by my enthusiasm rather than working out carefully what is practicable
- [ ] Not really understanding the complexity of the issues – not having looked into the topic sufficiently before deciding on my proposal
- [ ] Failure to understand the implications for finding material or collecting the data
- [ ] Failure to check whether the literature already available on the topic would be too advanced – or too basic – for the level of study.

I'll manage this potential risk by ...

- [ ] Using a good decision-making process for choosing my topic and title (pages 67–76)
- [ ] Evaluating my proposal carefully to check it is feasible (pages 113–18)
- [ ] Comparing my proposal with those undertaken successfully by previous students, to check for comparability in scale
- [ ] Working out, in detail, the timescales for each aspect of the intended research process, such as how long it would take to set up and conduct each interview or experiment, analyse each documentary source, etc.

Reflection: Meeting deadlines

How else might you manage this risk?

Reflection: Level of challenge

How else might you manage this risk?

Identify and manage potential risks

Risk 4: Falling in academic integrity

☑ *Likely to be true of me?*

☐ Copying and pasting from online sources for reference purposes or as reminders of what I found, and then mistaking this material as my own work

☐ Copying information such as tables or sections of text which I meant to attribute to the original source, but then forgot to do so

☐ Paraphrasing too closely from books, rather than extracting the key points and summarising these in my own words

☐ Not fully understanding the rules about copying, plagiarism, and attributing sources

☐ Working too closely with other students, so that there are too many similarities in our work.

I'll manage this potential risk by …

☐ Using good study methods, such as not cutting and pasting from sources or copying work from friends

☐ Reading the academic integrity statement at the start of my project, so that I know what it entails

☐ Being clear how my own project differs from what has gone before

☐ Talking through with my supervisor, straightaway, if I am at all unsure of the boundaries of what is permissible, such as discussing work with other people working in similar areas

☐ Writing my whole project in my own words, using any quotations sparingly and with due attribution.

Risk 5: Understanding the challenges

☑ *Likely to be true of me?*

☐ Being successful in the past at getting shorter assignments done at the last minute – and assuming this will work for dissertations

☐ Not realising how long it takes to write, and rewrite, successive drafts

☐ Being dismissive of soft issues such as managing motivational issues

☐ Not recognising the value of social contact with other students when studying independently on such large projects

☐ Assuming it will be relatively quick and easy to find the right topic

☐ Not planning in sufficient detail, so not realising how much there is to do and plan.

I'll manage this potential risk by …

☐ Thinking through the project in detail from the beginning, planning in fine detail

☐ Making arrangements to meet up regularly with other students

☐ Giving some thought to the self-management issues, so that I am not caught out by these if they arise

☐ Planning time to write and rewrite drafts.

Reflection: Academic integrity

How else might you manage this risk?

Reflection: Recognising the challenges

How else might you manage this risk?

Managing risks specific to my project

Apart from the generic risks identified above, there are likely to be risks that are specific to your project, context or personal circumstances. Think through what these are, and the action you will take to ensure that they do not derail your project.

Potential risks	How I will manage them

Chapter 4
Managing yourself for the task

Larger-scale assignments require more of the mentality of the marathon runner than the sprinter. It is quite likely that there will be times when your levels of enthusiasm and interest dip, and it may feel hard to keep going. This calls for skills in self-management which are often overlooked.

Independent study

Students often have difficulties that arise from managing independent study on this scale. These arise for the following reasons.

Significance: typically, the assignment carries a significant number of marks that count towards the final grades, creating added pressure to do well.

Duration: the independent study takes place over a longer time scale, making it harder to maintain a sense of direction and connection with the course.

Lack of structure: there is less tutor guidance, contact and direction, which can feel disorientating.

Complexity: to complete such assignments requires high levels of planning, thought and engagement, all of which you have to develop for yourself, and it may not be obvious how to do so.

Isolation: there is less frequent, organised contact with other students, which can make it hard to maintain a sense of what you should or shouldn't be doing at any given point – and it can feel lonely.

Level of autonomy: it is up to you to keep it all going, and you may not always feel up to the task.

Preparing yourself for the challenge

Being prepared for what might arise helps you to:

- keep difficulties in perspective
- think ahead about how to avert problems
- and/or manage them better if they do arise.

Be prepared for times when …

- you find it difficult to get down to study
- your interest in your research wanes
- you find it hard to motivate yourself to undertake tasks that you know need doing
- you feel isolated in your studies
- you can't see where your research is heading
- you feel you have got it all wrong
- you seem to have either too much time or too little time on your hands
- you need to work on managing yourself just to keep going.

Fortunately, you are not studying in a hermetically sealed box. Help, support, inspiration and guidance are available – and in many different forms. This chapter encourages you to consider some of these. You can draw on the experiences of others as well as your self-knowledge to help you anticipate, and manage, potential difficulties.

Managing yourself for the task: what students say

It was all great at the start. I love the subject. I wanted to do this project – I chose it. I loved the reading – most of it. I didn't want to have to go onto campus every day so it suited me … but, somehow, despite all that and even though I was genuinely interested, I just couldn't bring myself to do the work. It's hard to explain why.

Working on my own – there was no-one there week by week to make me get down to work. Once I got down to work each time, I enjoyed it. The problem was simply sitting down and doing it.

Although I do like this project, I am not used to studying the same thing all the time. It wasn't exactly boring, but I was bored.

I am very competitive but there was nobody there day by day to show off how much I knew and how much work I was doing, and I found that I was losing momentum.

I never thought of my lecturers as entertaining, as such, but not seeing them at least once a week, and all the group too, I missed their input.

I was looking forward to the dissertation and then, when I got started, I found it quite frightening at first. When you are studying the rest of your degree, you don't really think about just how much the weekly lectures and classes organise your thinking. You take it for granted. The lecturers have given you a sense of what is important, what to include, they break things down so you can see more clearly what you are doing. It didn't feel like that at the time. Then when you start the dissertation, you have to do all of that thinking for yourself and you don't know for sure whether you are doing it right or not. That made me anxious.

I lost my sense of why we were doing this – what was the point? Why so many words? Why just one big assignment? Did anyone care? Was there anyone still out there? It's hard to do the less interesting bits if you start to feel adrift from the project.

I am usually good at driving myself to do things but I wasn't prepared for how much you have to do, at times, to keep yourself motivated – and then motivate yourself again. And again.

I was slow to start, then got energised and then slacked off again. I was panicking by the end, but it all felt very sluggish for a long time in the middle. Looking back, I could have approached it differently so that I worked more steadily, maintained a more even level of interest, and reduced the pressure on the last few weeks.

Reflection: Self-management

- What insights can you gain from these comments?
- How would you plan your assignment so as to take these on board?

Developing the right mindset

One of the hardest aspects of undertaking a dissertation or other large assignment is developing, and then maintaining, the right mindset. Although it may seem obvious to prepare yourself mentally for the task, in practice it is not as easy as it sounds. If you find that you do struggle to remain engaged with your research project, it can help to know that you are not alone and that there are some practical things you can do.

Actions you can take

Maintain interest and motivation

1 Focus on the benefits
2 Nurture your intellectual curiosity
3 Choose the right project

Perspective and confidence

4 Maintain a balanced perspective
5 Tap into your expertise
6 Build confidence in yourself as a researcher
7 Be prepared for all possibilities
8 Build motivation: incentives and rewards

Harnessing support

9 Intellectual
10 Social
11 From the educational institution
12 From colleagues in the workplace
13 From family and friends

Be organised

14 Manage time and timing (Chapter 5)
15 Project plan your assignment (Chapter 3).

These actions are itemised below in more detail. Select those that would benefit you – not all will be needed. Then work out:

● What would be useful to do now
● What may be useful later.

1 Focus on the benefits

One way of connecting with your research project is to consider it in terms if its broader potential benefits, to you or others, as well as its importance to your grades and qualification. Return to this if you find your motivation needs a boost.

Identify wider benefits

Large-scale pieces of work can bring a range of benefits. The value of these varies from person to person. Select ☑ which of those listed below you value for yourself.

☐ To study in depth a topic that really interests me
☐ To take on greater intellectual challenge
☐ To become an expert in the subject
☐ To have the chance to study independently, with more control over the totality of the work
☐ To develop research skills
☐ To test out whether I would want an academic career
☐ To research an issue relevant to my current employment
☐ To help resolve an issue relevant to the lives of people I know or a cause that matters to me
☐ To make a difference as a result of my project
☐ To speak confidently on a specialist topic at job interviews
☐ To develop skills that transfer into employment
☐ To develop project management skills on my CV
☐ For the sense of achievement
☐ Other benefits:

Maintain intellectual engagement

2 Nurture your intellectual curiosity

On the taught parts of a course, there is a steady stream of input – new material, tasks and questions – that serves to stimulate your brain and broaden your thinking. Once you begin your project, it is largely up to you to keep stimulating your intellect. Although you cover a great deal of material, it tends to be in a narrow area. Your work will benefit from gaining fresh inspiration and wider perspectives.

Exercise your mind and curiosity

Select ☑ items from the suggestions below.

☐ **Follow leading academics** in my field online, such as on Twitter, Facebook, or iTunesU. See Cottrell and Morris (2012); Thorne (2013).

☐ **Listen to podcasts** by respected experts using media channels, or visit their webpages or read their blogs.

☐ **Set up a discussion thread** to debate issues or discuss things I have read (though not my core research question).

☐ **Read more broadly around my subject** for interest, rather than only the most obvious material.

☐ **Read outside my subject**; draw comparisons with my own.

☐ **Take a questioning approach** to what I find, linking it to broader issues in the subject, or more globally.

☐ **Challenge** the way that others define the questions in material I read, watch or listen to.

☐ **Challenge my position** on an issue. See Cottrell (2011).

☐ **Browse the 'origins'** – who were the first people to research this issue and what concerned them at the time?

☐ **Look for more than one way** of resolving an academic question – don't settle for the first answer.

☐ **Consider my work from a new perspective** – such as its political implications, cultural significance, historical roots, its impact on specific groups globally or on the environment, or how it is depicted in other countries or in the arts.

See also: *Intellectual input from peers*, page 49.

---

3 Choose the right project

Books on long assignments emphasise the importance of choosing a project that really excites and 'enthuses' you (Levin, 2005). This is sound advice, although it is often the case that either the range of topics open to you doesn't include anything that inspires you or, alternatively, you are undertaking a dissertation with little interest in doing so.

When deciding on your project (see pages 67–76), consider this from the perspective of longer-term motivation.

- Are there any angles that you could develop that would sustain your interest more than others?
- If a topic inspires you, is this sufficient to carry you through to the end?
- Are there weighty debates or controversial issues that provide additional interest?
- Will you enjoy the reading material? If not, what might interest you more?
- Do the research methods allow a sufficient diversity of tasks to reduce chances of boredom? Is much repetition involved?
- Does the project have the right level of challenge for you to maintain a balance between being over-stretched and under-stimulated?
- Do you have any special connection to the project to draw on for inspiration when needed?

Perspective and confidence

4 Maintain a balanced perspective

Don't let your anxieties and concerns get the better of you, especially if the going gets tough. Although these assignments are designed to be challenging, they are also meant to be manageable. It is important to maintain a sense of proportion if the work starts to feel overwhelming or difficult, whilst also planning carefully how you will manage a task of this scale.

5 Tap into your existing expertise

If you go adrift on your project, it can be easy to forget to call on what you already know. Your project is meant to build, at least to some extent, on your previous study, such as particular content, theoretical or methodological approaches, work experience, or academic skills.

If there are times when you feel you don't know where to start or can't see where material is leading, anchor yourself by going back over your previous coursework. Take note of what you already know and think about how you could make use of it.

6 Build your confidence as a researcher

The word 'research' can be off-putting to some people, suggesting a task that can only be undertaken by a special kind of expert.

Researcher confidence

Identify ✔ *any approaches that might be helpful to you.*

- [ ] Recognise that finding some aspects of research problematic is not the same as not being any good at it.
- [ ] Consider ways that I use similar skills in everyday life to those used for research, and build from there.
- [ ] Don't feel anxious about whether I am an 'expert' at the outset. By the end, I will be an expert simply by the amount of time, reading and thought that I have given to the topic compared with anyone else.
- [ ] Consider myself part of a learning community: all the previous work on the subject is there for me to draw upon to help with my own research.
- [ ] Seek out the excitement in investigating a topic that no-one has looked at in quite this way before.
- [ ] Allow myself to think forward to where my research could lead: how might I follow it up with further research if I had the opportunity?
- [ ] Share experiences with others.

7 Be prepared for all possibilities

Knowing the kinds of things that typically go wrong means that you will be less surprised if these occur, and you can think ahead about how you would deal with them.

Things that go wrong ...

Consider how you might take steps to address each of the following issues. Sign each one off ✔ *once you have planned for it in your risk assessment (pages 39–42).*

- [ ] Lack of supervisor availability
- [ ] Waiting for inter-library loans
- [ ] Other people using the documents or texts that I need at the point I had planned to use them
- [ ] New publications in my field that mean changing my methods or interpretations
- [ ] Computer problems or loss of files/folders/data
- [ ] Participants letting me down in some way
- [ ] Friends, family or work colleagues needing me
- [ ] Delays in getting the assignment bound (if relevant)
- [ ] Illness
- [ ] Other assignments needing to be handed in at the same time.

Motivation: incentives and rewards

8 Incentives and rewards

Although it can be helpful to outline the broader benefits of your research (see page 45) at times, these may seem to be rather distant goals and you may need to give your motivation a boost.

Identify your key incentives

People generally need an incentive to perform well. If your motivation starts to wane, spend about 15 minutes identifying incentives relevant to you.

☐ **ONE big incentive.** What is the ONE most important reason for completing your assignment? Write this down and put it where you can see it. If it ceases to inspire, come up with a new reason.

☐ **Key gains.** Make a quick list of anything that you consider to be of real benefit to you, personally, for completing the assignment well and on time.

☐ **Potential lost opportunities.** Make a quick list of every potential benefit that you might miss out on if you don't complete on time.

☐ **Inspiration.** Who or what can provide a source of inspiration to increase your motivation? Why do you find this inspiring?

Plan your rewards

Plan frequent small rewards

Build in frequent treats as rewards for completing set tasks. Keep these brief so you return to work quickly. These might be 5–10-minute breaks, a hot drink, a phone call, playing a game, watching TV, a snack, tweeting progress, or anything that works!

Plan big rewards

☐ Give yourself something to look forward to at the end of the day, as a reward for your hard work.

Once I get started, it is better for me to keep going rather than stopping for small rewards. I promised myself a bigger treat once I finished study planned for the day. For me, that was watching a DVD, having something nice to eat, going out to meet friends, reading graphic novels. If I stopped working before these rewards, well basically, it was doomed.

The big reward for me is always good quality chocolate. The only way I got anything done was making sure I didn't break into my chocolate treats until I finished what I had scheduled for the day.

The final reward

Once you have completed your assignment, it is likely that you will feel that that is reward enough. Until then, it may help to promise yourself an additional reward for once it is submitted. What kind of reward would motivate you to complete?

Everyone has their own way of getting through a long assignment

Reflection: Motivation

- How will you ensure that you get down to work when deadlines seem a long way off?
- What will you do to keep yourself motivated if you find your interest or energies waning?
- Which rewards would work best for you as real incentives to study?

Keeping in touch with others

Why would I need to do this?

It is not unusual for students to struggle with the effects of working alone on long assignments. If you find this, then check ☑ whether you are experiencing any of these common responses.

The impact of studying in isolation

- ☐ social isolation or loneliness
- ☐ feeling generally adrift from the course
- ☐ boredom
- ☐ feeling alone with my study problems
- ☐ lacking inspiration and exposure to ideas
- ☐ distress from the emotional content of the material I am covering
- ☐ overwhelmed by the amount of work to do
- ☐ torn because of the multiple demands of the project and other life commitments
- ☐ unsupported by my family or friends.

Most students become used to this way of studying and find ways of dealing with these issues. Nonetheless, the process can often be made less stressful and more manageable by maintaining contact with others.

9   Intellectual input from peers

It is easy to become stale in your thinking when working alone. Take steps to gain intellectual stimulation from others.

- Other people's questions about your work can motivate you to keep going.
- Others on your course will be struggling with some of the same intellectual issues as you and, together, you are more likely to devise better ways of tackling these.
- Take up opportunities for attending taught sessions, so as to broaden your thinking, even if the topic doesn't seem relevant.
- Attend study or support groups to develop your general understanding of the research experience – and to bring variety to your week – whether or not you like the group.

Intellectual input from peers

Consider which strategies would work best for you.

- ☐ Attend sessions already provided for students undertaking research projects
- ☐ Ask tutors to organise sessions to talk through issues related to managing my research
- ☐ Help to organise a study group to fire my interest and imagination and broaden my perspective
- ☐ Check whether I can attend lectures provided elsewhere in the college, for background.

10   Maintain social networks

- ☐ Arrange to meet up once a week with one or more students from my course
- ☐ Arrange to meet with friends from outside the course at least once a week
- ☐ Meet friends for a walk, sport or exercise at least twice a week, to manage the sedentary aspects of study.

11   Support from your institution

Apart from your supervisor, there will be facilities that you can use to maintain contact with others or to receive particular support. Consider:

- ☐ the student union
- ☐ student services or support desks
- ☐ library staff
- ☐ student counselling
- ☐ graduate school facilities (if you are a graduate).

Support from family, friends and colleagues

12 Support in the workplace

If you are in employment, your work colleagues may notice a change in your behaviour. It is entirely up to you whether you wish to discuss your study at work, unless, of course, your project is a work-based study. You may wish to discuss the following strategies.

Support at work

- ☐ Identify at least one colleague as a confidante so that there is someone who is on your side if others resent your having less time for them.
- ☐ Request study leave from your employer, as part of your personal or professional development.
- ☐ For work-based assignments, check whether you can have additional supervision time to talk through relevant issues – especially if your work or study has a high emotional content.

---

13 Support from family and friends

Longer assignments can take their toll, not just on you but also on your circle of friends and family. It is difficult for people not working on such tasks to understand the level of discipline that you need to bring to the task. They may feel you are not interested in them any more or that you are letting them down. This is especially the case if you are a parent or carer, or have returned to study as a mature student, but can be true for any student. It is up to you to help them to appreciate what the demands of the dissertation will be, what you need from them and what they can expect from you.

Below are some common issues that you may find it helpful to discuss.

Family and friends: issues to talk through

- ☐ Why the assignment is important to me
- ☐ What we will all gain from my doing this (if relevant)
- ☐ What the assignment will demand of me
- ☐ The support that I will need from them at different stages in the assignment
- ☐ When and where I will be studying and the implications of that
- ☐ What all this means for them. How they feel about my not being so available for them for that time
- ☐ How long this stage of my study will last
- ☐ How we will make this work best for us all
- ☐ Which events or times are most important for them, when they would want me to be available. Will it be feasible to meet these requests?
- ☐ What they need from me in order to provide me with the support I will need
- ☐ When I will be able to make time for them
- ☐ When and how we will discuss issues that arise from my study as we go along
- ☐ How we will make best use of time I have available in order to do things with them
- ☐ When and how they can interrupt me for what kinds of matters, if they know I am studying
- ☐ How we will celebrate together at the end, doing something that everyone will enjoy.

Be prepared …

Despite talking through the issues, be prepared for times when those around you forget what has been agreed, want your time, and show anger, resentment or loss. Talk this through – they may well come back on side before long.

Chapter 5
Using time effectively

Time is your most valuable resource

For most students, the time provided for completing a long assignment will seem far greater than for any previous project. People experience that additional time in different ways. For some, it can feel as if there is far too much unscheduled time weighing on their hands, at least at the beginning. For others, the scale of the assignment leaves them worrying that they will not have sufficient time.

Although it may not feel like it at the start of your project, time is your most valuable resource for long assignments. You are given the additional time for a reason – you will need it in order to do justice to the project.

Despite any natural tendencies to put off thinking about 'time' when there seems to be lots of it available, it is well worth considering 'time' and 'timing' from the start of your project. If you use the project management approaches outlined in Chapter 3, these will take you a long way in managing your time effectively.

Personal time challenges?

Students vary in which aspects of long assignments they find most challenging in terms of time management. Recognising the issue is already a step towards addressing any problems that might arise. Identify which of the following are likely to be issues for you.

What are my own 'time' issues?

☐ 1 Underestimating how long things take to do.

☐ 2 Getting started.

☐ 3 Not settling down to study on particular days.

☐ 4 Not pacing the work across the time available.

☐ 5 Losing momentum; finding it hard to keep going.

☐ 6 Not writing up in time.

☐ 7 Not bringing the assignment to an end.

But I have a whole year to do this dissertation!

Yes, but you have been saying that now for 364 days!

UNI Café

Dylan generally found it best to remain in denial about the passage of time

How long will it take?

Time from multiple perspectives

For a project of this scale, it pays to map out the time requirements at different levels of detail and from several perspectives, such as:

1 the course requirements
2 everyday time requirements
3 broad project processes
4 your chapters or report sections
5 your diary and planning tools.

1 Course requirements

Count the hours

A year of study (120 credits in the UK) is the equivalent of 1200 hours of study. If your project is worth 40 credits, it is the equivalent of a third of a full-time year of study (400 hours). This represents 10–12 weeks of full-time study. Some students will put in much less time, and others a great deal more.

If you are studying part-time for the equivalent of 50% of a full-time degree (600 hours or 60 credits in the UK) a 40-credit project or dissertation would represent two-thirds of a single year's study.

If you are studying full time for a Masters or doctoral thesis, this is the same as working for a full-time job.

2 Everyday time requirements

Make a list of everything you have to do across the project lifetime apart from the project itself, such as:

- your job
- family events
- travelling
- socialising
- leisure
- holiday
- everyday life tasks
- sports and fitness
- unforeseen emergencies.

Plan time for each into your diary or planner. Indicate clearly the items that cannot be changed, and those that could be moved.

3 Broad project processes

Allocate a broad percentage of your available time to each part of the process. This isn't an exact science. A typical allocation is as indicated below.

Allocating time across the project

Preparation and planning – 5%

Developing a proposal/research design – 15%

Background reading/Literature review – 15%

Gathering and analysing data/information – 40%

Writing and fine-tuning – 25%

---

4 Chapter or report sections

- Identify how many sections or chapters there will be to your report. See pages 185–96.
- Work out how long each section will take you.
- Give each section a number or colour.
- Map the work for each section of your report onto a time chart or schedule (page 36). Use colour or numbering to help you see clearly when you are to undertake the work that relates to each section of your report. This should correspond to the time you have identified for each task.

Your diary and planning tools

It is likely that you will use one or more planning tools such as charts, schedules, timelines and checklists as well as your diary or planner. Select one planning tool such as your diary or planner as a means of mapping out all demands on your time, whether study, family, work, health, leisure and other aspects of family life. Use this to coordinate your various planning tools, such as by cross-referencing to your checklists.

- Set yourself regular times in the day for checking the diary; develop the habit of checking it frequently if you don't do this already.
- Sort out time conflicts straightaway – don't assume they will manage themselves.

Getting started

What's the rush?

When a deadline is looming, it is more evident that there is no time for excuses for putting off work. This provides a sense of urgency which gets the adrenaline flowing and helps you to focus on what needs to be done.

One of the key challenges of longer assignments is that the deadline is, for a significant proportion of the time available, a long way off. This means that there is much less of a natural sense of urgency. Although it is essential that you use all the time available effectively and efficiently, there is little immediate incentive to do so.

Start early …

- so that you have the maximum possible time to dedicate to your dissertation
- so that anything needing advance booking or consideration is addressed in good time.

Address your excuses

Examine your excuses for putting off the work – do they stand up to scrutiny? Some examples are given below.

☐ 'I always leave things to the last minute and have always met the deadlines in the past.'

Assume that the project is not like former assignments – it is unlikely that a sudden burst of work near the deadline will pay off in ways that can work for a shorter assignment.

☐ 'There's loads of time left yet.'

Even if that is so, use that time well including the immediate future. Take seriously the scale and complexity of the task.

Form an overview of the work ahead

If you haven't done so already,

☐ **Browse the whole of this book**: develop a sense of how much you have to accomplish and how to go about it.

☐ **Read the early chapters**: these provide you with an overview of how to manage your project.

First steps

☐ **Make your schedule**
If you haven't already drawn up your schedule, do so now. You will then have accomplished, already, an essential task.

☐ **Schedule tasks from now**
As you make your schedule, plan in tasks starting straightaway, rather than next week.

Getting started each day

☐ **Just 15 minutes**

If you are not in the mood to work on the assignment, set out to do just 15 minutes. That will seem more manageable than several hours. Once you have started to work, it is generally easier to keep going than if you had planned a longer study session from the outset.

☐ **Study with a friend**

Arrange to meet with a friend to study alongside each other. Your commitment to them may help you to keep your 'appointment' to study.

☐ **Choose the right place**

Work in a location that reduces distractions, such as the library or a space you have set aside for study.

☐ **Specify the task exactly**

Avoid sitting down to work with only a general intention to study. Jot down a list of specific tasks to complete in a given time, to provide focus as soon as you sit down to study.

Pacing the work

Good pacing

Good pacing helps you to feel in control of the project and that you can complete on time without unrealistic demands at particular times in the year. Consider whether you could make use of any of the following strategies ☑.

☐ Little and often

It may feel tempting to wait until you have a clear space in your diary so as to accomplish major sections all at once. In practice, this is rarely realistic. Large-scale projects cannot be rushed over a weekend towards the end of the year. Each section of the work is likely to take a considerable amount of time.

This is easier to manage if, from the beginning, you are prepared to:

- break the task into more manageable sections with several steps to each; assume that you will return to each task more than once
- chip away at the larger tasks bit by bit, if need be, so that you are continually moving forward towards the end point.

Take it in small pieces ...

☐ Develop a regular work habit

Plan regular and frequent time slots into your diary or organiser to develop the habit of working on your project. This should be proportionate to the scale of your project: every day for a full-time Masters or doctorate; at least twice a week if you are a part-time undergraduate. This helps to ensure that you:

- keep the topic 'live' within your thinking
- settle to work more easily
- put yourself in a better position to manage setbacks if some stages take longer than expected
- keep adding incrementally to your project over a long time, avoiding last minute emergencies
- meet essential deadlines.

☐ Front-loading

Aim to front-load your project, doing more than you think may be strictly needed early on. This gives you more leeway later, if you underestimate the time needed.

☐ Contingency planning

Plan for unforeseen emergencies to help with pacing in the later stages of the assignment, and to avoid stressful last minute rushes.

☐ Plan in at least 10% more time than you think you need, as contingency.

☐ Over-compensate in your planning rather than take risks with running out of time.

☐ Pay particular attention to drawing up lists of tasks for your schedule (page 36). Include the fine details in your schedule and planner rather than just the headline tasks.

☐ Expect uneven progress

Be realistic about the pace of progress. Be prepared for an uneven pattern of success. Some aspects may run much more smoothly than expected, and no setbacks may materialise for whole sections of the work.

Conversely, aspects which seemed relatively straightforward may unexpectedly take much longer than planned. You may write pages of your report without a hitch, and then find a few paragraphs that you need to do several times before they are right.

Keeping going – maintaining momentum

Early stage change of direction

If you are bored in the early stages of the project, consider a different topic, or a new approach, while there is still time. This won't be feasible later.

Stick with it

Once your project is underway, it falls to you to maintain momentum. If you get bored and can't settle down to work, you will need to find strategies to keep you going, depending on what you think will work best for your personality and attitude. Below, are some strategies to use as starting points.

Develop a strict routine. See page 54.

Jumpstart. Once you complete a task, spend a few minutes on the next task on your list. For example, read through your plan to check what to do next, or jot down ideas for the next task.

Acknowledge achievements. Give yourself credit for tasks and sections completed so far.

Power of persuasion. Persuade a friend or family member why your research project is of value. This isn't always easy to do. Arguing your case may not convince them but it may remind you of why you chose it in the first place.

Accept setbacks and move on. If you find that you have, despite your best intentions, allowed things to slip, avoid dwelling on lost time. Focus on the time left, and reschedule tasks.

Avoid catastrophic thinking. Boredom is natural when things take a long time or if repetition is involved. Sometimes students look for escape from the work by reading more into the boredom, assuming it means the project was never right and they should somehow try to find something else to study, even when little time is left.

Create a sense of urgency

Set yourself challenges. Formulate goals to achieve over a week, day or session, adapting the timescale to suit your need. 'Competing with yourself' in this way can provide a sense of urgency, raising adrenaline levels and giving additional interest to your study. Keep challenges realistic and relevant to the study task, such as:

- reading a given number of pages, writing a set number of words, or finishing a set of calculations to a tight schedule
- finding the answers, in a given time, to a series of questions you have set yourself
- making notes within a given word limit or to a fixed number of pages in a given time.

Ask for a 'push'. Ask someone you trust to give you gentle reminders if you deviate from your schedule.

Create points of interest in your day

Keep up your social life. Keep in touch with friends and family. Ask what they have been doing. Go out and enjoy yourself – though not all the time available for study.

Share inspiration. Maintain links with other students. Find out what they find interesting about their projects. Identify at least one interesting thing you can tell them about your own.

I'm bored with my project. It must be the universe is trying to tell me to change the research topic.

Hermione wasn't one for taking personal responsibility for her own decisions

Writing it up and completing the project

The scale of the writing task can be off-putting. It is very common for students to procrastinate either on

- starting to write up their report, or on
- undertaking other aspects of the project, because they put off having to write it up.

It is also easy to find excuses, such as about the need to read more material, collect further data, or think more about your findings.

Chapter 22 looks in more detail about managing the writing of your assignment. If you have time, browse that chapter too. Below, are some ideas about things you can plan in from the beginning of your assignment, to help with later stages of the writing process.

Write an early draft of the conclusion

Students often put off writing the conclusion. All of your research should be leading towards your conclusion. Your sense of what that conclusion is should be developing as your project proceeds.

Unless it is contrary to the research philosophy itself, aim to write a rough early draft of your conclusion as soon as possible. For many projects, you could write this draft within the first few hours or days. Keep returning to this as you work on your project, updating it in line with what you find out and developments in your thinking.

Writing this early on will help to avoid procrastination later when it comes to completing the assignment.

- [ ] **Write as you go**: don't wait until you have completed all of your research before starting to write. Write each section as you go. See pages 186–93.

- [ ] **Set deadlines for yourself** for completing writing up specific sections or chapters: the larger the word limit, the more important this is.

- [ ] **Set yourself word targets**: plan to write a set number of words or pages during a particular writing session for completing sections of your project. Stick to these.

Bringing the assignment to an end

Many students struggle with identifying how to bring closure to their project. It is tempting to keep finding other things to do rather than acknowledging the point where either further work will make little difference, or handing it in has become the most essential aspect of the project.

- [ ] **Give yourself a 'sense of the ending'.** Think through the different tasks that you will complete for the final 5–10% of your project.

- [ ] **Good enough?** Excessive perfectionism creates a barrier to completion. There is always something extra that could be read, summarised, used within the dissertation. There are always better ways of writing up sections of the report. That is the nature of both research and writing.

At some point, you have to decide that, despite improvements that you can still see, this project is as good as it can be within the time available. Decide what 'good enough' will look like.

- [ ] **Plan backwards from the deadlines of your project.** Set yourself clear dates for the final tasks.

Chapter 6
Working with your supervisor

Typically, when you are conducting a research project, very little is provided as formal teaching. You may receive some training in specialist research methods prior to starting your project or, occasionally, alongside it. Otherwise, you are largely on your own, except for your supervisor.

What is a supervisor?

The term 'supervisor' can be misleading as it may suggest that you will receive the kind of day-to-day supervision that is sometimes provided in the workplace. Supervision for dissertations and similar projects is not like that. It is usually:

- infrequent – you may receive only 2 or 3 short sessions
- provided on an individual, face-to-face basis, although it could be offered through phone or other contact, if needed
- provided in order to steer you broadly in the right direction, not to teach you how to undertake the project you have selected.

For very large projects that extend across a year, you may meet with your supervisor several times in the year.

A key to success

The support of your supervisor can make all the difference to succeeding with your assignment. A good supervisor can, with apparently little input, provide just the right amount of guidance to enable you to avoid potentially poor choices and to find good solutions to apparently intractable problems.

Squeak

Jocelyn was embarrassed to find that she was sometimes intimidated by her supervisor

However often you meet your supervisor, it pays to:

- have realistic expectations
- make full use of whatever meetings and support are offered
- form a good working relationship, so that you then feel more confident to ask for advice or check details that are concerning you
- manage the relationship sensibly.

This chapter provides a brief overview of what it is reasonable to expect from your supervisor and ways of managing this working relationship effectively.

> ### Find out: Guidance
> What background information is provided to help you to understand what is required? Is anything provided on the VLE or department website?

What to expect from supervision

What you can expect

This will vary depending on the level of study, the subject and the institutional regulations. Broadly speaking, it is reasonable to assume the following.

- Clear guidance about how much supervision time you will receive and details of how to book supervision times
- Details of who to contact, and how, if you are struggling with a particular aspect
- A steer about how to find the help or resources you need
- At least one meeting (in person, by phone, using Skype or other video conferencing) where you can discuss your proposal
- Guidance, either in person or through group communication, on what is expected, where to find the marking criteria and how to interpret these
- Guidance on whether your initial suggestions for a research proposal or topic are likely to be accepted and whether your methodology is appropriate
- A steer on where your proposal has strengths or needs further work
- Some direction on where to start looking for some of the background research material
- Responses to occasional enquiries you might have about aspects of your assignment
- At least one meeting (in person, by phone, using Skype or other video conferencing) to discuss progress on completing the assignment.

Depending on the context and the scale of the assignment, you may also receive:

- some taught group sessions on core methodological issues
- group sessions to enable mutual support and sharing of tips in managing the process
- individual or group sessions on difficult areas.

It is not reasonable to expect your supervisor to:

- see you on a day-to-day basis
- tell you what to do
- find things out for you rather than pointing you in the right direction
- be a particular kind of person or your friend – although they should provide a constructive, friendly working environment.

What your supervisor may expect

It is reasonable for your supervisor to have the following expectations of you. Consider which of these you are very likely to meet. Then note which items you have not yet marked. Decide how you will go about meeting such expectations.

- ☐ Show an engaged, interested approach to your subject.
- ☐ Arrive on time and well-prepared for each supervision session.
- ☐ Be responsible and self-reliant, working out what you need to do and when, and planning out your work.
- ☐ Think about your work between sessions and undertake further work on the assignment.
- ☐ Be clear about what you need from them – ask for expert input.
- ☐ Prepare questions in advance of meetings or group sessions (if relevant).
- ☐ Check that the answers to your questions haven't been provided already, through the website, handbook or handouts.
- ☐ Make notes, during meetings, of recommendations and agreed actions.
- ☐ Complete any work that has been agreed and follow up on their suggestions.

Managing time with your supervisor

As only a limited amount of supervision time is available for each student, use it to best effect.

Take advice seriously

Supervisors are experts in the subject and/or in guiding students through to successful completion of research assignments. They can provide invaluable insights into what will work. If they do give you a steer, you do not have to follow their advice to the letter, but it is in your interest to give it proper attention.

Ask for their input

Do ask your supervisor such things as:

- whether they consider your project to be manageable
- whether your project is pitched at the right level for your stage of study
- whether there are important studies that they are aware of, relevant to your subject, that you haven't included in your literature review
- whether your title or hypothesis is worded well
- any concerns you have about ethics or health and safety issues
- whether you are likely to be in breach of any regulations, or might affect the reputation of the course or the university in some way.

Manage supervision time well

Identify ☑ which of the following suggestions would be useful for you to apply – then plan these into your scheduling. The checklist overleaf may help to draw information together.

☐ Be prepared to make first contact – don't just wait for your supervisor to contact you.

☐ Prepare a list of questions before each session.

☐ Organise these in order of priority, in case you run out of time during the session.

☐ Check through notes of the previous session. Make sure that you have followed through on everything you had agreed to do.

☐ Check the guidance you have been given to see whether there are particular aspects of the work that you should have completed before the next meeting. If so, be prepared to report on these or to submit whatever is required.

☐ Clarify whether your supervisor wishes to see (or is prepared to accept) sections of your work to read in advance of meetings.

☐ If so, how far in advance do they need this?

☐ What, specifically, do they want to see and when?

Ask for help

Do ask for help if you need it. However, before asking for help, make a serious attempt to resolve the problem for yourself. Be ready to talk through what you have tried out already, as well as what has, or hasn't, worked so far. This will help your supervisor to focus more precisely on where you really need help – and they will take your work more seriously. Don't expect your supervisor to keep answering questions on minor issues.

Maintain contact

Keep appointments that have been arranged; request further contact if needed. If you have agreed a direction of travel with your supervisor and then decide to do something different, keep them in the loop.

If you are keen to study a particular subject, it may be tempting to avoid advice. Often, when students decide to ignore such advice, they then feel less comfortable meeting up with their supervisor and problems can mount up.

If you do feel you have damaged the relationship with your supervisor, or just not followed up on their suggestions, do still maintain contact. They may be frustrated at times, but it is risky to lose contact. If you do have problems later, it can count against you if you missed supervision sessions or didn't keep your supervisor informed of changes in your plans.

Supervision

Who is my supervisor?	
How frequently will we meet for supervision? How many meetings in total?	
When and where do we meet?	
What are the arrangements for booking individual sessions?	
How long does each session last?	
Are group sessions provided? If so, what are these for?	
What am I expected to do before supervision sessions?	
What am I expected to bring to sessions?	
What happens during supervision sessions?	
What am I expected to do after a supervision session?	
What kind of help is my supervisor prepared to offer?	
What kinds of help won't be offered?	
What is specified about supervision in my institution's regulations or code of practice?	

Part 2
Developing your proposal

What is the proposal stage?

The proposal stage of the project is critical. If your proposal is good, the rest of your research will fall into place. Its purpose is for you to:

- draw together your initial ideas into a workable project outline
- have an agreed project outline in place early enough to give you reasonable time to complete it
- clarify to yourself and, if necessary, to others, that your research plans are feasible
- prepare the groundwork for gathering the data or material that you need
- gain formal approval, if required.

What do I need to do?

The formal requirements for a research proposal vary enormously from one course to the next. For some, a detailed proposal with results of a small pilot must be submitted to the course team and/or an ethics panel for approval. For others, only a title and a broad outline are required – or the submission of a literature review or summary of the proposed chapters.

For your own purposes in planning your research, it is helpful to consider the proposal stage as encompassing the whole process from analysing the assignment brief through to that point when you are clear, in your own mind, what you will research and how. Even if you are not formally required to write up such a detailed proposal, it is advisable to do so.

Aspects of the proposal stage

Know your brief, to ensure your proposal meets it.

Research the background, from literature search to a first draft of your literature review, to ensure the proposal is grounded in research in your field.

Settle on a topic, title and/or hypothesis, so that your research is suitably focused.

Decide on a methodology, so you are clear why you are approaching your research in the way chosen.

Select your methods, piloting them so you know they work before finalising the proposal: see Part 3.

Think through ethical implications, so you know that your research complies with ethics policies.

Plan and prepare in detail, so you know that the project is feasible and that you are ready to begin.

Write up the proposal to meet requirements.

Contents of Part 2

The following chapters offer help in thinking through the issues and practical details of preparing and writing up your proposal.

7 Understanding the assignment brief
8 Choosing your topic and title
9 Literature search and review
10 Principles of good research
11 Methodological approaches
12 Ethical considerations
13 Writing the research proposal.

What students say

I couldn't wait to get on with my 'real research', analysing visual material in films.

My supervisor kept insisting that I get a proposal down on paper. Back then, it seemed to me to be a waste of time to write a detailed proposal – the writing was supposed to come at the end, wasn't it, not the beginning? All his words about 'scale' and 'scope' and methods and 'methodology' went over my head. I just wasn't that bothered about what anyone else had written about 'my' subject or how they had done it. My work was going to be so original so what was the point? Anyway, I had to do it. Then, bit by bit, it dawned on me how much research had been done, how much was already out there, and there were quite a few things I did really need to know! It is quite scary, now, to think what a total mess I could have made of the dissertation without the sweat of the proposal.

Plan! Plan! Plan! That was my supervisor's message. So I did a load of planning but for some reason, I just didn't want to write anything down. I think I was scared I didn't know enough. I got a final warning so reluctantly I wrote up the proposal and handed it in. When I got it back, my supervisor talked me through loads of points. They weren't major, but they did make me see where I could do better. The main thing was she showed me short cuts that were really useful and saved me a lot of time.

I am one of life's natural planners and am always making lists so I was happy enough working away on my research proposal.

I actually felt quite smug when our tutor warned the seminar group that people needed to put more thought into their proposals. I smiled too soon, as it turned out, because I spent too much time on it. When everyone else had rushed in their proposals and had them all approved, there I was, still happily colouring in my planning sheets and browsing interesting things on the website. In the end, I had less time for the actual research and despite my lovely 'plans', I was very rushed at the end.

The main thing that caught us out, in our group, was the ethical side.

We assumed that because we are all very nice mature students and wouldn't hurt a fly, our proposals would definitely be ethical. It came as quite a shock to find out that we had to dot the 'i's on so many issues to show we had considered everything.

I was sure that my research would be fantastic once completed but that the 'wonder' of it would not shine through in a proposal.

I kept putting off doing it because I was worried I wouldn't be able to get my message across. As it happens, it did get returned for rewriting. My supervisor said my rationale and ideas came across as muddled, and it wasn't obvious how these all fitted together. I had to think hard about what my concept really was and saw that there were some inconsistencies in my thinking. The reason for these was that I was trying to squeeze in too many interesting things that didn't quite belong together. I found it hard to cut some out but the proposal worked better when I did.

Reflection: Developing your proposal

What, if anything, can you learn from these students' reflections about their research proposals?

Chapter 7
Understanding the assignment brief

What is the assignment brief?

The 'brief' was introduced on page 31. It provides the formal set of requirements that you must meet to pass your assignment:

- what you will need to submit
- arrangements for submitting your work
- standards and marking criteria
- general guidance about the assignment.

What to submit

The brief typically specifies such things as:

- **Which items to include**: as well as the final piece of work, you may be asked to submit one or more interim items such as an outline plan, literature review, results of a pilot and/or a formal project proposal
- **Details about content**: it may provide guidelines on the choices of topic open to you, and any limitations on what you can choose
- **Details about length**: the word or page limit and whether that includes diagrams and appendices
- **Details about approach**: methodologies, methods, techniques, equipment or software that you are expected to use.

Arrangements for submitting work

- How: to whom, where and by what methods
- Timescales: deadlines for hand-in
- Presentation: format, structure, layout and binding.

Standards and marking criteria

Either your course materials or the departmental or institutional website or virtual learning environment (VLE) should provide details of:

- what achieves good marks at this *level* of study
- what gains good marks for this *kind of assignment*
- the *criteria* that examiners use to mark or grade work.

Assignment guidance

You may also receive guidance on such things as:

- details of any taught sessions provided, such as in specialist research methods
- source materials or websites that are likely to be good starting places
- statistical packages and other specialist equipment available to you
- details of when and how to meet with your supervisor
- any peer support arrangements available.

Making full use of the assignment brief

Use the brief fully

Mark off ☑ each task once completed.

- [ ] Read the brief at least twice.
- [ ] Examine it closely, following the guidelines below and the checklist on page 65.
- [ ] Highlight or underline key terms.
- [ ] Highlight requirements you must meet.
- [ ] Highlight, in different colours, the aspects over which you have some choice.
- [ ] Summarise the brief in your own words.
- [ ] Reorganise the brief into a checklist, unless the checklists here will suffice.
- [ ] Plan into a diary when to look at the brief again to check that essential aspects are not forgotten.
- [ ] Plan into a diary when, at the end of the project, you will check that your work complies with all aspect of the brief.

Examine the brief

Analyse the brief carefully. Note the fine details about what you need to do. Consider whether your proposed project can follow these to the letter. Read the brief in combination with marking criteria and any guidance provided. Find out:

The purpose Why was this kind of assignment and/or brief set as part of my course? Page 23.

Outputs What exactly am I expected to produce? An extended essay? Dissertation? Project report? Other outputs?

Interim submissions Do I have to hand in anything for approval at a stage earlier than the final submission, such as the title, outline proposal, proposed reading, pilot results, early drafts or specific sections?

Rules, regulations and formal requirements
What parameters are set? What am I allowed or not allowed to do? Can I choose the topic myself or is it provided? Do I propose a title or is this set? What is the word limit?

Ethics Are guidelines provided about ethical considerations? What are the main issues I would need to take on board? Is there an ethics panel that will consider my proposal? If so, what will it be looking for?

Deadlines What has to be handed in, by when?

Standards What would 'good', 'bad' and 'indifferent' look like? What would get good marks? What is needed just to pass?

Use the marking criteria

Check that you understand all the marking criteria. If in doubt, ask your supervisor.

Consider carefully what each criterion means in the context of your project proposal.

Display the criteria where you can see them throughout your research.

Use them to guide your work.

Refer back to the criteria regularly, including when you start and complete a section or chapter.

Match your work carefully against the criteria.

Amend your work if it does not meet them, even if that means considerable changes or rewriting.

Checklist and project log

- Use the details on the checklist below to clarify the assignment brief.
- To focus your attention, draw out the relevant details for yourself. Jot down your observations in a project log.

Reflection: The project brief

- For previous assignments, how much use did you make of the assignment brief to guide your work?
- How might you make best use of the brief and any guidance provided?

Analysing the assignment brief

Check off ☑ each item once you are confident that you have considered it in full and are clear about the requirements for that aspect of the brief. Keep detailed notes for each response.

Purpose	☐ Why have I been asked to undertake a research project or dissertation? *Why would the course set such an assignment?* *What kind of skills and knowledge are they expecting me to demonstrate through it?*
Outputs	☐ What exactly am I expected to produce? *Extended essay? Dissertation? Thesis? Project report? Client brief? Other outputs?*
Criteria	☐ What are the marking criteria? *What are examiners looking for in order for the work to pass?* *What do I need to do in order to achieve the best marks?*
Research Proposal	☐ When and how do I agree the research proposal with my supervisor? ☐ What am I expected to submit at the proposal stage?
Other interim submissions	☐ Do I have to hand in anything else for approval earlier than the final submission? *If so, what exactly do I need to submit, to whom, in what format?*
Deadlines	☐ What is the final submission date? What do I have to submit at that point? ☐ What is the deadline for the research proposal? ☐ What are the deadlines set for any interim submissions? ☐ If the work needs to be professionally bound, what is the deadline for this?
Length	☐ What is the minimum permissible word length? ☐ What is the maximum permissible word length? ☐ Do these limits include references, diagrams, appendices and abstract? ☐ Is there a maximum number of illustrations or diagrams that I can include? ☐ Is there a maximum page limit?
Topic	☐ What kind of research topic is typical for my subject discipline? ☐ Is the topic pre-given or can I choose this for myself? ☐ Are there any restrictions on what topic I can choose?
Title	☐ Are there any typical ways that titles are formulated or phrased in my subject? ☐ Does the title have to be approved before I can proceed further?

Analysing the assignment brief continued

Hypothesis/ research question	☐ Am I required to formulate my own research hypothesis? *If so, how should it be set out?* ☐ Am I required to provide a research question or statement? *If so, what should this include? How many words are allowed for this?*
Data and resources	☐ What kind of data and/or source materials would I need to collect? *Numerical data? Documents? Images? Films? Photos? Interviews? Etc.?*
Methodology and methods	☐ Am I expected to draw on any particular research methodologies? ☐ Am I expected to take a qualitative or quantitative approach? ☐ Am I expected to make use of any particular research methods (techniques)? ☐ Am I expected to pilot my methods? ☐ If so, do I need to submit the results of the pilot at the proposal stage?
Ethical considerations	What kinds of ethical issues am I expected to consider? *How I collect and store data? How I work with participants? Privacy and confidentiality issues?* ☐ Do I need to make any submission to a research ethics committee? *If so, what must I submit, to whom and by when?*
Structure	☐ Is there a specific structure that I am expected to follow? ☐ How many sections/chapters should I include? What would these be? ☐ What is the relative length of each? ☐ What kind of abstract is expected?
Style	☐ What writing style is expected? Should this vary from one section to another?
Citations and referencing	☐ Which style of referencing is expected? ☐ Am I required to produce a separate bibliography?
Presentation	☐ How should the work be laid out and presented? ☐ Does it need to be bound?
Viva	☐ Will a viva be set? ☐ If so, when does this take place? Do all students have a viva or only some?
Understanding of the brief	☐ Have I really understood this brief? If not, what do I need to clarify? *Check carefully through course documentation and your institution's website to see if the answers to your questions lie there. If not, ask your supervisor.*

Chapter 8
Choosing your topic and title

The most important task?

Making the right choice of topic is, arguably, the most important aspect of the project. It merits attention and considerable thought. It also requires a hard head: you need to think through not just what you would like to study but what is practicable, achievable and likely to meet your longer-term needs.

Some students have known for years what they want to research for their dissertation, at least in broad terms, and are fired with enthusiasm when the opportunity arises. For them, the key issue tends to be in finding the exact focus for their energies. However, it is more typical for students to have little or no idea about what to choose, or even how to start thinking about this.

A winding path ...?

Finding a topic that is just right for you is important. The path towards that topic may be unexpectedly easy to navigate or it may be long, winding and adventurous. There may be many false starts. Topics that looked exciting may prove less so on closer observation, or are too big, too small, too popular, too expensive, too time consuming, require too many participants, or fall before some other barrier.

Such circuitous routes can be irksome if you are keen to get started on a suitable subject. However, if you plan in enough time for investigating potential topics, and approach the hunt in a constructive and open-minded way, then this aspect of the project can be enjoyable in its own right. In searching for your topic, you are likely to gain a great deal of background knowledge and broader understanding of your subject as well as valuable insights into what has been researched already and how. In the longer term, that may prove more valuable than landing on a topic too easily.

This chapter provides some ideas for arriving at the best possible topic for you to research at this time. It suggests different ways of addressing this challenge so that, if one route doesn't work, another may. It also provides some guidance on what, in broad terms, constitutes a good research topic and what it may be best to avoid.

Anton realised his research idea might not be as original as he thought

What makes a good topic?

Motivating

You are more likely to stick with your research project if …

- it fires your imagination
- it is one you find genuinely interesting and worthwhile
- you can see its relevance to your career, workplace, identity, family or life interests
- you wanted to know more about the topic when you studied the broader subject area
- you have an interest in studying it in more depth later, such as for a research degree.

Look for a topic that is likely to keep you inspired and engaged over a long timescale. A typical final year dissertation or research project involves a nominal 400 hours; a Masters or doctoral thesis several years. That is a long time to work on a topic if you lose interest in it.

Challenging

Your research topic should have a suitable amount of difficulty for the level of study. It needs to be sufficiently complex for you to feel stretched intellectually, and should add to your previous knowledge and skills. However, consider the practicalities of researching the topic and writing it up on time. The best topics strike a balance between being over-ambitious and under-challenging.

'Over-ambitious' means that, however fascinating and important the topic, you cannot reasonably expect to complete it within the set time and word limits. If you have such a topic in mind, then consider how you might scale it down or focus on a specific aspect. You could use this assignment to test out what it would be like to research the topic in greater depth in future.

Irma's problem wasn't that she lacked ambition …

Grounded

Aim to select a topic in which you already have a good foundation. It is easier to keep the project or dissertation manageable if the topic:

- goes deeper into a subject that you studied recently on your course
- is one for which you have already undertaken some background reading
- is one for which you have a good grasp of the main debates, theories and methodologies.

Feasible

Scale The topic is not so immense or complex that you could not do justice, within the time available and the word limit, to the necessary background reading, information gathering and analysis of your research findings.

Ethics The research will meet ethical requirements: Chapter 12.

Finance You can afford the travel, materials and resources needed and have thought through potential hidden costs.

Originality The topic is not so ground-breaking that there are few sources to draw upon for your literature review: pages 22 and 69.

How original does it need to be?

Make a contribution to knowledge

Your dissertation, essay or report needs to be original. That means that nobody has studied this topic in *exactly* this way before, using your participants, data, sources and methods to make the same kinds of interpretation as you. In that sense, you add to, or take forward in some way, what is already known on the topic.

Keep 'originality' in perspective

If you do not have a topic already in mind, the idea of 'original research' may seem daunting. Keep this in perspective. Originality, in this context, does not mean that you have to reinvent the wheel. In practice, it would usually be a disadvantage to choose a topic that has not been previously researched because one of the skills you need to demonstrate is how you draw upon, and add to, existing knowledge and understandings. 'Original' generally means finding your own angle on what is previously published on the subject.

Build on what has gone before

You will be conducting your research within the context of your academic discipline(s). It is assumed that you identify a topic:

- ideally, that is in an area in which your lecturers have some expertise
- that already has good published research for you to draw upon as background and for your literature review (see pages 77–8)
- where you can track the development of thinking and research into the topic through key pieces of published research
- where there are established methods that you can adopt or adapt.

Find your own angle

You take knowledge forward by bringing something new to the way the topic is understood. There are a number of different ways in which that might be accomplished. Some are listed below.

Replication – setting out to see whether you can replicate the results of previously published research, and whether previous results hold true for your own research. Your originality of concept may be limited but this is a distinct piece of research. Your dataset or findings will be original, as will be your analysis of whether, how, and why they differ from previous research.

Selecting new variables – varying one or more of the variables used in previous published research, such as the temperature, location, time, speed, etc.

Changing the population – focusing on a different demographic from that used for previous research. This might mean selecting participants from a local community, people you work with or, as often happens, a particular sub-set of students in your institution.

Client-based – undertaking a project on behalf of a particular client, such as an employer or a local business or charity.

Product-based – applying research findings to produce a leaflet, poster, website, toy, design, tool, or industrial or commercial items.

Comparative evaluation – researching which of two items or theories is better.
See also: 'Finding inspiration', page 70.

Reflection: Originality

How confident are you that you understand what originality means within the context of your own project brief?

If you are uncertain, speak to your supervisor before advancing your proposal.

Finding inspiration

Starting places

Consider areas you have found especially interesting already, such as from:

- material covered in class
- an article or chapter in a book that you used as background reading
- a podcast that you found online
- an angle of a previous assignment you would like to study in more depth
- a topical item in the news
- a topical issue in your workplace
- a theme emerging on a discussion board.

Think about how you might follow it up in more depth, using original sources or through gathering your own data.

Using your reading to identify a topic

When investigating the background, be active in looking for a suitable topic.

- Watch out for recurrent themes within the research, especially for areas of research in which similar hypotheses are tested under slightly varying conditions. Consider whether you might be able to undertake similar research of your own, with a new set of conditions. If so, how, precisely, would yours differ?
- Browse journals and book reviews for ideas about what is topical in the subject. Consider what the next logical step would be in extending that research, and whether that might be something to which you could contribute through your own research project.
- Look at other dissertations in your subject. What kinds of topics have other students chosen? How might you take a different approach to such topics?

Gaps in the research

Watch out for passing references to areas that are still under-researched. These may be indicated by your lecturers, in book reviews, journals, TV programmes, or your own observation.

The results or discussion sections of research articles often refer to limitations of the research or state ways that further research could throw more light on the topic. These gaps may provide a lead on a topic where you could make a contribution.

Recommendations for action

Consider whether you would prefer to undertake research that leads to a practical outcome. This is often possible with research linked to a workplace. If you are employed, this might be of value of your employer and might support your career prospects. If so, speak to your employer. Alternatively, the Careers Service at your college or university may have contacts and projects that link you with employers (see page 135).

Identify your niche

Look for an angle that is relevant to you, your family, employment, background or community. For example, consider whether a theory that was covered on your course is equally applicable to everyone that you know, or to situations that you have encountered. If not, that might open up an avenue to research.

Clarify your purpose or rationale

Clarify your rationale for considering a topic, so that you can explain its relevance and significance to your supervisor/tutor. What lends it importance? What makes it a good topic? In what way would it be original? What interests you about it?

Broadening out – narrowing down

Although you may be fortunate in finding, instantly, the perfect topic and the ideal title, it is more typical for students to arrive at their final decisions after a long process of searching, thinking, reading, trial and error, false starts, talking to others, fine-tuning and, possibly, some sleepless nights.

Broaden out

- Don't jump into choosing a topic too early. Be open-minded, initially, about considering a range of possibilities.
- Look for inspiration in many places, not just the most obvious.
- Conduct an initial literature search to broaden your ideas (Chapter 9).
- Make a 'long list' of themes that hold some interest or which offer potential for further investigation. Consider the kinds of questions or hypotheses you could research for each of these.

Reflection: What kind of topic is expected?

- What kinds of research topics are typical for student dissertations within your subject discipline?
- Are there any restrictions on what topic you can choose?

Narrow down

Once you have a good range of options, consider which ones engage your interest more than others.

- Devise criteria by which to choose between topics.
- Eliminate topics one by one from the list.
- Settle on one broad area to research.
- Select one area of interest.

Broaden out again

Once you have narrowed your choice of themes down to one, explore that theme from many different points of view. Read about it. See what research has been done already. Make a new 'long list' of all the questions and angles that interest you.

Eliminate

Eliminate items on your list that are likely to be:

- too complicated to explain
- too complicated to research
- too expensive to research (page 38)
- too time-consuming to research

and/or which would

- be likely to raise complex ethical questions
- violate your department's ethical code
- be difficult to address within the word limit
- be unlikely to sustain your interest
- be popular with other students.

Specify

- Settle on one topic to research.
- Specify exactly which aspect of that topic you will research: to what question will your research contribute an answer?
- Find a manageable focus, such as a particular population, timescale, set of items, as relevant to the subject.
- Keep formulating your topic more precisely until you have a clear research question to investigate and/or can formulate your research hypothesis.
- Then, focus your reading specifically on material relevant to the title.

Continue to define your topic more precisely until you arrive at a sufficiently challenging but manageable topic for the assignment brief.

Developing an idea

Read widely

There are few substitutes for reading widely. Even if there is little that is exactly on your chosen topic, reading around your subject provides your brain with ideas and new angles, some of which will be worth pursuing. If you find that your thinking process has come to a halt, or you feel stale in your ideas, just browsing texts in a bookshop or online can stimulate a new line of enquiry.

Free association

Jot down everything that comes into your mind when you reflect on the topic. Leave this for a few hours. Then, re-read your initial notes. Select any gems that you can develop further. Add your new thoughts, leave again, and repeat.

Walk and note

Take a break from study and take some exercise. Go for a walk, talk to a friend about your ideas, listen to their comments. This uses a different part of your brain. Keep a notebook handy for jotting down any ideas that are generated.

Networks

The brain operates as a large network of connections – and it can help to organise your material into networks of associated material too.

- Make a visual network or chart to capture and organise your thoughts. You can do this on your computer and add to it as you go.
- Alternatively, make a huge wall chart for your room, so that you can stand back and reflect on developing networks of ideas, references, and pieces of information you gather.

Add items to your chart in such a way that you can move them about, rearranging them in new combinations. Working with your material like this can help you to see connections or angles that might not have been so obvious otherwise.

Put it into writing

Although it can be tempting to put off writing until you sense that you know exactly what you want to say, many people find that the act of putting thoughts down on paper helps ideas to flow.

Even when the writing process seems difficult, just getting something down on paper gives you something to work with. It can help you to:

- identify what you know already – it may be more than you thought
- spot gaps in your knowledge or in the logic of your thinking
- see the directions in which your thinking or your material are leading
- think through ideas that are still not fully formulated.

Choosing your topic: Do ... and Don't ...

Have a clear rationale

Make sure you can provide good reasons for studying the proposed topic and in the way you intend.

- List your reasons.
- Read them back and consider whether they are convincing.

Jot down your answers to the following core questions:

- What is the purpose of your research? What question(s) does it set out to answer?
- How does it throw further light on what was already known?
- Within the context of your discipline, why does this matter?

Have clarity of concept

Consider whether your research idea might come across as confusing to your reader. In particular, consider whether you are attempting to do too much, such as by incorporating disparate ideas in one project. If so, separate these out and consider whether your research concept would be strengthened by focusing on fewer strands – or just one of these.

Be clear about methods

Before settling on your topic, think through the practicalities of how you will gather and work with the data or sources you will need (see Part 3). Avoid choosing a topic for which the methods are unclear or over-complicated. Otherwise, you may need to change topic later, making it more difficult to complete a good assignment before the deadline.

Over-ambitious projects

If your interest lies with a topic that is too demanding, select only a more manageable aspect of it. You might pursue this in more depth later, through a research degree.

Confusing levels of complexity

Although you will need to synthesise ideas from many sources, be careful of the choices that you make when drawing on methods from different kinds of research. Check that the methodologies are compatible and that your objectives don't come across as vague or confused. Avoid topics that are so complicated in concept or design that you use up much of your available word limit to explain them.

Topics that lack a research base

It may seem comforting to find that there is little to read for topics that interest you: you can cover all there is to know. However, such topics are hard to pursue, even for experts. The risks are that:

- It is harder to demonstrate that you are building on previous knowledge.
- You lack the advantages that come from being able to refer to a previous body of knowledge, such as facts already established elsewhere.
- It is difficult to find sufficient useful background material to choose from, and you are likely to end up using material that is not directly relevant.
- The theoretical basis of the topic may be underdeveloped so that your topic then feels lightweight, or you have to develop this for yourself.
- You may have to compensate for such gaps in background knowledge and theory, which is difficult to do well, takes time, and uses up your word limit.

Choosing a topic just to work with friends

If you are not genuinely interested in the topic,

- you are less likely to stay motivated
- you may be less likely to find your own angle, so your work may not be regarded as original
- you risk copying from others.

Choosing a topic: what students say

Contributes to knowledge

My lecturer said: 'there is nothing new under the sun'. I found this quite helpful as it made me realise that everything is related to something that has gone before, but varies from it in some way. This encouraged me to look at what already existed as research papers that I could use as a basis for my own project, and how I could bring my own angle to these.

Originality

I didn't really get what was meant by doing 'original' research. I got myself worked up because I thought it had to be something nobody had ever thought of in any way before. I couldn't imagine how I could come up with something that had never entered anybody else's mind before. I assumed everyone else could and that I was deficient in some way. It would have been helpful if someone had talked to us more about what 'original' does and does not mean in the context of a student dissertation.

Fits the brief

I got an idea for our project on land conservation very quickly – about my home town – and I got very excited about it.

I had loads of ideas and immediately typed these up. That led to other ideas, and I just kept writing away. Then I heard other students on my course talking about their dissertation and I got this horrible feeling that I might not have read the requirements quite closely enough. I went back and read it and it was only then that I realised that my ideas didn't fit the brief. One thing was that the project had to be based on a coastal area, and my home town wasn't coastal. I don't know why I didn't see that earlier.

Body of evidence

I knew exactly what I wanted to study for my Masters dissertation.

I was really excited about it and dug my heels in, although the reception from the Institute was pretty lukewarm. They thought it was an interesting idea but that there weren't any previous papers published on the subject that I could use as background. There wasn't an evidence base. They weren't sure that I would be able to make a whole dissertation out of it … It turned out they were right. I struggled to find anything for the literature search or to use as the basis for developing my ideas further.

Scale

I had always wanted to study hydroponics and assumed that my dissertation would be about that.

I could see myself growing all these vegetables up all the walls of the college, maybe starting a food revolution. I was so excited by it. There were all kinds of other practical and cost issues that I hadn't thought about at all and I wasn't allowed to do it. I felt very flat. Then, one of the other students suggested that I do a more theoretical dissertation on hydroponics that would help me in future and wouldn't cost me anything. That was a genius idea and even though I don't usually enjoy theory much, for this topic, because I'm interested in it, I got really fascinated by it.

Specifying your title

Choosing your title

Your title is the first thing that your readers will see; it may also be used for entries onto databases, so it is important to get this right. It is best to start simple. Aim for a core statement or question that expresses, in a straightforward way, what your research will address. If you can't do so, this may indicate that you are not yet sufficiently clear what you want to find out. You can elaborate on the core statement later, such as through the use of a sub-title.

A good title ...

- **is clear**: it makes sense to the reader and indicates what your research project or dissertation is about
- **is specific**: it sets the parameters of what your research will address, defining the boundaries by time, place or population so that you are not committed to delivering more than is feasible
- **incorporates a question** that your research sets out to address (even if the title itself is not worded as a question)
- **is precise**: it is as short and crisp as it can be whilst still being clear
- **fits conventions**: it is typical of titles used in dissertations undertaken in previous years and/or the titles of journal articles.

Wording the title

The wording of titles varies according to the subject, so check how these are styled in your subject. Look at the phrasing of titles of journal articles to see what is typical. Talk to your supervisor if your title seems to break the mould.

> **Example**
>
> The Use of Chemical X in Promoting Growth in XYZ-strain rice. An experiment to test whether the results of Smith and Bloggs (2010) with ABC-strain rice hold true for other strains.

Use of sub-titles

Sometimes the titles of dissertations and long essays consist of a statement or quotation, generally one that is eye-catching, topical or controversial, followed by a sub-title that grounds the research in specifics. This is especially the case in arts, humanities and social science subjects.

> **Examples**
>
> *'Too little, too late.'* An analysis of the failure of local government interventions to improve levels of water pollution in New Acid Town, 1986–95.
>
> *Wild winds and weeds.* The use of nature imagery in the poetry of Fern Growing and the London Pavement Poets 1920–39.
>
> *'The mystery of the vanishing houses'*. A case study of two houses demolished by unknown causes in the territory of The Three Little Pigs in the period of 'Once upon a time ...', with a consideration of the role of the Hungry Wolf.

Next we have '*The Elephant in the Room – The Inside Story*'. Now whose title is this?

How good is my topic?

Check off ☑ each item once you are confident that you have considered it in full and are satisfied that your title meets that criterion.

1 ☐ The topic inspires and interests me.

2 ☐ I already know something about the subject.

3 ☐ I have reasonable grounds for believing that I can sustain my interest in this topic for the duration of the research project.

4 ☐ I have a reasonable idea about what my thesis/research hypothesis is likely to be.

5 ☐ I have a good idea how I can turn this into a sensible research proposal (see page 73).

6 ☐ It will be evident that the proposed research falls into an area that would be recognised as belonging to my subject discipline.

7 ☐ My supervisor or other tutors on the course would be suitably expert in the subject to advise me on it.

8 ☐ It fits the brief set by my course.

9 ☐ It enables me to meet the marking criteria used for the award of high marks.

10 ☐ I can see where I will be able to make an original contribution to the field.

11 ☐ It offers a different angle, or uses different data, from that used in previous research.

12 ☐ I can provide a clear and convincing rationale for studying this topic.

13 ☐ There is a pre-existing body of research literature on the topic that I can draw upon.

14 ☐ There is an established theoretical framework to which I can refer.

15 ☐ There are established methods that I can draw upon.

16 ☐ It provides challenge appropriate to this level of study.

17 ☐ The data/information I need will be reasonably straightforward to collate.

18 ☐ The information I need is available in the public domain (if relevant).

19 ☐ The topic lends itself to interesting argument and debate.

20 ☐ I could do justice to the topic within the given word limit.

21 ☐ I could do justice to the topic within the given time limit.

22 ☐ I have a good title in mind (see below).

Evaluating my title: checklist

Strengths of my proposed title are ☑

1 ☐ It is clear, so the reader is in no doubt what my research is about.

2 ☐ It is specific: it sets out what the parameters of the research will be – it has defined the boundaries.

3 ☐ It fits the material covered by the project.

4 ☐ It contains the question, implicitly or explicitly, that my research will address.

5 ☐ It is precise: it isn't over fanciful or wordy.

6 ☐ Its phrasing is typical of my discipline.

Chapter 9
Literature search and review

As part of any research project report, you would include a section or chapter that engages critically with the most significant material written on the topic. This is generally referred to as the 'literature review'.

The purpose of the search and review

You undertake a review of previous research for a number of reasons. These include:

- developing the breadth of understanding about your field
- understanding how research is conducted in your subject
- gaining ideas for a topic of your own
- identifying what has been covered in depth already, so that you are clear how your own project can contribute in an original way and where it fits
- putting your own research into context for yourself and your reader.

Aspects of the literature 'review'

Your review of the literature is addressed primarily towards the beginning of the project and is written up as a specific section or chapter towards the start of the report. It consists of three main steps:

- searching for relevant material already published on the subject
- formally 'reviewing' that material – analysing it and deciding what to include
- writing it up in a critically analytical way.

A staged process

Your engagement with the literature continues throughout the project. The experience is likely to be that of a staged process, as outlined on page 78.

I can't remember all of the texts I read at the start of this dissertation – it's so embarrassing; everyone expects it of me.

A staged process

Part of the process	Aspect of the literature search and review
	Initial browsing to scope what is published ↓
	Recording details of potential useful databases, journals, etc. ↓
	Detailed searches for relevant material, checking its quality ↓
	Making careful choices about what to read ↓
	In-depth engagement with key reading matter ↓
	Decision-making about how to draw upon previous research for ideas, theory, methods, background material ↓
	Understanding the connections between different items that you read ↓
	Decision-making: what to include in the literature review, at what length ↓
	Writing up your literature review ↓
	Referring back to aspects of the literature about methods and methodologies as you evolve your own methods ↓
	Referring back to aspects of the literature when you have analysed your own data or material, for purposes of comparison ↓
	Drawing on the literature in your discussions of your findings ↓
	Referring back to aspects of the literature as you draw conclusions and/or make recommendations ↓
	Maintaining reading, to ensure your work is up to date when you submit it ↓
	Adapting your literature review and possibly other aspects of your research, if feasible, in the light of any newly published material

Making a literature search

Early stages

The early stages of the literature search are more of an adventure in exploring the field. At the start of your project, browse widely, dipping into the literature to gain a broad sense of the field in which you are working. Look for what has been written, by whom, and when. Don't focus your reading too early. Avoid getting drawn into spending too much time reading in depth on issues that may not be relevant to your choice of topic.

Initial searches

Use your initial searches to give you:

- a way of getting started, in general
- ideas about potential topics
- a sense of the quality and depth of research in the field, to reassure you that there is sufficient material for you to draw on for your literature review
- a steer on where to look for the best information when you come to do your literature review – the digital repositories, journals, special collections
- a sense of the names of experts or 'big names' that recur in the searches and reviews, so that you are aware of these for further reading later.

Look for

Before starting to read in depth on a particular topic, aim to gain a sense of:

- the possible research topics that might be open to you
- the research journals relevant to that topic
- whether there is already a strong research base in the subject, with relevant materials that you can use and refer to when you come to write your literature review
- the debates or issues that are pertinent to your discipline
- the ways in which research is conducted in your field
- how the main schools of thought and theoretical perspectives within your subject discipline influence the way that issues are conceptualised and investigated in your field
- the direction of travel of thinking within the subject: what is topical? Are new ways of looking at issues starting to enter the field? If so, who is leading the way? How are such views being greeted by experts?

Keep records from the start

Take accurate, precise notes as you go along, in case you wish to refer to the material in your work later. It is easy to waste time searching for information that is poorly noted or labelled.

Keep details for your references

Keep a complete list of the full details of all sources which you read or to which you refer. You must provide a bibliography that includes all of these, and a reference list for all sources that you cite in your work. See page 109.

- Use reference tools to keep details of all the sources you use. See page 28.
- Retain details for references according to the conventions required by your course. Follow your department's directions exactly – including the finer details specified for sequencing items, abbreviating, punctuating and capitalising. This may seem tedious, but marks are usually deducted for inaccurate details in references, and work is sent back for these to be corrected before archiving.

Finding information

Where to look

- If you have been provided with reading lists, start with these.

- Follow up the list of references in items that you read from that list or in items by known experts in your field.

- Use Google Scholar to identify the experts in the field. Google them to see what they have written. Check their recent publications in specialist repositories and journals.

- Find out about the range of specialist journals in your discipline. Check whether there are specialist journals devoted to topics that interest you.

- Browse book reviews in journals to find out what has caught the attention of experts in the field.

- Look up the items you identified in references, and then look up the references in these too. Develop a trail of leads that you can follow up in more detail.

- Browse the main journals in your discipline to gain a sense of what kinds of research have been undertaken in the last 10 years.

- Ask the college or university librarian about specialist repositories, collections or archives relevant to the topics that interest you. Find out which are online or, if they are not, how long they take to arrive if ordered, and at what cost.

Keeping the reading manageable

It is likely that, by this point in your course, you have the expertise that you need to read, note and record relevant information. If you do start to feel overwhelmed by the task, return to basics.

- Focus your reading on your literature review, and the principles outlined on page 84.

- Be ruthless in selecting to read just those parts of texts that you really need.

- Read for understanding and to find what you want for your project – rather than getting distracted by other interesting material.

- You may need to read some articles in full so as to understand the context and conclusions. For other items and for books, it may be sufficient to select only the passages that provide the exact piece of information that you need.

- Make notes only of material you intend to include.

- Avoid cutting and pasting text from any source.

- Use bookmarks, tabs, colour highlights, or similar means to mark up those areas that you consider are likely to prove most useful. This can help with being efficient in finding them quickly and easily when you need them.

Evaluate for relevance

Evaluate everything you read in terms its relevance and significance. Consider material from two angles:

The field: Gain an understanding of why a text is regarded as significant in the field. This will usually be evident from other texts or research that refers to it, or from reviews of that research.

Your topic: Why, specifically, it is the text relevant to your own topic?

Using specialist resources

Quality

For work at this level, it is expected that you use expert sources, and that you can differentiate between peer reviewed material and that produced for popular interest or commercial purposes. You should also make use of primary sources for yourself rather than referring to what others say about them.

Peer reviewed material

Specialist journals in your subject would not normally publish an article before subjecting it to the scrutiny of other experts, or 'peers', in the subject. Although that is not a guarantee that the material is accurate and free from bias, such peer review helps to ensure that the material is more likely to be reliable.

Good sources for material

It should be relatively easy to track down good quality materials if you set out to look for them. You can find high quality resources online, many designed for researchers. For a general research search service, see
http://zetoc.mimas.ac.uk
http://scholar.google.com

Other useful starting places are:

- Bibliographic databases
- Subject gateway services
- Specialist collections
- Copyright libraries
- Digital repositories.

Bibliographic databases

There will be bibliographic databases relevant to your subject, which you can access from your library catalogue or the internet. Generic databases that can help start a search include:

- www.webofknowledge.com
- www.pubmed.com (medical subjects)

Subject gateway services

These are maintained by subject experts and can be accessed through your library website.

Specialist collections

These collections of documents, artworks or other specialist materials may be located at a single site, such as a museum, gallery or university. You may need to travel to that site to use the sources. Using these in the original brings a different angle to research and can help to bring your subject alive. However, many collections are becoming available online.

Copyright libraries

If there is a source that you are finding difficult to track down, there may be a copy at one of a few copyright libraries, such as the British Library, the Bodleian Library or the Library of Congress.

Digital repositories

These contain digital versions of books, journals, theses, government papers, medieval manuscripts, photographs, video and other sources. These repositories are growing year on year, making all kinds of materials easier to access. You may not be able to search the contents of the repository before entering it, but many are free to use and material is tagged to help with searches.

- **www.ulib.org** – the University Digital Library
- **www.jstor.org** for a wide range of journals and other sources material
- **http://arXiv.org** for sciences and statistics
- **Digitalgallery.nypl.org** – New York Public Library
- **Wikipedia** – 'List of digital library projects'

Know your field

The literature review is important for getting to know your field and examining this from multiple perspectives. Work with your material, considering it from different angles so that you develop a good understanding of what and who are important in your subject, and why. The higher the level of your work, and the longer it is, the more attention you should give to this.

Consider your field from the following angles. Check off ☑ each once you have considered its relevance fully in relation to your project.

☐ Origins

Undertake a preliminary broad survey of the material on the topic you have selected, tracing research on the topic and or specific issues back to their origins.

☐ Who or what started research into this area?

☐ What did they establish as important foundation points, facts or theories?

☐ Breadth

Read widely around the subject, selecting texts that represent well the various perspectives taken by experts in this area.

☐ Recurrent issues

Note recurrent themes and issues that might have a bearing on your own project.

☐ What are the recurrent issues or debates?

☐ What are the main points of disagreement between experts and why do these arise?

☐ Who disagrees with whom, and why?

☐ How has research into these issues taken forward our understanding of them over time?

☐ Whose position seems to be most respected in recent articles or reviews? Do you agree?

☐ Schools of thought

Note how the issues in the field are treated by the key schools of thought in your discipline.

☐ What are the main schools of thought in your field?

☐ What differentiates these? Are their differences mainly about ideology? Theory? Method? Politics? Other things?

☐ What position is taken on key issues by those who favour each of the main schools of thought?

☐ How do different schools of thought address the main issues that relate to your project?

☐ Which positions on the issues do you find the more convincing, and why?

☐ Journals

☐ Find out the specialist journals that cover material relevant to your chosen topic.

☐ Do any journals focus more on research for one school of thought rather than another?

☐ Browse abstracts of a range of journal articles.

☐ Identify relevant articles to read in full.

☐ People

Find out the leading figures writing on issues relevant to your selected topic – those whose primary research, theories or writings are regarded by academics as essential to know about, even if you do not read their work in detail.

☐ Who are they and what did each contribute?

☐ Which schools of thought are represented by their position?

☐ What do others find to be strengths or limitations in the research of each?

Know your field

☐ **Topicality and currency**

☐ What issues are most live in recent research publications in your field?

☐ How are these relevant in your topic?

☐ Which specialist articles cover these issues?

☐ **Pendulum swings**

Sometimes the pendulum swings backwards and forwards, with different perspectives or interpretations coming into favour or being rejected. If that is the case for an issue you are hoping to research:

☐ What are the alternative positions on the issue?

☐ Where does the pendulum lie at this point?

☐ **Methods**

☐ Are there standard methods for researching topics similar to the one you have in mind?

☐ Are there current methodological issues or problems in researching in this area? If so, what do you need to be mindful of for your own project?

☐ Are there particular challenges facing researchers in this field? If so, what are these and why do they arise? How will you address these in your own research?

☐ **Ideology**

☐ Are there ideological differences in the way the topic is written about? How does this affect the way the research is undertaken or received?

☐ How does this reflect your own position on the issue?

☐ How will you ensure that your own work is conducted in an objective way?

☐ **Application**

☐ How is research in your area being applied within the field, in industry or in everyday life?

☐ Do any of these inspire you to research such applications further?

☐ **Gaps**

☐ Which aspects are not yet fully researched?

☐ What do researchers point to as future research that will help advance understanding of the topic?

☐ **Trajectory and links**

How has published research in this area changed in direction over time? Be clear in your own mind how understanding of this topic has developed through successive pieces of research or theoretical works.

☐ Consider how each piece of research or set of ideas influenced others.

☐ Note how each piece of research picks up where previous research left off.

☐ Note the literature review section of the books, articles and theses that you read. Which previous pieces of research does each refer to, and how?

Note the chain of contributions …

- Who contributed to the topic?
- What was their contribution?
- What was the title of the research paper/text, and where were its full reference details?
- Was their work reviewed? If so, what strengths or limitations were identified?
- How did this get picked up by any further research, and by whom?

Reflection: Understand your field

Which of the aspects above are ones that you are most and least familiar with in your field – and which do you need to address?

Principles to inform the literature review

Once your literature search has given you a sense of the field, you will have to start to make choices about:

- where to focus the rest of your search
- what to follow up in depth
- what to include in your written review.

The following principles can help to make this part of the process more manageable.

Become increasingly focused

As you become clearer about your likely topic, your reading should become increasingly:

- specialist in content
- relevant to your title
- reflective about what you are finding and how this might be useful to you
- analytical and critical of the material you are considering for inclusion.

Include specialist material

Read at least some material that has been published in specialist journals, conference papers or as monographs. Look out for what is at the cutting edge of research in your subject. This is an area where your supervisor should be able to provide good leads for you to follow up.

As such material is written for experts, it can be difficult to read at first. If so, it can help to:

- read some general background first
- make use of any available reviews of the research, in journals or online.

For seminal research (that is, work which had a fundamental influence in the field), there will be many texts that provide background, explanations and analyses that you can draw upon.

Demonstrate your understanding

When considering what to include in your literature review, be careful to make choices that enable you to demonstrate that you have:

- a breadth of understanding of the field; this will be revealed partly through the intelligent way that you discuss the literature and also in the breadth of your references
- a depth of understanding of your specialist topic; this will be indicated by the kinds of specialist material to which you refer
- a good grasp of what is the most significant, and what is less so; this will be reflected in both your choices of what to include and the use you make of the material.

Be selective

As you read, start to make decisions about how, exactly, you will make use of the material in your own work. Ask yourself such questions as:

- Am I really going to use this at all?
- To which section, chapters, or themes of my work does it relate?
- Am I going to agree with it or challenge it?
- What do I want to say about it?
- Just how important is it compared with other things that I am reading?
- Is there a short quotation that I want to use from it? Will I be paraphrasing any section of it? Will I just be alluding to it in passing?

Decide on how much you will use

Consider whether you will refer to the material:

- simply as a passing reference (which will be the case for most of what you read)
- in a sentence, for more significant pieces of work
- in several sentences, if especially important
- in one or more paragraphs, if the research is really of exceptional importance and if your word limit permits.

The checklists on page 85 can help to focus your thinking about if, and how, to make use of material in your own work.

Selecting material to include

Clarify your purpose

As you uncover new material, make decisions about what to read, note or include in your own work – for what purpose and at what depth.

1 **Purpose.** How, specifically, will you draw upon it in your research? In which section of your report or dissertation will you refer to it?

2 **Depth of coverage.** How much will you write about it? Just briefly in passing, such as part of a list of citations? A line or two? In greater depth?

Using the checklist below

If it isn't immediately obvious why, how and where you would make use of material, browse through the following checklist to focus your decision-making.

It isn't likely that you would need to use this checklist for everything you read. The left-hand column helps decide how you would use it; the right-hand column how much to include.

Checklist: How would I use this material?

1 Purpose

Indicate ✓ all uses that apply.

I would use this material to:

1 ☐ indicate a key phase in the development of previous research in my field

2 ☐ draw attention to developments in, or limitations of, the theoretical base

3 ☐ identify developments or limitations in the methodologies used for researching the topic

4 ☐ show how my own research will draw on insights from its methodology or make use of its methods

5 ☐ make reference to its findings

6 ☐ demonstrate how it has contributed to the evidence base that I am drawing upon

7 ☐ draw upon its critique of relevant research, methods, theory, or interpretations of findings

8 ☐ show how it contributed to the general understanding of issues relevant to my project

9 ☐ replicate the work or test out an aspect of the research for myself

10 ☐ build further on that research in a particular way

11 ☐ illustrate a point that I am trying to make

12 ☐ indicate how it supports, or contradicts, my own findings or conclusions.

2 Depth of coverage?

I would make reference to this piece of material …

☐ Just in passing?

☐ In about a sentence?

☐ As a short paragraph?

☐ In several paragraphs?

Add any other ways you would use it.

Connecting it up: synthesis

Chart it out

To clarify your thinking, as you read, draw up a flow chart or table that makes clear to you the journey taken by research in the field. This may involve some complex links between several pieces of work. Note that you wouldn't normally include such a chart within the dissertation, long essay or report itself.

The origin: Who started the line of enquiry that leads, directly or indirectly, to your research?

Direction of travel: Who were the main theorists or researchers who built on that original piece of work, either adding to it in a major way or taking the line of enquiry in a different direction? What new perspectives, insights, or findings did they contribute? How are these relevant to your proposal?

Contributory players: Note short details of anyone whose work added to the direction of travel in some way. You may wish to refer to these, in passing, in your review or in the body of your dissertation.

Most recent contributors: What has been published in the last few years, if anything, that throws further light on the subject? How does this affect the way you are approaching your own proposal?

Themes: As you chart the information, take note of themes and issues to take into consideration, such as ideas about where to focus, what scale is likely to be manageable and how you might conduct your own research.

Work back along the chain

At as early a stage as possible, start to evaluate everything you choose to read in terms of its relevance and significance to your own selected title or hypothesis.

- Organise the material in such a way that you work back from your own hypothesis or research question to each piece of research that came before.
- Consider how each piece of research that you are thinking of including in your review built on previous research and theory. If it isn't relevant, don't include it.
- List those pieces of research, or developments in theory, that have had most influence on the subject.

The purpose of this is to keep your reading as manageable as possible, isolating the most relevant research to read about.

Follow the chain forward

Once you have worked back through the chain and you are clear what is relevant, you can then work with the material from the opposite direction. Consider your 'chain' forwards from the earliest research through to your own. This is the order in which you will write about it.

- Draw these out as a history starting from the earliest piece of research.
- Chart briefly how each influenced others in the chain, as outlined above, but now including only items relevant to your research.

Reflection: Connecting it up

- How can you best organise your material so that each of the most important links in the chain stands out clearly to you?
- Do you have a good sense of how the 'chain' of research developed for your topic? If not, how will you address this?

Writing your literature review

What is it for?

Your review of the literature provides the reader with background on the key aspects of previous research that have a bearing on your own project. The way this contributes to the assignment is detailed on page 187.

How long should it be?

You include this towards the start of your work, and it would normally take about 10–15% of the word limit.

When should I write it?

Start writing the first draft of your literature review alongside your reading; capture anything that is relevant from your early reading. Unless you are required to hand in your literature review as part of the approval process for your proposal, do not finalise your drafts too early. It is better to wait until:

- you have decided on the title or hypothesis – and this has been agreed by your supervisor
- you complete the overall proposal, and this is accepted by the ethics panel (if relevant)
- you have completed the bulk of the reading that you expect to do.

If you do this, it reduces the likelihood of needing to rewrite the review substantially later on.

What should I include?

Provide a succinct summary of previous research and theory. Include only that which has a bearing on your own project. If you charted the trajectory of that research as recommended on page 86, then this should be relatively easy to write. Include reference to:

- the research that, originally, started off this line of enquiry
- milestones in the research that deepened understanding or took it in a new direction
- the findings from that research that influenced the way you have designed your own research.

By the end of the review, it should be clear to the reader how your project both:

- draws upon previous research, *and*
- differs from what has gone before, building upon it in some way.

What style should I use?

Aim to write the review so that it provides a sense of:

- key issues and debates
- why these are meaningful
- the 'story' of research into the topic to date, rather like a relay race, up to the point where you are taking up the baton.

Avoid

- lengthy descriptions of the literature
- summarising literature without clarifying what it contributes to the field
- writing up your review more or less as a list, without engaging with debates and without drawing out the significance of material included.

Examples: writing style

✗ ☹ *Jones (1997) said oil-based products were 'dangerous for those with heart and liver conditions'. Xiang (2001) said oil-based products could be used for those with heart conditions. This illustrates differences in opinion.*

The above example is poor because it lists only 'what' was found. The better example, below, gives a more precise sense of significance and of the relationships between pieces of research.

✓ ☺ *Jones (1997) demonstrated the risks of oil-based products for heart and liver patients. Xiang (2001) showed that grape seed oil did not have the cholesterol effects predicted by Jones; this led to the extension of the treatment to heart patients.*

The literature review

It is an art to select and cover the literature in a way that addresses the various requirements for breadth, depth, brevity, relevance and understanding. Consider the checklist below before writing your literature review and return to it as you write. Check off ☑ each item when you are satisfied that you have addressed it as well as you can.

Breadth and depth

☐ I incorporate reference to a broad range of sources within my review.

☐ I include reference to specialist sources or articles that are relevant to my project.

☐ These sources all appear in my bibliography and/ or list of references.

☐ I make brief, 'passing references' to many sources relevant in some way to my research.

Understanding and judgement

☐ My literature review demonstrates that I understand my field (see pages 82–3).

☐ The items that I refer to in the literature review demonstrate that I recognise which sources are most significant for my topic.

☐ I have given due recognition to seminal pieces of work in this field.

☐ The way I make use of the literature indicates that I understand what I have read.

☐ I have allocated the most space (or words) to those sources that are most relevant to my own project.

☐ It is clear that my reading is up to date and covers the most recent publications.

Organisation, relevance, coherence

☐ All the literature to which I have referred is relevant in some way to my research.

☐ There is a logical order to the way that I introduce sources.

☐ The way I present my sources 'tells the story' of the development of research relevant to my own project.

☐ I have made it clear how each item contributed, in some way, to developments in the debates, research or theory relevant to my own research.

☐ I have made clear the connections between different items included in my literature review.

☐ I have made clear how previous research leads up to the point where my own research will begin.

Style, brevity and criticality

☐ I refer to sources in a critically evaluative way, focusing on their specific contribution and/or limitations.

☐ I make every word count – wordy sentences are rewritten more concisely so that I can make reference to more pieces of relevant research.

☐ I avoid describing sources at length.

☐ I avoid long quotations (of more than a few words).

☐ I have stayed close to my planned word limit for this section.

☐ I have edited out irrelevant matter such as interesting tangents and anecdotes.

Chapter 10
Principles of good research

Discipline differences

Each academic discipline approaches research in a different way. Those differences are core to what defines the discipline as a distinct, specialist area of study. Your course of study will draw upon one or more such disciplines.

The research in each discipline varies along a number of key dimensions such as:

- *the subject matter*, or topics and research questions that each considers suitable for its domain of knowledge
- *the philosophy*, or the principles that underlie their preferred research methodologies
- *the raw material*, or primary sources, used as the basis of analysis
- *the techniques* or methods that best suit the subject matter, philosophy and raw materials.

It follows from this that there isn't a single universally accepted set of approaches for academic research. Depending on your subject and the research question, there will, of necessity, be characteristic ways of collecting and working with information. These in turn, generate particular methodological and ethical issues.

I had been going to use a mixed methodological approach of interpretivist, phenomenological, ethnographic, critical analysis, with a smattering of empiricism ... but the methodology section then took up my whole word limit.

Yet again, Cassie was full of excuses ...

What makes good research?

Despite differences from one discipline to another, there are some broadly accepted principles of good research. Key considerations are outlined here.

'Fit-for-purpose' research design

Good research chooses the most appropriate method for yielding the most accurate results, in the most ethical and efficient ways, to answer the research question and meet the overall research brief.

Precision and clarity

Precision and clarity are essential to every aspect of your work:

- in defining your terms
- in measuring only what you set out to measure
- in how careful and exacting you are in controlling for variables
- in how you record methods, observations and findings
- in how you present what you find out
- in how you write up your findings and phrase your conclusions.

Integrity

Research should:

- build on previous research (pages 81–6)
- attribute fully anything drawn on from other people's work (page 79)
- adhere to ethical codes (Chapter 12)
- aim to avoid prejudice and bias
- avoid any kind of cheating or deception in gathering material and analysing it
- avoid misrepresenting findings.

Respect for the discipline

Even experts within a subject discipline grapple with the philosophical and methodological issues that confront researchers in that field. This makes it advisable for those newer to research to draw on the principles of research already established within the discipline. If you draw on methods from other branches of knowledge, find out about the broader methodological and ethical issues that inform them.

If you do wish to draw on approaches and methods from other disciplines or to invent your own methods, always talk these through with your supervisor first.

Theoretical underpinning

Academic research is grounded in theory. Any one piece of research builds on existing understandings, interpretations and explanations. A good piece of research identifies the theories that are most apposite to the topic and research question, and teases out how these throw light on the issue. Your own report, dissertation or thesis then needs to be clear about the extent to which your research findings support or challenge existing theory.

Congruence

Congruence means that there is consistency and coherence between different aspects of your research. Your choice of topic, methodology, methods and participants as well as the way you design materials, apply ethical codes, carry out your research and report it should all be mutually supporting and make sense in terms of each other.

Find out about your discipline

Read closely the methods sections of research articles in your discipline's specialist journals. Notice how they design the research to achieve precise and accurate findings. The checklist on page 96 can help you to focus your analysis of journal articles for this purpose.

Research design

Your research design is the way that you set up and conduct your research to find out the answer to the question implicit in your research title – or to test your research hypothesis (page 116).

The design includes such aspects as:

- *your methodology*: the principles that inform the way you make choices and decisions in designing, undertaking and writing up your research

- *your choice of raw material*, whether documents, data, or the characteristics you look for when selecting participants

- *your chosen methods* for collecting data, including any conditions you create for undertaking your research

- *materials you develop*, such as information provided to participants

- *your methods of recording information* at each stage of your research

- *analytical methods you employ*, such as the statistical approaches, formulae or analytical techniques that you apply to your raw data or source materials.

Good research design

A well designed project brings together all of these aspects so that they are mutually supporting: the techniques you use for gathering information and the way you use and interpret these are consistent and congruent.

In a poorly designed project, the thinking is inconsistent or incoherent. Separate aspects pull in different directions or undermine each other. For example, the methods might not match the philosophy that the research purports to espouse, or are unlikely to provide the kinds of information needed to answer the research question.

Fit for purpose

In effect, the quality of the research design is determined by whether it is fit for purpose, taking on board such factors as the brief, the context, ethical considerations and any constraints. This is important for any research but is a particular consideration if your brief was set for a client such as an organisation or employer.

Examples: 'fit for purpose' design

Below are employers' views of how well students designed research projects. Note the strengths and weaknesses that they spotted.

Employer 1

The best project I have seen was where a social work student used a methodology which was risky and quite unusual but it fitted the brief perfectly. She used rich picture methodology to depict people's experience of using our day services for older adults. The methodology resulted in a very visual representation of the service users' experiences. It was immediately understood by other workers at the centre and much more effective than if she had presented us with a summary of findings on a 1–5 scale.

Employer 2

We wanted the student projects to provide methods that had a good chance of testing our hypotheses. It seemed to us that some just stuck to methods they were comfortable with even if these weren't a good fit with what we needed.

Employer 3

I see a lot of projects struggling because of poor questionnaires. What I mean by that is, the students used a lot of closed questions because it was easier for them to work with that kind of data. In fact, all this gave us was a limited set of responses that didn't help our understanding of the issue at all.

Objectivity and subjectivity

Both objectivity and subjectivity can be appropriate to good research, depending on the discipline and the nature of the research.

Objectivity

Objectivity is both an intention on the part of the researcher and a method that forms part of the research design.

- **Intention**: the researcher sets out to be as objective as possible, as an ideal.
- **Research design**: the researcher draws on, or devises, methods that are carefully thought through to ensure that the results are not skewed, either deliberately or accidentally, by personal preference or bias.

Often these two aspects go hand in hand, but not always: you might aim to be objective but use methods that allow personal bias to enter without realising and acknowledging this.

The aim of objective research is to remove your personal feelings and responses from the equation so that the findings could be the same irrespective of who carried out the research. This is easier to attain for hard sciences and other subjects which focus on the physical world and/or measurable items, in the search for 'universal' laws. It is more difficult to attain this fully in social sciences, arts and media.

Methods used for objective research

For objective styles of research, the researcher specifies their hypotheses or informed judgements about what is likely to occur, or be discovered, under certain conditions. The researcher then sets up the conditions to test these out, using methods such as carefully defined terms, controlled experiments or observation, close measurement, or surveys with closed questions. As little as possible is left to chance or to alternative interpretations.

Subjectivity

Subjective approaches acknowledge that the methods and results will vary as a result of the researchers themselves – the results would not be exactly the same without their personal input. Subjective approaches are used across all disciplines, including sciences, but are valued differently depending on the discipline.

For some, such as counselling, psychotherapy and the arts, subjectivity is held in high regard: you are encouraged to take note of your own emotional or aesthetic responses. However, you would usually be expected to interpret these by drawing on relevant theoretical frameworks. In other words, you need to make sense of personal experience within the context of research within your subject.

Checklist: objectivity/subjectivity

In my subject disciplines, it is assumed that research methods will be

☐ Objective (always)

☐ Subjective (always)

☐ More objective than subjective

☐ More subjective than objective

☐ Combining objectivity and subjectivity

☐ All of the above are acceptable.

Activity ⟳ Objectivity and subjectivity

Browse through the methods sections of at least ten dissertations and/or journal articles in your subject discipline.

How do the authors design their methods so as to reflect the degree of objectivity/subjectivity that would be expected?

Jot down your thoughts and ideas about what you learn from browsing these items. Check that your own research meets requirements in similar ways.

Quantitative and qualitative approaches

Quantitative approaches

Quantitative research focuses on what can be measured in an objective way, using data such as that drawn from experiments; structured observations; closed questions in surveys, questionnaires and structured interviews; published data sets.

Advantages

- They enable study on a broader scale, such as through online surveys, generating large amounts of data which can be analysed relatively easily using relevant software.
- The research questions or hypotheses tend to be very precisely articulated, allowing the possibility of precise answers.
- The scale of the research makes it easier to draw reasonably valid generalisations in a relatively short timeframe.
- They help establish patterns such as trends in behaviour or, in science, 'universal laws'.
- Projects that use quantitative approaches are generally easier to plan and to contain in size, making them ideal for student projects.

Disadvantages

- Not everything is easily measured. There is a risk of gaining skewed understanding of a phenomenon as a result of omitting those aspects that can't be measured.
- There is a risk of gaining rather banal results.
- The results can lack ecological validity.

Qualitative approaches

Qualitative research endeavours to extend our understanding of human behaviour, individually and collectively, by investigating the underlying causes for people acting and thinking as they do. Such approaches entail a greater degree of subjectivity, which is either controlled for in the research design or acknowledged as a feature of the research.

Qualitative approaches draw on methods such as in-depth case studies, open-ended survey questions, unstructured interviews, focus groups, or unstructured observations. These can be used to investigate such things as attitudes, attributes, features, qualities, comments, images, feelings, themes in narratives, or the particulars of individual events and occurrences. These can be applied usefully to a range of subject disciplines where the material is more difficult to reduce to a set of measurable entities.

Advantages

- They tend to more open-ended, allowing a greater set of responses to emerge.
- They are useful for in-depth analysis of individual people, businesses, events and occurrences.
- They have greater ecological validity.

Disadvantages

- Findings may be useful to the particular case but not more generally applicable.
- They can be unpredictable, making them harder to manage and contain.

Composite approaches

In arts, media, business and social sciences, it is not unusual to combine these approaches. Creative approaches can be used to find ways of measuring soft data such as feelings, attitudes and responses. Some social scientists are critical of the distinction between qualitative and quantitative approaches (see Pring, 2000).

Checklist: quantitative/qualitative

My subject discipline tends to:

☐ use quantitative methods
☐ use qualitative methods
☐ use a composite of these
☐ repudiate, philosophically, a division between quantitative and qualitative methods.

Validity

Ensuring validity

A key task for you as a researcher is to ensure that your research measures or investigates exactly what it claims to do. Generally, this means creating conditions that enable you to have as much control as possible over anything that might interfere with your results. To do this, you eliminate, or at least reduce to a minimum, any extraneous factors that might lead to confusion about what your results mean. Your aim is to set up your research in such a way that you reduce to a minimum the chance that your findings could be open to more than one, equally valid, interpretation. (See Chapter 16, Experiments.)

For many topics, there will be a limit to how far you can control the conditions. Where people form part of the material to be measured, human individual variability means that it is impossible to control for every variable. To keep the research manageable and clear, you make decisions about which factors you wish to isolate and 'control' in some way, and which to ignore for that particular piece of research.

Ecological validity

One disadvantage of controlling for variables is that, although the results may be clear, precise and more easily measurable, they may not hold true outside of the controlled research conditions or in the 'real world'. For example, if you measure the growth of a plant under coloured filters in controlled laboratory conditions, those conditions may eliminate other variables such as trace elements in the soil or the behaviour of pests that would impact on the plant under natural conditions. This means that results gained in controlled conditions may lack ecological validity.

This can be even more of an issue for research into human behaviours. Humans in everyday life respond to complex sets of conditions such as peer pressure, family influences, the weather or the season, trends in thinking or taste, the pressures of everyday life, items in the news, and myriad other factors that might give rise to a different set of responses from those gathered under controlled conditions.

The relative importance of ecological validity versus the advantages of results gained under precise, tightly controlled conditions depends very much on what you are trying to find out. It may not matter very much at all – or it could be significant.

What kind of validity?

For my research project, it is better to:

☐ control for variables for more precise results

☐ aim for ecological validity.

Reliability and replication

For disciplines that value objective approaches, conduct your research in such a manner that, if the research were to be repeated under exactly the same conditions by yourself or others, the findings would be the same. In other words, you should aim to set up the research so that you, or someone else, could replicate it.

This means conducting it in such a way that

- exactly the same resources or types of participant would be available
- the methods could be repeated in identical ways
- controlled conditions are used, if feasible.

Attention to process and detail

Why does it matter?

Good research pays close attention to the details of each step in the process. This is for a number of reasons:

The integrity of your findings: Your findings, conclusions or recommendations are premised on your methods being appropriate, your measurements being accurate and/or your judgements being well-based. You need to provide precise details in your research so that it is evident that this is the case.

Making your case: Your dissertation or report should demonstrate exactly what you did and why, or why you drew the conclusions that you did. You cannot demonstrate that well if your thinking is imprecise and if your methods lacked precision, system, order, clarity and accuracy.

Retracing your steps: If something starts to go awry during the research, or if your results don't make sense, you need to be able to retrace your steps and locate the problem quickly and easily.

Verification: At the end of your research, your records should make it possible for you or anyone else to verify your results for themselves, either by tracking your process as written in your report, or by replicating your research to test your findings.

Careful controls

For many kinds of research, careful controls are put in place to ensure that the data that is collected will provide the kind of evidence base that is needed. Depending on the discipline, this might mean taking care with such things as:

- controlling the experimental conditions (pages 125 and 138–40)
- selecting an unbiased sample
- ensuring the provenance, authenticity or dating of documents, artefacts or sample materials.

Recording the exact conditions

For your research to be verifiable or open to replication, there must be an excellent record of how you conducted it at every stage. Include close details of anything which might have an effect on the results or your findings, such as:

- which documentation and sources you used in order to piece together an event or incident, such as a historical or political event or an incident in the workplace
- details about how you selected your participants, how you briefed them about the research, exactly what you asked them to do, and any other salient characteristics of the research conditions
- details of every step in setting up, conducting experiments and recording observations and results.

Controlling for variables

Controlling materials and environments

It is relatively easy to control some aspects such as the amounts and types of materials used; the technology, equipment and software used; the conditions under which the research is undertaken, such as location, time of day or year, light, temperature, pressure, atmosphere; current, or other factors of the physical environment. Even slight changes in the amounts of chemicals, light or other factors might lead to different results.

Working with participants

When working with participants, it isn't possible to control for every variable but you need to be clear about which variables were controlled for. This is examined in more detail in Part 3.

Journal articles: methodology and methods

Use specialist journals in your subject to develop your understanding of methodological frameworks, methods and approaches relevant to your subject discipline, participants or raw materials. Check off ☑ each aspect once you have considered it. Jot down notes that will help you in designing your research and selecting methods to use.

☐ **Methodology**
- Do the authors refer directly to the philosophical or methodological principles that inform their research? If so, in which sections of the report do they do so?
- If not, what can you tease out about methodological thinking in your subject discipline?

☐ **Data/raw material/sources**
- With what kinds of materials do researchers in your field work with most commonly? (Pages 121–8)
- What kinds of data/information are generated through using these materials or sources?
- What kinds of methodological issues do you think are raised by working with such data or sources?

☐ **Methods and techniques**
- What kinds of methods are used for gathering material or data in your subject?
- Which of these appear to be the most typical?
- What tips did you pick up on techniques you could replicate or adapt for your own research?

☐ **Ethical considerations**
- What kinds of ethical issues are referred to with respect to the methods used?
- How are such ethical matters addressed?
- What considerations does this raise for how you would conduct your own research?

☐ **Equipment, software and tools**
- What kinds of equipment or software, if any, are used for gathering, collating or analysing the kind of data that you aim to collect?
- What kinds of tools do researchers in your subject design for themselves?
- What ideas do these give you for collecting and recording information for your project?

☐ **Critique of methods and techniques**
- How did the authors critique their own methods? What kinds of issues did they raise?
- For your subject, where does that critique appear in the report? (The Discussion section? The main body? The conclusion?)
- What insights does this give you about how to critique your own methods in the relevant section of your own report or dissertation?
- What lessons can you learn from what the authors say about the research methods that they used? How would you use those lessons in devising your own research methods?

☐ **Style for writing about methods**
- What kind of writing style is used in writing up methods sections of reports/articles?
- How succinct, or wordy, are these sections?
- What kinds of specialist terminology are used? Are you comfortable using such language?

☐ **Any other observations**
- What other observations did you make from your browsing and reading of journal articles that would be useful for your own dissertation, research project or long essay?

Chapter 11
Methodological approaches

Methodology

The methodology is the overarching approach to the research. Dawson (2012) describes methodology as 'the philosophy or the general principle which will guide your research'. When deciding on your methodology, you are considering the bigger 'how' and 'why' issues from which should flow, logically, your other decisions about how to conduct your research.

These big issues will be nuanced differently depending on your subject, but they include factors such as:

- the research paradigm(s) that influence all research in your field
- the theories about research that inform research in your field
- the role of the researcher – and how your own behaviours might impact on the outcomes of the research
- the ethical considerations that are most salient to your area of study
- the research methods best for gathering particular kinds of data or testing particular kinds of hypothesis.

From such understandings, you will be better placed to make methodological choices such as whether qualitative or quantitative, subjective or objective approaches are most appropriate to answering your research question.

Terminology

There isn't complete consistency in research terminology. Some variations to be aware of are:

- how far writers, and lecturers, distinguish between 'methods' and 'methodology'
- terms such as 'design frame', 'research design, 'research framework' or 'approach' may be used differently from one publication to another. The general meaning is usually still evident.

Research paradigms

'Paradigm' is a term coined by Kuhn (1970) to refer to a broad overarching framework, or integrated set of assumptions, about how research should be conducted. Two key paradigms to be aware of are:

- scientific (or, in social sciences, positivism)
- interpretivism.

Even if you do not need to write about these in your work, it is worth knowing what they are so you understand references to them in seminars or your reading. It is worth noting that some authors, such as Atkinson (1995), find research methods too varied to be encompassed by these paradigms.

Methodological approaches

This chapter looks at several of the most common methodologies.

- Empiricism
- Historical
- Action research
- Phenomenological
- Grounded theory
- Ethnographic
- Critical theory

Research paradigms: scientific and positivist

Scientific approaches

Scientific research is based on a set of shared assumptions, developed over hundreds of years, about how the physical, or natural, world should best be studied in order to derive an objective knowledge of the 'laws' that govern it. The assumption is that, at least above the quantum level, these laws are universal, coherent and mutually supporting. They are arrived at through:

- maintaining a neutral, disinterested stance in the pursuit of indisputable, objectively established, 'facts' or truths

- testing theories (explanations of why things happen)

- building systematically on theories that have best withstood previous rigorous testing

- aiming to establish cause and effect

- comparing only 'like' with 'like', making only justified, valid comparisons

- precision and exactitude – in terminology, use of language, definitions, methods, recording, reporting, and conclusions

- controlling research conditions, such as the type and quantity of material, heat and light, so as to isolate the object of study; this makes it manifest which variables are being manipulated and what occurs as a result.

Scientific voice

The style of scientific writing is consistent with the research methodology. Text is written in an objective way:

- there is no reference to the researcher as a person – there is no reference to 'I' or 'we' or 'you' – you wouldn't write '*I mixed two substances …*'

- the research seems to conduct itself or to be conducted by an invisible character in the background: '*two substances were mixed …*'

- interpretations, too, appear to be made by a neutral entity rather than by a researcher or author that feels 'present' to the reader:
'*the results indicate*' rather than '*I think the results indicate …*'

Positivism

Positivism asserts that the social world can be studied using methods akin to those in the physical sciences. It is characterised by:

- a belief that the social world can and should be studied objectively

- a search for generalisable findings

- use of quantitative approaches

- defining terms and units of study precisely so as to enable measurement of these and to enable justified comparisons

- the removal of the individuality of the researcher from the research process: the aim is that findings would be the same irrespective of who conducts the research

- the assumption that a researcher's own ideological beliefs, points of view, values or personality, do not need to affect the results of research – and should not do so.

Choice of positivist paradigm

The application of scientific methods is more complex when humans are involved, not least because of the difficulties in tying down the impact of variables such as 'choice' or 'consciousness'. When people are the object of study, the research does not always lend itself to investigation based on clearly definable and measurable units.

However, it is often possible to isolate variables such as age, gender, disability, parental status, or occupation that allow for a more 'scientific' analysis of data. The 'right' paradigm depends on the field of study and the research question.

Research paradigms: interpretivism

The interpretivist paradigm offers an alternative way of understanding knowledge within social sciences and in areas such as health studies and counselling.

Interpretivism/Constructivism

Interpretivism is sometimes also referred to as constructivism, or social constructivism as it is interested in the way that people construct perceptions of the world. In its purest form, it lies at the opposite end of the spectrum to scientific research. It considers it unlikely, if not impossible, that a researcher could stand outside of the context in which they form judgements, and so they could not really be 'neutral' observers.

The basic tenets of interpretivism

Not 'out there': For interpretivists, knowledge isn't a neutral, external set of facts or laws that are waiting 'out there' to be discovered in a depersonalised or abstract way. Rather, knowledge is constructed through societies and through the act of research itself.

Social variability: What constitutes knowledge, and how it is interpreted, varies from one society to the next.

Immersion: Researchers should 'immerse' themselves in the context that they are studying, observing it in fine detail, from mass interactions down to minutiae of non-verbal clues – the nods, shrugs, coughs and stammers.

Contextuality: To make full sense of research, you would need to investigate the broader structures and rich contexts in which it is constructed; 'to know' means taking on board such things as the mental structures, belief systems, behaviours, and the range of social norms within which such knowing takes place.

Subjectivity: Knowledge, research and interpretations are necessarily subjective, as they are part and parcel of particular societies at particular times.

Personal insights: Researchers can call upon their own insights and experiences as 'people' to help understand how others think, behave and interact, acknowledging their own subjectivity.

Positioning: Researchers' thinking is constructed too: as individuals, they cannot stand outside of all ideological positions.

Researcher impact: A researcher's own position forms part of the process and, of necessity, has some impact on that process. That impact should be considered as part of the research and its reporting.

Inter-textuality: Sets of texts, including research reports, are informed by other sets of texts. A text cannot be understood in isolation from the society in which it was produced or texts that preceded it. Researchers' positions are similarly informed by previous texts.

Generalisations: These are not the goal of interpretivist research and you wouldn't be expected to draw any.

The impact on style

Unlike the 'scientific voice' (page 98), the researcher is more apparent in the process. The writing style reflects this by using:

- first person: I; we; our; us
- active voice: I found … (rather than 'it was found …')

Purity of paradigm?

In practice, paradigms cannot always be applied in their pure forms. For example, the potential or actual impacts of researchers' behaviours and position are acknowledged even in the sciences. Interpretivists vary in how far they consider that researchers can bring objectivity and distance to their methods and how far it is appropriate to call upon personal experience and insights.

Methodology: empiricism

Empirical research is based on data collection: on experimentation, observation and measurement. This is typical of science subjects and the positivist research tradition. The researcher formulates a hypothesis and then devises controlled conditions to test it out.

For experimental research, the research would be conducted through manipulating carefully isolated variables. For controlled observations, the researcher may not be controlling all variables in the same way, but would make a careful selection of what would be observed and how, in order to produce securely identifiable and measurable results.

Determinism and causation

Typically, experimental research in sciences and social sciences looks to establish cause and effect. It seeks to ascertain that whenever one set of conditions pertains (such as heated flame, oxygen and fuel), then the outcome will always be the same (a particular kind of fire). The conditions, or cause, determine the effect.

A key concern when designing and interpreting scientific research findings is to ensure that the variables can be isolated and conditions controlled in such ways that reasonable certainty can be established between cause and effect. There is, otherwise, the risk that because two or more things seem to happen in tandem, or are apparently associated in some way, the relationship between them is not one of cause and effect.

Researchers need to clarify:

- whether it is simply coincidental that two things seem to occur, or change, at the same time
- whether the incidence of, or change in, one thing, or variable, is related to changes in the other variables (umbrellas are opened; it rains)
- whether any connection between variables is direct, or indirect
- which of the two variables is the cause and which is showing the effect? For example, rain and the opening of umbrellas occur together, but putting up an umbrella doesn't cause it to rain.

Advantages and opportunities

- The methodology can be adapted to suit many kinds of student project, from the most basic through to a thesis.
- It can be scaled to suit the time and resources available for student projects.

Disadvantages and risks

- Closely controlled experiments can lack ecological validity (see page 137).
- Experiments often do not go to plan.
- They can demand a great deal of patience, waiting for the experiment to run its course and to collect the data.
- When people are involved, it becomes harder to control the conditions (see page 140).

Gita went to extraordinary lengths to control every possible independent variable

Methodology: historical

Historical methods can be used to research the background of issues in any discipline, rather than only by those studying history.

Use of evidence

You can draw on a range of primary sources to work out what is likely to have happened, in what order and why. Sources might include anything from written documents, letters, laws, film, artefacts and architecture through to oral testimonies, published material (used as a primary source), film, etc.

Typically, you would triangulate evidence across many sources in order to build up a rich and accurate construction of the time period, theme, historical event, or life of a particular person. You would also look to work with the original source, wherever possible, rather than with facsimiles or later printed editions.

Characteristics

Unlike empirical research, historical research:

- examines the past, so is not based on direct observation (though it may draw on other people's observations as raw material)
- is generally concerned with the 'particular' rather than the 'universal', with unique events and the impact of individuals
- looks, where relevant, for common themes and patterns but not usually to establish universal laws
- is highly conscious of the complexity of events, so is cautious about attributing direct 'cause' and effect in a deterministic way
- normally focuses on what did happen, as far as we can tell, rather than hypothesising about 'counterfactuals' (that is, what might have happened if conditions had been different)
- uses a range of sources and methods to piece together a picture and draw likely conclusions and explanations
- constructs a narrative that provides the most logical interpretation of the evidence.

For original research, given the time it takes to find and piece together the data, you may need to focus the subject very narrowly, such as to a short timeframe and/or a particular locality and/or theme.

Advantages and opportunities

- Almost anything can be studied from a historical perspective.
- You can be creative in drawing on many different resources.
- Vast resources are available, generally without charge.

Disadvantages and risks

- It can be difficult to select the most relevant material from the large amount of primary material available.
- There are often gaps in the records and data, making it difficult to know how much weight to give to the material that is available.
- For more recent history, resources may not be as readily available, as many sensitive documents are not made available to the public until a certain number of years has elapsed.

Objectivity and subjectivity

There is an aim to be as objective as possible in historical research – which means removing any unnecessary bias rather than assuming that 'scientific' objectivity can be achieved. It is evident that the historical narratives that have been created are reflective of the ideologies and assumptions of the times when they were written.

Methodology: action research

Characteristics

Action research, based on the work of Lewin (1946), is generally undertaken as participant research by practitioners into an area related to their own work, with a view to improving professional practice. It is typical of areas such as education, social sciences, health, and caring professions but can be applied within other fields.

For action research, the researcher:

- identifies an issue or problem that needs to be resolved
- involves co-workers or other relevant people as co-researchers
- works as part of this group in a 4-stage cyclical process of (1) planning for action; (2) undertaking action; (3) observation; and (4) reflection
- uses the reflection on the first cycle to review how far the solution is working, still pertinent or applicable to other contexts, and develop the idea for further action through a second cycle of active research; this might continue for many cycles
- is part of the change process rather than an outside investigator
- devises ways of measuring the change that occurs as a result of the action taken, evaluating its impact
- can utilise diverse research methods, as relevant to the project.

Advantages and opportunities

- There are several different models to choose from (see Hart and Bond, 1995).
- It is useful for research into the impact of service delivery such as through measuring the social return on investment.
- It is useful for providing a chance to research in a way that makes a difference to your own workplace or community.
- It is useful if you are in work already, to add interest and build links with like-minded colleagues.
- It can give a sense of 'shared ownership' of the research, as usually it involves a group working together.
- It can develop reflective and team-working skills, as these are core to the methodology.

Disadvantages and risks

- It is more difficult if you are not already skilled to some extent in working collaboratively with others.
- It is challenging, as you are seeking to effect change as well as study it.
- It is demanding in terms of your own integrity when describing results.
- Findings will be specific to that group, so are unlikely to lead to generalisations.
- Group research might not meet the assignment brief, especially for the autonomous study usually required for student dissertations and projects.
- The results of the action, or the decisions of others involved, may mean that the research veers away from the assignment brief.
- Workplace conditions tend to change for a variety of reasons outside of the researchers' control. This makes it hard to sustain the research and/or to demonstrate clearly that change is the result only of the actions you took.
- There can also be difficulties in gaining permission to conduct research, access data, use work premises, or report on conditions in the workplace.

Methodology: phenomenology, grounded theory

Characteristics of phenomenology

Phenomenology has its origins in the philosophy of Husserl (1962). It values an individual's subjective experience, focusing on emotions, feelings, beliefs and perceptions, presenting these in ways 'true' to the individual. It prioritises description and interpretation over analysis, and uses methods likely to elicit rich, nuanced material:

- open-ended interviews
- unstructured observations
- diaries, blogs, journals, letters,
- drawings, stories and other creative material.

It eschews methods which, by defining questions or making any kind of assumption in advance, could limit the findings of the research. It avoids:

- testing hypotheses, as these state an assumption as to what the research will find
- closed questions or structured interviews, as these set limitations on potential responses.

Some phenomenologists want to understand why an individual came to understand their experience the way they do, and so draw on contextual information relevant to that individual. They value the fusion of the perceptions of both individual and researcher (Gadamer, 1990).

Advantages and opportunities

- Provides rich data, allowing researchers to study individual experience in depth.
- Useful in areas such as health and medicine, where the lived experiences of patients or practitioners are of key interest.
- May have practical outcomes that make a real difference to the life of individuals.

Disadvantages and risks

- Can generate much unusable information that is time-consuming to work with.
- The experience of an individual may not be representative of that of others.
- It is more difficult to identify the impact of the researcher's own subjective role.

Grounded theory

Most research in the social sciences starts with a theory or hypothesis, which is then tested though gathering data. Grounded theory turns that method on its head (Glaser, 1995; Glaser and Strauss, 1967).

The approach is based on generating data first and then using it to derive theory inductively (Strauss and Corbin, 1990). The data can be quantitative, based on close observation, or qualitative, derived from talking to participants through interviews and focus groups. The approach is responsive to emerging findings, so that, in practice, methods and theory develop organically as the researcher goes along. This continues up to the point where new information becomes redundant – that is, adds nothing further to what has been discovered.

Advantages

Grounded theory is more common in education and health-related disciplines. It is open to unpredictable results, which can themselves lead to unexpected findings and applications. This means that new areas of enquiry can emerge. It also doesn't prescribe how much evidence is needed in advance, so can keep extending its reach until a pattern is established.

Disadvantages and risks

Its strengths can also be disadvantages for time-bound, resource-limited student assignments. Students may have to bring their research to a premature end, rather than letting the research run its natural course. They may also be required to be more specific in their proposal than this method requires.

Methodology: ethnography

Ethnography

Ethnographic research originated in anthropology (Malinowski, 1922, 1935; Mead 1928). Anthropologists typically study peoples and cultures other than their own. The approach has been adopted more broadly, especially in health and in education, for research into local community settings such as hospitals or classrooms.

Ethnographers participate as fully as possible in the life of the community or the group being studied, rather than standing back in a purely observer role. The aim is to gain a holistic understanding from the society's own point of view (Spradley, 1980). The researchers observe everyday life and/or particular events, looking for patterns and generalisations, making notes and writing these up so that others can gain an insight into that culture.

There are particular ethical issues to consider when making yourself part of a community whilst simultaneously researching it as an observer, not least those of trust and confidentiality. Reflexivity, or heightened introspective self-awareness, is an important aspect of this approach (Woods, 2006) in order to understand how your own beliefs and interests might affect the way you make sense out of what you find.

Ethnographers lay great emphasis on the nature of the written report or text, and the ethics of what to include or omit, given that this purports to depict a particular group. Generally, it would be argued that the report represents just one interpretation or 'construction' of the society rather than, necessarily, a 'true' representation in an absolute sense.

Advantages and opportunities

- It can be undertaken in a wide range of settings, from classrooms to work-based settings, focusing on a particular group.
- It can yield rich data and a holistic understanding of the society.
- Researchers can gain a good understanding of the broader context that leads to phenomena or behaviours arising, and the consequences of these.
- It offers high levels of ecological validity.

Disadvantages and risks

- It can be a time-consuming process, which creates practical issues for student research projects, where there may not be sufficient time to form part of the group.
- You might not be accepted into the group.
- Your presence in the group might disrupt what would otherwise have happened.
- Immersion in a society may make it difficult to remain objective.
- You might not be aware of how far the group is acting differently simply because of your presence or actions as a researcher; this makes it harder to know whether your findings are accurate and valid.
- It can generate a 'pixilated' view of a community or society based on disparate stories and pieces of research, rather than a coherent evidence base.

Useful reading

Reading seminal anthropological texts, such as those by Mead and Malinowski, provides important grounding in this approach. However, thinking has moved on a great deal since then. For an introduction to ethnography, see Hammersley and Atkinson (1983).

Life history approach

This looks to understanding a community via descriptions of the lives of a few of its individuals, possibly drawing on phenomenology.

Methodology: critical theory

Many disciplines within the arts, humanities and social sciences draw on critical theory in order to bring close critical analysis to the object of study.

There is a nuanced variation in how critical theory is applied in each discipline. However, experts in critical theory tend to be relatively familiar with developments in other disciplines: there has been significant application of theory across the boundaries of subject disciplines.

Characteristics

The research methodology is characterised by:

- an interest in social constructs such as identity, meaning and ideology, especially constructs that may be less easy to identity because they are woven into the fabric of everyday thought, communication or relationships
- identifying how particular theories or tools of critical analysis will be applied in the research
- applying theoretical perspectives in order to make a close critical analysis of the material
- investigating the relationships of component parts to each other, their context or other texts
- drawing broader conclusions about ideology, political positions, social consequences, ethical implications or similar.

Semiotics/Semiology

This is the study of meaning – or how societies and cultures represent themselves through systems of signs and symbols. Signs or symbols might by anything from how social status is represented through fashion to how ideological positions are unconsciously communicated through body language or use of imagery. For a classic introduction, see Culler (1981) or Leitch (1983).

Discourse analysis

Discourse analysis, or content analysis, is differently nuanced from one discipline to another. Broadly, it consists of close analysis of small units of communication, whether spoken or written or acted out socially. Usually, analysis consists of:

- selecting a given context, piece of work, set of actions, texts or equivalent as representative of a broader range (such as all texts of that time, or of a particular segment of society, etc.)
- defining units precisely, so that occurrences can be identified accurately and like can be compared with like
- identifying and mapping the units in terms of when and how they occur in the material
- establishing meaningful patterns such as how sets of occurrences of one kind of speech or image relate to other sets of occurrences, such as a political event or the social status of participants
- interpreting the significance of the findings, especially by drawing on existing theory or presenting new theories.

Use of theory

Critical theorists draw widely from a range of theory across the disciplines. These include:

Structuralism: drawing from Jakobson's (1980) and Saussure's (1998) analyses of languages in terms of their internal structures, and the anthropologist Lévi-Strauss's structural analyses of societies (1964).

Psychoanalytic theory, drawing on the work of Freud or Lacan. A useful critique of the use of this within arts and humanities subjects can be found in Minsky (1998).

Deconstruction, intertextuality, post-modernism, especially the pivotal role of language in making sense of the world and shaping perceptions of identity (Leitch, 1983; Kristeva, 1980; Kvale, 1992; Allen, 2011).

Feminist: a collection of theories and approaches that seek to understand women's experiences, inequalities and gendered power relationships (Greer, 1970/2006; Walters, 2005).

Methodologies: making choices

If you can choose which methodology to use, it may be difficult to select from the options on offer. If you are unsure which approach to take, you would need to prioritise according to the following considerations (and usually in this order):

- the requirements of your research brief
- the circumstances in which you will be conducting the research
- the topic you have in mind
- your personal preferences.

Note: The methodologies suggested below are true in most circumstances. However, depending on the project brief, there may be good reasons for drawing on a methodology that is atypical for your subject discipline. For example, scientific methods are usually based on direct observation in the present, but can be applied to material remains from the past.

Which of the following is most relevant for you and your research project?

Ways of working

- [ ] To test a hypothesis through gathering data (empirical; action)
- [ ] to have clear delimitations on your research before you begin (empirical)
- [ ] to piece together how something came to be as it is (historical; phenomenological)
- [ ] to build a picture based on the experiences of individuals (phenomenological; historical; critical theory)
- [ ] to work with other practitioners to arrive at a practical solution (empirical; action research)
- [ ] to work in an open-ended way to see what kinds of results might emerge (phenomenological; historical; grounded theory; action research; ethnographic)
- [ ] to conduct research based on observation and close recording (empirical; ethnographic; phenomenological; grounded)
- [ ] working with theory, especially focused on texts, artefacts, secondary sources, other people's thinking and philosophies (critical theory)

Context

- [ ] work-based research (most methodologies are applicable, depending on the context)
- [ ] research where you could work mainly with documents and material resources (historical; phenomenological; critical theory such as discourse analysis and semiotics)
- [ ] research where you would be interacting closely with people (ethnographic; action research; phenomenological; potentially empirical)
- [ ] to investigate a community from within (ethnographic)
- [ ] controlled environments (empirical)
- [ ] working out in the field (empirical; phenomenological; grounded; action research)

Focus

- [ ] physical sciences (empirical)
- [ ] societies and communities in the present (empirical; ethnographic; action research; grounded theory; critical theory)
- [ ] societies in the past (historical; critical theory; empirical – such as carbon dating or DNA testing of ancient bones)
- [ ] individuals in the present (phenomenological; critical theory)
- [ ] individuals in the past (historical; empirical; critical theory)
- [ ] arts, artefacts, media and performance (critical theory; historical).

Chapter 12
Ethical considerations

Ethics in research is about following good moral principles. As an academic researcher, it is expected that you will be strongly principled, with an aim to:

- bring integrity, fairness and honesty to your work
- and to do right by all potential stakeholders, treating them with dignity, and with respect for their welfare, rights and safety.

In effect, this means thinking through from a moral, or ethical, perspective:

- what you research
- how you research it
- what you do with the findings
- the potential consequences of these.

You need to look at your project in the round, considering in some depth:

- what its impact or effects might be on people, life forms and the environment
- whether that impact is morally right and just
- the potential costs and benefits
- how you will manage your project in order to ensure that it is conducted in an ethical manner
- and seeking the right information and advice to help you make the best decisions.

Why is this important?

Even if you are not formally required to do so, it is valuable to consider the ethical implications:

- for the sake of others – so that you don't harm or distress them inadvertently
- for yourself: it helps to protect you from legal consequences and gives you peace of mind.

Too late, Cornelius realised he should have presented his proposal to the ethics committee for health and safety approval

What is required at university or college?

Most student research proposals have to gain the approval of the Ethics Committee, or equivalent, at the college or university. This is especially so at higher levels of study and/or when potentially vulnerable participants are involved. You need to demonstrate that you have addressed the ethical implications of your proposed research in full. If not, it is likely that your proposal will be sent back for further work or else be rejected.

You may also be asked to sign a statement to say that you understand your responsibilities and to agree to work in line with the spirit of the department's, or profession's, ethics policy.

What do I need to consider?

Typically, you need to ensure that you can demonstrate the following.

No harm

No one will be harmed as a result of the project – physically, psychologically or otherwise.

Legal requirements

The project will meet all legal requirements such as health and safety, data protection, financial practice, child protection, libel, slander and any others that relate to your subject. If you are researching or publishing in more than one country or state, the legal issues are likely to vary. You need to be aware of what those differences are and how they might apply to your research.

Signed consent

Gain the signed consent of all participants before they take part, and also for using or publishing their data, photos or other personal information. It is advisable that consent covers:

- their understanding of what the research is for
- what they will be asked to do
- agreement to take part
- agreement that you can use their responses and data as part of your research.

Full understanding

You will take every possible step to ensure that participants understand fully what they are consenting to. They should do this before they sign their agreements and consents.

Anonymity and confidentiality

This includes every aspect of confidentiality from electronically stored data through to not including proper names in documentation and not including any details that would identify a participant without their permission. This issue may need some careful thought if you are using:

- images and audio-visual material, especially those collected in group contexts
- participants or sources of information that refer to third parties, such as their employer, colleagues, family or teachers
- groups or individuals whose characteristics could make them easily identifiable
- sensitive material such as medical samples, DNA or highly personal information
- material offered by people whose contribution you wish to acknowledge but where it would mean exposing the identity of others to do so.

Give thought to how you would, realistically, conceal participants' identities, such as by changing their names or blurring faces in videos.

The environment

You should take steps to ensure that you do not cause unnecessary harm to animals, wildlife, and natural habitats, or generally damage the environment. In some instances this might mean thinking through the choices you make about routes through the countryside on a field trip, so as not to disturb animal breeding grounds, or where you dispose of waste arising from experiments, so as not to pollute the environment.

Academic integrity

Attributing your sources

When you draw upon other people's work in your research, whether as background reading, inspiration, methods, phrasing or for other purposes, you must attribute this fully and correctly. This is usually undertaken through:

- citing the source in your text, and then
- providing full details of the source as a footnote and/or in a list of references or bibliography, depending on the practice used on your course.

This should be familiar to you from previous assignments, but it is especially important at this level to be:

- comprehensive in your coverage
- precise in the way you write your references
- compliant with the format required by your course.

If you need to refresh your skills in referencing, see

- Cottrell (2013) for an overview of what to do and why
- Pears and Shields (2010) for formats to use for a wide range of sources, in both Harvard and Vancouver styles.

Intellectual property

Even when you have attributed your sources, you also need to ensure that you have the right to use the material. If you have been given access to information that is not published or which affects patents, for example, do not assume that this automatically gives you permission to use it in your own work. This could arise if you are working in a research-based setting either at work or in a university, with access to other people's research.

Conflicts of interest

Vested interest and bias

The integrity of your work is dependent, in part, on your commitment to investigating and reporting your topic objectively – at least within the conventions of your subject discipline.

It is best to avoid research projects where you have a vested interest of some kind, and especially where there is any chance that your judgements would be clouded by bias. Vested interest is typically understood as financial gain, but could also refer to emotional, ideological or other kinds of investment.

As a student, for assignment purposes, avoid research where your personal interests, such as loss of job, income or reputation, might infringe upon your capacity to be objective. The same is true of research that affects the finances or reputation of people you know – such as a relative, friend, employer or your academic institution.

Declaration of interests

If you do undertake research in which you have a vested interest in the outcome, you should always declare it at the start of your research report. This can arise, for example, where you undertake research with a commercial purpose, or if you want to prove the efficacy of a medical treatment or educational approach from which you stand to gain or lose personally in some way.

If you are uncertain whether this applies, then:

- talk it through with your supervisor at the point where it arises as a possibility, and well before launching into the research
- provide details within the proposal, if you proceed to proposal stage with the idea
- raise this as an issue for consideration by the relevant ethics committee (such as that run by your department or institution)
- include in your proposal some details about how you would inform participants and others about any such vested interests.

Thinking about the issues

Bring a thoughtful approach

Taking an ethical approach is about more than simply going through a checklist, useful though that might be as a prompt. It is more about the attitude of mind that you bring to your research and the way you evaluate its impact on the world around you.

Being ethical isn't simply a question of not infringing the 'rules', or the law, but of considering what is the right thing to do – and that isn't always straightforward. One way of doing this is to generate questions such as those below, adapted to your own area of research.

- What is meant by 'harm' in this context? Would others take a different view?

- Would any aspect of the research betray the trust of participants or sponsors?

- Is it likely that the research data or findings would be used later in ways for which it was not intended, and that would cause harm to others at that point?

- Would the participants find any aspect of the research offensive or unnecessarily intrusive? Could this be addressed – or should the research use different methods altogether?

- Is the privacy and dignity of participants respected fully and is every effort made to take care of small details that matter to individuals?

Question your motives and interests

Much research is undertaken for commercial reasons or to support work-related improvements or sectional interests, such as to support the work of a political party. This is not necessarily unethical. However, there are different ethical considerations when commercial and financial interests come into play.

Participants and any co-researchers, sponsors and your university or college should be informed about the interests involved and be able to decide whether they wish to be involved on that basis. That means that they need to know such things as:

- what you intend to do with your findings

- whether you or others would make a personal profit

- what other companies, organisations or agencies (if relevant) intend to do with your research

- whether the research is intended to further the interests of a particular group or organisation, whether religious, political, community, lobbyist, business, educational, environmental or other.

Reflect on consequences

This means looking at your research project from many angles, and in a reflective way, to identify potential issues, considering whether any unintended outcomes could arise.

Rights: Consider in what ways your research might be thought to infringe upon anybody else's rights. From an ethical perspective, the 'rights' of an issue may look different from both legal rights and common practice.

Distress: Consider whether anybody might be unduly distressed by the way you conduct your research, even if the research is legal in technical terms. Could this be avoided?

Fairness: Consider whether you are being fair to others in the way you select, conduct or report on your research. Copying the idea of a fellow student would not demonstrate a good understanding of research ethics.

Inclusion: Consider whether the way you set up the research is appropriately inclusive of people from different backgrounds and circumstances.

Thinking about the issues

Safeguarding: what special care might be needed when working with more vulnerable groups such as children, the elderly or those with particular medical conditions or disabilities?

Conservation: whether you might be unnecessarily wasteful of resources.

Preservation: are you working with rare documents that require handling in a particular way? If so, are you honouring the rules so that you help to preserve them?

Transparency: whether the way you ask questions could be considered to be deliberately misleading or deceptive in some way.

Honesty: if you made promises such as about the outcomes or benefits of the research or the timescales or costs for completion, can you deliver on them?

Security: whether there might be any risks to participants if data were not kept private. (The levels of risk arising from leaks of apparently trivial material are not always immediately apparent.)

Dignity and respect: how might you avoid your research adversely affecting others' dignity? Will you be asking questions or requiring actions that might cause unnecessary embarrassment?

What if I uncover difficult issues?

If ethical concerns arise early on, this doesn't mean that you can't research the topic in some way. Identifying the issues is a first step towards finding ways of resolving these. It is likely that if you intend to conduct your research ethically, and consider the issues, you will find a way to do so.

If there are more serious ethical concerns and you cannot find a way of addressing these, raise this immediately with your supervisor. There may be a different route that you could take to achieve the objectives of the research by more ethical means.

Benefits v. risks

There is always some element of risk, and there may well be some individuals who might take offence or be upset by some aspect of most research. Whilst this should be taken seriously, it does need to be balanced sensibly against the bigger picture:

- How great is the risk or level or harm?
- How likely is it to occur?
- What would be the benefits of the research?
- Do the benefits really outweigh the risks?
- If you consider that the benefits do outweigh the risks, be prepared to present the case for that position in your proposal.

Complaints procedure

Provide a procedure for participants or other parties to make complaints if they feel these are justified. For example:

- provide details of a website that outlines the department's or institution's complaints procedure
- give details of your academic department on handouts or materials that you provide to participants or their parents/carers
- include the name of your college or university within your research report, as well as that of your department. It is useful to include the address of its main site and/or a website.

Ethical considerations

Both at the proposal stage and at each stage of your research, check that each of the relevant ethical issues are fully considered, as relevant to that stage. Check off ☑ once fully addressed. Put a line through any that do not apply.

I have given careful consideration to each of the following and taken due measures to ensure that each is met.

Children and vulnerable people

- ☐ The needs of any vulnerable participants such as children (page 134)
- ☐ Meeting ethical codes with respect to working with vulnerable participants
- ☐ Signed permission of the participants and/or their carers (as relevant)

Anonymity and confidentiality

- ☐ Guaranteed anonymity
- ☐ Guaranteed confidentiality
- ☐ Guaranteed security of data
- ☐ No false promises about anonymity, confidentiality or security

Academic integrity and intellectual property

- ☐ Acknowledgement of all sources
- ☐ Necessary permissions and licences for use of materials and sources
- ☐ No material used if permission was refused
- ☐ Respect for other people's intellectual property (in spirit as well as within the law)

Conflicts of interest

- ☐ Full awareness of potential vested interests
- ☐ Full awareness of potential conflicts of interest
- ☐ Declaration of vested interests (own or those of family members)
- ☐ Unbiased reporting of findings
- ☐ Careful consideration of the consequences for others (e.g. reputation of employer/ institution)

Conservation and Environment

- ☐ Care of fragile and rare resources/materials
- ☐ Consideration for animals, wildlife, natural habitats, water, etc.
- ☐ Consideration of environmental choices (environmental footprint; green miles; etc.)
- ☐ Environmental impact

Health and safety

- ☐ Health and safety issues thought through from the perspective of different stakeholders
- ☐ Consequences of research thought through from the perspective of different stakeholders

Signed informed consent

- ☐ Participants receiving the information they need in order to give informed consent
- ☐ Participants' understanding of the purpose and nature of the research
- ☐ Participants' understanding of what they are required to do
- ☐ Participants' signed consent for taking part
- ☐ Participants' signed consent for use to be made of their responses, data, images, etc.

Overall

- ☐ The concept of 'no harm' is upheld.

Useful Resources

National Research Ethics Society (NRES) at **www.nres.npsa.nhs.uk**.

Chapter 13
Writing the research proposal

The purpose of the proposal

The rationale for writing a detailed research proposal is that it helps you to:

- work through, and clarify, your thinking about your concept
- synthesise your early ideas and reading
- prepare the groundwork well
- identify potential problems at an early stage, while there is still plenty of time to manage the implications of these
- demonstrate the feasibility of the research from all angles
- make a case for gaining formal approval.

What happens at the approval stage?

Your supervisor, or a designated panel, reads the proposal to consider whether:

- it is likely to meet the required brief
- it looks broadly sensible and manageable
- there are legal, ethical, or health and safety issues to address
- there are potential problems that you might encounter, so that they can offer advice and steer you in the right direction
- they can agree to your proposal.

The approval process does not guarantee:

- that the project is feasible, as that will depend on how you then conduct it
- that further ethical issues will not arise
- that your project will be successful.

A good supervisor will be persistent in asking you to write up your ideas

What should I have done by now?

Before submitting your proposal, consider for yourself whether it is likely to work. There isn't any point in seeking approval for a proposal that you don't really believe you can carry through or in which you can already see major flaws. If it is rejected, or returned with recommendations for change, this reduces the time available to you for conducting and writing up the research.

If you have worked through the various sections of the book so far, and can complete checklists on pages 76 (topic) and 118 (proposal), then you should be in a strong position to gain approval.

Developing your research proposal

Demonstrate that you know the field

Include indicative reading that you have undertaken already or that shows you are aware of the key works relevant to this topic.

Indicate the foundations

Either summarise, or demonstrate that you are clear on, what has already been established, or is generally accepted, as the foundation upon which you are building your own research.

Identify your 'issue'

From your background reading, you should have identified some gap, problem, unexplored issue or area of doubt that forms an opening for your own research. Provide a brief outline of what this is and how your research will go about addressing that issue, at least in part.

State your thesis/hypothesis

Summarise what you expect to find, stating this as your research thesis or hypothesis.

Indicate the parameters

Specify exactly what your research will cover. Be as precise as you can. The level of precision should, of itself, indicate to your supervisor what you are not going to address. If any ambiguity might still remain, state briefly what the research does not cover.

State your methodology

Indicate or outline the approach you will take to the research. Make use of the specific terminology that is used within your subject discipline for referring to the methodology and research design that you intend to use. If relevant, provide brief details of the statistical methods that you will apply and/ or the theoretical framework that you will be drawing upon. There isn't usually a need to go into detail of these at the proposal stage.

Include ethical considerations

In developing your proposal, evaluate your proposal against the ethical guidelines of your department or institution. Refer to this within your proposal. Include, if required, a signed statement that you adhere to the ethics policy (page 107).

Demonstrate how it can be achieved

Outline briefly the methods that you will use. Give an indication of the scope and scale of the research and the likely timeline for each stage. This helps your supervisor to tell whether it is likely to be manageable (page 52).

Evaluation checklist (page 118)

Before starting to write the proposal, use the checklist to help ensure that you cover all angles. Make sure that, when you sign off an item on the checklist, you do so based on careful checks and planning rather than guess work or wishful thinking. Do this for each statement, even if a particular aspect is not required formally as part of your submission.

Risks

- Demonstrate that you have thought through any potential risks (pages 39–42).
- Raise any issues with your supervisor.

Expert guidance

Talk through the draft proposal with your supervisor, leaving plenty of time to make substantial changes if recommended.

Test it out: conduct a pilot

If you can, conduct a pilot to test your proposed research methods (see page 117). Go through this with your supervisor and/or submit details of this with your proposal. Your proposal needs to show that you have a good grasp of:

(a) what you are going to research
(b) why
(c) within the context of research in your discipline
(d) and according to the brief that was set.

Formulating your thesis statement

Stating your position

Unless this is contrary to your research methodology (Chapter 11), then as part of the process of drawing together your proposal, formulate a clear, brief, statement of what you assume your research will uncover and/or where you stand on the issue. It need only be a sentence or two, to sum up your position. This represents your expectations of what you can deliver through your research. Your position may well change during the course of your research.

For phenomenological, grounded theory and similar methodologies, provide a statement of the purpose of your research and the methodology that you are using.

For experimental topics, especially in the sciences, draw up a hypothesis rather than a thesis statement (page 116).

The function of the thesis statement

Your thesis statement should:

- summarise your core message, making it clear to the reader where you stand on the issue
- be precise, clear and succinct, typically consisting of just one or two sentences
- form part of your initial proposal, so it is clear what you are setting out to find
- be included in the introduction to your report, essay or dissertation. Depending on your research findings, you may be able to cut and paste the position statement from your proposal, assuming your position remains the same. If your findings lead you to change your position on the issue, you can state this in the introduction to your work
- be the point to which you return continually within your dissertation, essay or report, to focus your writing and orientate your readers
- shape your argument.

Benefits of a good thesis statement

Clarity. Formulating your position requires you to distil and clarify your thinking, helping you then to provide a well structured argument.

A clear reference point. The thesis statement provides a point to which you can keep returning to check that you are not drifting off subject, either in terms of your research or of your writing up. This can be invaluable for larger-scale assignments.

Formulating your statement

By the time you come to write your statement, make sure you have developed a solid knowledge base and understanding of the topic.

Read widely. Examine different perspectives. Think about these. Jot down ideas. Weigh up options. Continue these activities until your thinking is clear.

The best projects tend to be those where the authors' position on the issues and their understanding of others' different positions enables them to provide a strong argument. Your report or dissertation will read better if you can debate your statement, drawing on different points of view, whilst remaining convincing that the evidence supports your position (assuming that it does!).

Evaluating my thesis statement: checklist

Strengths of my thesis statement are:

- [ ] it fits the assignment brief
- [ ] it is short and precisely worded
- [ ] my stance on the issue is clear
- [ ] it will allow me to develop a strong line of reasoning/argument
- [ ] it matches what I assume, at this point, will be the conclusions of the report.

Formulating your hypothesis

What is a hypothesis?

A hypothesis is a theory or, in effect, your own 'best guess' of what will happen in particular circumstances, and for what reasons. It is a proposition, or initial premise, that condition A will result in outcome B for reason C.

Your research then sets out to test your theory, or hypothesis, to see it if stands up completely or in part, or not at all. This might be through a range of methods, such as an experiment, survey or observations. You design your research in such a way that it tests out your theory as closely as possible, to see whether it can be supported by evidence that you collect.

The hypothesis is formulated *before* you start the research and states precisely what you *expect* to find. In order to arrive at your hypothesis, a considerable amount of thought and background reading is usually needed. You need to be aware of which similar hypotheses have already been tested, what the results were, and where there are gaps for you to formulate a hypothesis of your own. The results of previous research help you to extrapolate what results you are likely to find and, therefore, to formulate a sensible hypothesis.

Objectivity and integrity

When testing a hypothesis, your research should be objective. The point is not to prove that your hypothesis was right but, rather, to test it. Your research should have integrity. It is important to demonstrate that you can devise rigorous, reliable and valid ways of testing your hypothesis and provide the results with clarity, transparency, and honesty, whatever the outcome. If your results do not prove your hypothesis, that is an outcome in itself, and still contributes to knowledge.

The nature of a hypothesis

You can't 'prove' a hypothesis.

You can disprove it – if your research findings do not support it. This still adds to our understanding of the issue. Be aware that your hypothesis may have been correct, but your sample size too small to demonstrate this (see page 122).

You can provide evidence that supports it
Be aware that this does not prove that you are right. Your research findings relate to a specific set of conditions. It is often the case that further research does not support earlier findings. This is why it would be risky to say a piece of research 'proved' something conclusively.

Using your hypothesis

Your hypothesis serves as the focus of your research and as a spine for your written report.

- Results section: in this, you state whether your research findings support the research hypotheses, or not.

- Discussion section: in this, you examine the reasons for, or conditions that gave rise to, your findings, and why the hypotheses were or were not supported by the evidence.

- Abstract: state your hypothesis, whether the results support it and at what level of significance.

Evaluating my hypothesis: checklist

Strengths of my hypothesis are:

1 ☐ it fits the assignment brief
2 ☐ it sums up exactly what it is that I am setting out to research
3 ☐ it is precise
4 ☐ it is not open to more than one interpretation
5 ☐ it is clear what I assume will be the outcomes of my research
6 ☐ it will be clear to others why, on the basis of previous research, I have formulated the hypothesis in this way.

Wording the research proposal

Your proposal should be written so that it sounds convincing:

- based on a good foundation of background reading and investigation into the topic
- making reasonable assumptions about what can be achieved within the brief.

Clarity of purpose

Set out the case for the research clearly and in ways that do not stretch the truth, nor call for a stretch of imagination on the part of the reader. In particular, make sure that there is no room for doubt about the purpose of your research project and the questions you aim to address. If these come across accurately, then, even if the proposal has some weaknesses, your supervisor is better placed to provide you with good advice.

Express action

Write the proposal using verbs that express the action you will take, using the style used by your course. This may include active verbs in the first person, as in:

- 'I will test what occurs when X ...'
- 'I will demonstrate that ...'

Alternatively, for science subjects and those that favour an objective approach, either use the passive voice, as in:

- 'A survey will be conducted ...'
- 'This will allow direct comparisons to be drawn between X and Y'

or write in the third person, as in:

- 'It is expected that this will reveal that ...'
- 'The project will investigate ...'
- 'The results will clarify whether X ... or Y ...'

Avoid hesitancy and vagueness

Avoid using a style that implies that the research might not go to plan (even though that is always a possibility) or that suggests you are unclear about your focus. For example, avoid phrasing such as:

- 'I'll try to examine ...'
- 'The research will explore the area of ...'
- 'The general aim is to ...'
- 'Every effort will be made to provide accurate results ...'

Writing up the pilot

Write your pilot as a factual report, stating exactly:

- what you set out to do
- what you did
- the results
- a succinct, critical outline of what worked, any flaws that were apparent and what would improve or fine-tune the research
- how you plan to adapt your approach and methods for when you start to collect data.

Analyse your pilot in brief and keep to the point.

- Avoid praising the parts that went right.
- Don't apologise or make excuses for anything that needs to be improved.
- Do include copies of materials used, or data collected during the pilot.

Preparing a strong written proposal

Leave your written draft of your proposal aside for at least a day. Then, read it from the standpoint of your supervisor or Approval Panel, and with a critical eye. Consider what questions they would have as they read it, and whether you have provided the answers they would need in order to approve the project. It is likely that, the first time you do this, you will find quite a few things to improve. It follows, that it is important to do this with sufficient time to make such amendments.

Use the checklist

Return again to the checklist on page 118. Evaluate whether your proposal is ready to submit.

Evaluating my research proposal

Strengths of my proposal

Consider your proposal in relation to each of the following points. Check off ☑ each that applies already. If you can't do so, and if the item is relevant to your proposal, put more work into that aspect.

1 ☐ My written proposal meets the requirements set for my course and/or the assignment brief.

2 ☐ It has a strong structure, with clear sections and headings.

3 ☐ I have selected a good topic (page 76).

4 ☐ I have included a well-worded title.

5 ☐ I have included a well formulated thesis/ hypothesis or research question (pages 115–16).

6 ☐ I have written a draft review of the literature (whether or not I am required to submit this).

In the proposal, the following come across clearly and evidently:

7 ☐ my rationale for choosing this topic: it is clear why I think the topic worthy of research

8 ☐ what it is that I aim to find out

9 ☐ that I have a good understanding of my field and where my research fits into it

10 ☐ the ways my research will build on previous research and contribute to the field

11 ☐ that the proposed research would be seen as belonging within my subject discipline

12 ☐ the methodological and/or theoretical frameworks that inform the design of my own research

13 ☐ the nature of my sources and/or raw materials and/or participants

14 ☐ that sources will be accessible to me and/ or available when needed

15 ☐ my methods for collecting the data or information that I will need

16 ☐ that my methods will be consistent with the methodology or theoretical framework (if relevant)

17 ☐ the ways I will work with participants, and what materials I will use with them

18 ☐ that health and safety requirements will be met (if relevant)

19 ☐ that it is reasonable to assume that it will be a manageable task to collect and analyse the data/material required to prove the research hypothesis or answer my research question

20 ☐ that the scale of the research is proportionate to the time available

21 ☐ that the research will meet ethical requirements

22 ☐ that I can do justice to the research within the time available

23 ☐ that the proposed research can evidently be completed by the deadline

24 ☐ that the overall proposal is definitely achievable.

Use of pilot (if required)

25 ☐ I have used the pilot to test my methods.

26 ☐ I used the pilot to identify areas for improvement.

27 ☐ I have fine-tuned, or changed, my methods, to address the issues raised by the pilot.

28 ☐ I know that the improvements will work.

29 ☐ I have included details of the pilot in my proposal.

Part 3
Conducting your research

Once your research proposal has been agreed, you are committed to investigating the topic in the ways that you have suggested. As courses require the submission of research proposals at varied points in the research process, you may be starting this part of the book at one of several different stages in that process:

- your proposal may consist of a broad outline, and the details of the methods may yet to be worked out

- OR: you have already had to spell out exactly how you will gather information but are not yet certain whether your methods will work

- OR: you have trialled your methods, fine-tuned them and submitted these as part of a proposal, which has been accepted.

If you have worked on your proposal as outlined in Part 2, then it is likely that you are now ready to start collecting data. This can feel as if you are starting the research 'for real', although good work at the proposal stage would mean that your research is already well underway.

This section looks at some core considerations for gathering and using the information that will form the evidence base of your research.

Gathering information

- Decide which kinds of information you will use as your raw material – this will be your 'evidence base'.
- Decide on methods for collecting this.
- Organise information so that it is easy for you to use.

There were times Gordon wondered whether he had chosen the best method for research on recycling

Interpreting and presenting findings

- Make sense of what your findings are telling you.
- Draw out the key findings.
- Present these clearly.

Contents of Part 3

14 The evidence base
15 Working with participants
16 Experiments
17 Observations
18 Surveys and questionnaires
19 Interviews
20 Case studies
21 Interpreting your findings

What students say ...

Consistency and timing ...

I set out to collect my data, thinking I would have a nice time for several months conducting observations and interviews and then I'd sit down and make sense of it all. In practice, it didn't work like that. After a while, I started to be able to second guess what some participants were going to say. I told my supervisor who said it was really important not to let the participants see that, in case it influenced their responses. We discussed how I must keep on approaching each participant in the same way that I did at the start of the research, so that my results would be valid. I understood why this was important but I did find it quite hard at times.

She also said that if I could see emerging patterns, I could write her an interim report to help me to get going on writing up. I felt this might be a waste of time because I wasn't ready yet. But, actually, it turned out to be quite a good idea because it saved me time later. Also, when she read it, my supervisor pointed out some research articles she thought would be useful. These gave me new ideas about how to interpret my data and were good to add to the literature review. I probably wouldn't have read these if I had left the data analysis all to the end.

Enough is enough ...

There is always some other document to read – that's what I found. I wasn't sure how you know when to stop following up on leads within the sources and collecting more material. I assumed you were 'not allowed' NOT to read every word of every document that was even vaguely relevant. I didn't want to raise this with my supervisor in case he thought I was being lazy. Luckily, I found out I didn't have to do this.

Pilot ...

The biggest eye opener for me was piloting my survey. I didn't feel like doing a pilot because I thought my survey was pretty good as it was. I just wanted to send it out and get on with it. My supervisor said I had to do at least one trial run so I asked six friends to try it out. They did, sort of. Nobody answered all the questions. When I asked them about it, I noticed they were interpreting some questions in a completely different way to the way I meant. They didn't understand some of the questions so either didn't answer them or used the rating scale the wrong way. They showed me the rating scale didn't make sense for some of the questions. There was so much that needed a rethink. I had to change the wording of nearly half of the questions. I ended up running three trials before I was happy with it.

Combining methods

Everyone on my course was asking each other whether they were going to use questionnaires or surveys or interviews or experiments or official data etc., and I got sucked into that way of thinking. It didn't strike me until it was nearly too late that I didn't have to make an either/or choice. I could combine some of these methods and get a more rounded view.

Chapter 14
The evidence base

When you come to write up your research, you will be making assertions and drawing conclusions. The assumption is that these are based on a close critical analysis of a solid evidence base. You are responsible for gathering that evidence base. It falls to you, with guidance from your supervisor, to decide what would constitute an adequate evidence base to:

● answer the research questions and/or support the research hypotheses

● ensure a reasonable level of confidence that your findings, and any judgements you make based on these, are reliable.

Methods

An early task is to decide on the methods, or techniques, to use for gathering, collating and analysing information. These might be through such means as:

● Surveys
● Observations
● Case studies
● Critiquing texts
● Piecing together an event or incident

● Experiments
● Interviews
● Using documents
● Analysing official data
● Combinations of these

Methods: scope your options

It can be tempting to choose methods with which you are most familiar or that you enjoy rather than those that will yield the best results. Before launching into using the most obvious methods, consider different options. Keep returning to the question:

Will this method, or this wording, yield exactly what I am I looking for?

Decide on your raw material

Of necessity, your decisions about research methods go hand in hand with decisions about what kind of source material or raw data to use. Your methods would be very different depending on whether you used data from controlled experiments, historical documents, artefacts, rock strata and minerals, digital media, videos, participant responses, and so on.

Pilot your methods

If feasible, test out your methods in a trial run to check they deliver the kinds of information you want. Pilots are helpful for picking up flaws that are otherwise easy to miss, such as:

● whether participants understand instructions and/or questions

● whether you had been overambitious in how many themes you could follow up

● whether it is possible to maintain an accurate tally of the items that you had hoped to record during an observation

● whether your methods of recording interviews proved off-putting to the interviewee

● whether the way you collected data made it difficult to collate, interpret or present.

Avoid going through the motions simply because a pilot is required. Use the opportunity to check for ways of fine-tuning your research design.

Be systematic

Conduct your research with precision, in a methodical, planned way. Once you start collecting data or participant responses, continue as you began, carrying the research to its logical conclusions, even if you can see flaws emerging in your design. Alternatively, if there is time, start afresh with an improved design – using new participants if relevant.

Deciding on your data or 'raw material'

Data

It is sometimes assumed that 'data' is another word for statistics or numbers, but the term refers to any kind of information or 'facts' – verbal as well as numerical.
Note that 'data' is the plural of the Latin word 'datum'. When writing your report, this means you should refer to them in the plural, as in

- 'the data are unclear …'
- or 'the data indicate that …'.

How much material do I need?

This is a key question raised by students. This aspect of the project can be one of the hardest for you to judge accurately. It depends on what is needed to answer your research question.

Scaling your evidence base

Scale the size of your evidence base carefully in order to juggle these different demands:

- *The nature of your research*: What volume of evidence is typical for similar student projects in your subject?
- *For an appropriate evidence base*: What information will you actually need in order to gain significant results and/or to provide an answer to your research question, based on solid evidence?
- *Time demands*: How long will it take you to collect and process each piece of evidence?
- *Time resources*: How much time is available to collect and work with your evidence base? In practical terms, how much material can you really process in the time available?

It is best not to leave data collection to chance: avoid setting out to see 'just how much you can cover' and working from there. This is especially important for research methodologies that favour more open-ended approaches: it is essential to set parameters for the research in order to ensure that the evidence base remains manageable.

This means managing those factors that are most under your control, such as the number of case studies, events, themes, exemplars or participants included; the amount of time you allocate to each observation; or the timescales set for case studies or a piece of historical research.

Sample Size Calculator

The Sample Size Calculator is a free on-line resource, which indicates what sample size you would need in order to be confident in your results: www.surveysystem.com/sscalc.htm

Do …

- Investigate the typical evidence base for similar projects
- Plan carefully for what you collect
- Collect enough data for your results to be significant
- Manage the process so that you leave as little as possible to chance.

Don't

Collect more than you need or could use: too much information can be problematic.

It generally means using time collecting, sorting and selecting material that you cannot use. Too much material can obscure the key messages.

Primary and secondary sources

When you are discussing your research proposal with your supervisor or in a seminar group or viva, it will be assumed that you will know the difference between a primary and a secondary source. You may also be required to list these separately in your bibliography.

Secondary sources

What are they?

Secondary sources are the books, articles, papers and similar materials written or produced by others that help you to form your background understanding of the subject. You would use these to find out about experts' findings, analyses or perspectives on the issue and decide whether to draw upon these explicitly in your research. They are 'about' your subject, or related to it in some relevant way, and generally are referred to in your literature review or to throw light upon your analysis and discussion of your own evidence.

> **Example 1: secondary sources**
>
> If you were researching an aspect of how science affected art in the nineteenth century, you might draw on a range of background texts written more recently about that period in order to help your background understanding. These secondary sources might range from texts about art and science, to those about how ideas were communicated at that time, how the arts industry was organised, the impact of industrial exhibitions, technical changes in photography, or the production of artists' materials.

When would I use them?

For shorter projects conducted over a few months, you would use these sources mainly before starting your own research. For longer projects of a year or more, you would continue to read secondary sources in order to:

- ensure that you are up to date with what is being written in the subject
- browse, at the very least, material that looks relevant
- make use of the latest material where this is relevant, such as to add to the literature review or to inform your analysis and discussion of your findings.

Primary sources

Primary sources are your raw materials. They are the subject of your research, part of the evidence base itself, rather than sources you draw on to throw light on your own findings. Although these are usually data you collect or documentary materials that you select yourself, it is the way materials are used that makes them primary or secondary sources.

> **Example 2: primary sources**
>
> If you were researching how the relationship between art and science is represented in the early twenty-first century, then some of the textbooks that were secondary sources in Example 1 might be your primary sources, or raw materials.
>
> For more about secondary sources, see pages 77–88 on *Literature search and review*.

Primary source

Secondary source

About ART

Primary source

About ART

Secondary source

Theories of ART

Deciding on your raw material

Which source materials?

For the research topic I have in mind, my raw data or evidence base will be drawn from the following sources. *(Indicate any that you plan to use.)*

☐ Numerical data or material that I generate myself through experiments, surveys, questionnaires or interviews

☐ qualitative data or material that I generate myself through experiments, surveys and questionnaires or interviews

☐ records of my observations of individuals or groups in controlled or everyday settings

☐ easily accessible datasets already in the public domain, such as official statistics, meteorological records, financial records, or specialist databases

☐ data from private sources, such as family or company records not in the public domain

☐ published material such as literary texts, government papers, statutes, companies' online collections of printed historical manuscripts, legal documents, political papers, philosophical tracts, DVDs, musical scores, etc.

☐ largely unpublished documents, manuscripts, records, scores, such as those held in private, specialist or official collections

☐ my own records of live events, such as interviews or performances I attended

☐ other people's recording of live events, such as recordings of interviews, broadcasted performances, reviews of events

☐ rare objects or artefacts

☐ material sources, such as rocks, minerals or textiles.

Permissions?

Y ☐ N ☐ Will special permission be needed in order to make use of any source materials such as documents and artefacts?

Y ☐ N ☐ If so, is there a cost involved?

Y ☐ N ☐ If there is an application process for using the material, would I hear back early enough to make practical use of the source?

Y ☐ N ☐ Will the source be sent to me?

Y ☐ N ☐ Will I receive the source back quickly?

Y ☐ N ☐ Will I have to travel to use the source?

Y ☐ N ☐ Will there be a limit to how long I am given access to the source?

Y ☐ N ☐ Will I have enough funds to cover the full costs of using these sources?

Y ☐ N ☐ Will I have sufficient time to make use of the source in the way I would need, taking into consideration the time required from application to receipt to the end of the permission?

Y ☐ N ☐ Is this source essential: would my research project be viable without it?

Selecting and samples

The need to select …

Sometimes, the parameters of your evidence are self-evident, such as if your research focuses on a particular text, document or event. More often, you need to make difficult decisions about which data or materials to collect and analyse. Your selection of evidence must be on a well-reasoned basis, not arbitrary.

Typically, you make such choices in terms of:

- the most logical parameters, such as timescales, themes, geographical location, the work of a particular artist, the set of documents or texts, so that you can use all available evidence
- OR: a suitable sample taken from the total 'population'. (The full dataset or total number of instances, whether fish, rocks, patients, etc., is known as the 'population'.)

The assumption is that such a selection would yield similar findings to those you would have achieved from the complete set (of relevant documents, data, events, population, etc.).

Selecting a representative sample

Usually, you cannot include every single instance of a population in a piece of research. Instead, you choose a sample to represent the whole. If your sample is representative, then conclusions drawn about it allow you to make accurate inferences about the whole population.

The challenge lies in ensuring that the sample is truly representative and not skewed in a way that would invalidate inferences drawn from your results. Your aim is to ensure that deliberate and unforeseen bias and distortions are removed.

Random sampling

Random sampling can yield a representative sample. Random selection can be attractive as an apparently simple way of ensuring a neutral, unbiased, balanced sample. This might be by selecting every tenth house for a survey or the first 100 respondents. However, you must check carefully for 'selection bias' even in apparently random samples. With every tenth house number, houses with even numbers might be on the same side of the road, which might itself represent differing housing, social and financial circumstances. Early respondents to a survey might not be representative of others.

Purposive samples

These samples are selected for particular characteristics rather than on a random basis. Your results can be generalised only in terms of populations that share those characteristics. You would select the combination of characteristics relevant for your research, which might include age, gender, ethnicity, abilities, place of work, occupation, length of time in their job, month of birth, education, language, blood type, fitness, weight, and so on.

When working with people, you cannot control for every variable. Decide which characteristics are most relevant to your project. Typical ways of doing this are by:

- selecting participants who all share a set of specified characteristics, or
- if there is more than one group, ensuring each group is 'matched' for relevant characteristics: each group should share a similar profile, except for the variable that you plan to measure.

Examples: controlling for variables

(a) All participants were men aged 19–25 years, in full-time employment (37 hours a week or more), who drive 40–60 miles a week.

(b) All were aged 65–80 years old, non-smokers and resident in the area for over 10 years.

(c) Each of the 4 groups was matched for age, gender and body mass index. A different exercise regime was given to each group.

Sample size

Sample size

If your sample is small, it runs more risk of:

- not being representative
- yielding results that are more extreme, and where 'outliers' carry too much weight
- yielding results that suggest your hypothesis is wrong, when it might be correct
- your findings being overturned by similar research with a larger database
- any generalisations you make being invalid.

Size and statistical significance

Your sample should be large enough to ensure that the data are significant and that your results are highly unlikely to have occurred by chance. In other words, too small a sample can mean that your research is worthless. Kahneman (2011) argues that a great deal of even expert research uses overly small samples decided on poorly based intuitions of what constitutes a good evidence base, rather than computing it.

Probability of a chance outcome

The 'significance' of quantitative data is expressed in terms of how likely, or probable, it is that those results could have occurred by chance. If you were about to take a potential risk, such as investing or lending money or undergoing a serious operation, you would feel less confidence in a 1 in 10 chance of a bad outcome than a 1 in a million chance.

Probability is expressed as $p = < 0.0$ (number).

Examples

$p = < 0.1$ (a less than 1 in 10 chance that the outcome is random)

$p = < 0.01$ (a less than 1 in 100 chance)

$p = < 0.001$ (a less than 1 in 1000 chance)

$p = < 0.0001$ (a less than 1 in 10,000 chance).

What size sample is appropriate?

Official polls and surveys

Government polls and similar surveys aim for around 1000 participants to gauge national opinion or behaviours. Some medical and pharmaceutical trials are much larger.

Small projects

Smaller-scale student projects are set mainly to learn methods and it is understood that the results are unlikely to carry much statistical weight. Lower levels of statistical significance can be obtained with relatively small samples although it is best to aim for at least 20 participants for each experimental condition.

Larger-scale research projects

For dissertations and theses, you would scale your sample appropriately, weighing up:

- time: how time-consuming it will be to work with each item/person in the sample
- costs: large samples can be expensive to set up, although electronic media can sometimes reduce costs
- need: how large the sample really needs to be for relevant and significant results.

Great! A 66% success rate. My supervisor will be delighted.

Samples and project focus

Project title and precise sampling

Your project title and your choices of sources or sample are closely linked. Your sample is partly defined already by the project title, as illustrated in the example below.

Example: choosing a sample

Report title: 'Public use of antibiotics: A study of gender differences in completing a prescribed course of penicillin amongst the 18–30-year-olds living in Marsbley, UK'.

If this was your title, then whether you gathered your evidence base from talking to doctors, using official data, interviews of patients, surveys or other means, the sample would be limited to the following:

Only people living in Marsbley. You would need to decide whether your participants should have been resident in Marsbley for any particular length of time. Would recent arrivals bring different attitudes to taking antibiotics that might distort your survey?

Only those in Marsbley aged 18–30. You would need to define within which dates participants' ages should fall within that age range.

Only those in Marsbley aged 18–30 prescribed a course of penicillin. Your sample would exclude:
- those who hadn't been prescribed penicillin
- those prescribed other kinds of antibiotic
- those taking penicillin that hadn't been prescribed for them.

Representative sample
You would normally ensure that your sample was of a similar profile to that of the overall population – such as, for example, if your sample shared a similar proportion of each ethnic or socio-economic group to that of the general Marsbley population, or if the proportion of those with short and long-term illnesses matched that of the population prescribed penicillin.

Reviewing your focus

Once you start to identify who or what to include in your sample, you may find that you need to amend your title – with your supervisor's approval. Some reasons for doing this would be:

- *Available population*: there isn't a large enough population with the characteristics you need, to yield significant data. In the example above, Marsbley might be too small a village to provide enough 18–30-year-olds that match the criteria for the sample.

- *Unforeseen variables*: when you pilot your methods, you might find that there are unforeseen variables. For the example above, the age range is quite broad – so the older and younger participants might have received different health education at school. Educational differences might appear to be a critical factor. The research could be designed to check for both factors, if the sample is large enough, and balanced for gender across the age spectrum.

Tell your reader

Clarify for your reader which method you used to select your sample and the reasons for doing so.

Edith was shocked at the suggestion that her sample might be skewed in some way

---

The evidence base

Check off ☑ each of the following once you have addressed it in full. Give due consideration to each, considering the potential impact for your final dissertation/report if these aspects are not right from the beginning. Put a line through items that are not relevant to your kind of research.

Before

Appropriate evidence

☐ I have decided on the nature of my evidence base (see 'Raw material', page 122).

☐ I have decided on the criteria that I will use for selecting source materials (such as timescales, dates, origin, location, etc.).

☐ I have decided on the methods that I will use for gathering this evidence (see Part 3).

☐ I have checked that sufficient suitable evidence will be available to me and/or that gathering it will be feasible.

☐ I have talked through my planned evidence base with my supervisor to check that it is suitable.

☐ I am confident that I have the technical and/or analytical skills for working with my planned evidence base *OR* that support for acquiring these is available.

☐ I have piloted my methods to check that these yield the evidence base that I need.

Sampling

☐ I have a clear rationale for the sampling method that I am going to use.

☐ I have thought through all variables that could interfere with my results and set up conditions to control for these.

☐ I am confident that my planned sample size is large enough to yield significant results (if relevant) and have checked this with my supervisor.

☐ I am confident that it is possible to obtain participants or samples with the characteristics that I need for my research.

☐ I am confident my sample is representative of the population that I am studying.

Organisation of evidence base

☐ I have a system for recording, labelling and/or coding my evidence as I go along.

☐ I have designed a system for storing and organising evidence as I collect it, so that I can find and use it with ease as and when needed.

☐ I have designed a system for storing my evidence that enables easy retrieval.

During (for interim checks)

☐ I am maintaining a list of the evidence that I am using, with all the details that I will need for the References section of my dissertation/report.

☐ I am working systematically, using the methods I planned for gathering evidence.

☐ I am working systematically, using the methods I planned for labelling evidence.

☐ I am working systematically, using the methods I planned for storing evidence.

☐ My methods are yielding the data that I expected.

☐ My initial analysis of the evidence indicates that it is appropriate to the needs of my research.

☐ If my methods are not yielding the data that I need, I have spoken to my supervisor to consider the impact of this on my project.

After

☐ I have made a comprehensive list of documentary and other primary sources used for my research, using the required referencing system.

☐ I have checked that I haven't omitted from my list any primary sources that I have used.

Chapter 15
Working with participants

Participant-based research is typical of a wide range of subjects, from social sciences, education, medicine and health to business and business-related subjects, linguistics, media and performance, product design, tourism, social geography, politics and many others.

Gathering research material through working with participants can make an assignment particularly engaging. The results tend to be more difficult to predict, there are ethical issues to grapple with, and the organisational issues can be complex, all of which add extra interest as well as challenge. In addition, participant-based research calls for, and can develop, interpersonal skills and personal qualities that are valued by employers.

Overview of methods

If you are interested in conducting a project that requires participant involvement, many options are open to you. There are well established methods to draw upon, and plenty of research and specialist manuals available to help you to tease out the issues for the method you select.

For student research, the most typical methods are:

- Experiments
- Surveys and questionnaires
- Interviews
- Observations
- Combinations of these methods, such as in case studies.

More details of these are provided in Chapters 16–20.

Things to consider

Working with participants requires good planning and a great deal of forethought. It is advisable to put yourself in the shoes of your proposed participants in order to consider how to find them, work with them, and address their needs. This means thinking through such things as:

Presentation: how would potential participants view you as a researcher? What would be the implications of such perceptions for your research?

Safety and boundaries: how do you take care of yourself and others when conducting the research?

Communication: what are the best ways of clarifying to potential and actual participants the purpose of the research, and what you need from them?

Particular circumstances: what issues arise from working with specific types of participant, such as children, or those participating in their workplace?

Ethics

You will be expected to demonstrate that you have thought through the ethical issues relevant to your research and participants. Such considerations should be addressed at the proposal stage; see Chapter 12. Issues specific to working with children and employees are considered below.

Selection

One important factor to think through early on is how you will find the right participants. See pages 125–7 and 134–6.

Presenting yourself as a researcher

Managing perceptions

It is always important to present yourself and your research in a professional manner. This is especially so if you suspect that potential participants might not take the research seriously if conducted by a student. Manage perceptions through being efficient, well-organised, well-informed, and looking the part.

General considerations

Think through, in advance, the concerns and interests of those you will be approaching and how you will address these.

Time: Consider their time as precious.

Motivation: If you are approaching organisations, businesses or schools for help, research them first. Is it likely that they could help or would want to? Which angles of your research might spark their interest and make them want to be involved?

Questions: Be prepared for people to be suspicious about what you want from them. Have answers ready.

Reluctance: Don't persist if people wish to stop.

Phone calls

Prepare the content of phone calls before making them. Don't read from a script, but do prepare a list of items to cover. Give the impression that you have thought things through, are orderly, and won't take up their time a moment more than necessary.

Be clear how long the call will take and ask if they can give that time. Time yourself, and don't take longer than you promised. Avoid being drawn into more small talk than planned, as you won't then be able to complete the call on time.

Listen when others are speaking, interrupting only if essential to keep to time. Acknowledge what they say, returning to your list promptly and politely.

Face-to-face contact

- Arrive slightly ahead of time. Be prepared to wait but don't keep others waiting.
- Dress smartly or appropriately for the context.
- Be polite and friendly but retain formality.
- Avoid being drawn into personal anecdotes and reciting your own examples.
- Be clear what you need and why, and how long everything will take.
- Stick to the time schedule that you outlined.

Providing information

- Keep this as short as possible.
- Provide necessary detail succinctly.
- Use clear, straightforward, age-appropriate language.
- Explain any jargon or technical terms.
- Give full, accurate details about times, locations, etc.
- Word-process material, using informative headings. Don't overcrowd the page.
- Use high quality copies – not material that is blurred or printed off-centre.
- State your department and institution, with contact details, but not personal details.

Responsibility to your organisation

Whether or not you feel as though you represent your college, university or organisation, those that you contact about a student or work-related project will see you in an ambassadorial role. Avoid putting your institution or organisation into any awkward situation through actions of your own.

It is easier to avoid unexpected outcomes if you:
- follow guidelines set by your institution
- keep to the ethical guidelines
- keep to your prepared outline or script
- prepare brief handouts in advance
- work through the content of handouts with the participant as well as giving them a copy, so that it is clear what you mean.

Safety and boundaries

Safety

It is your responsibility to ensure that the research is conducted safely, for yourself, participants and anyone else that could be affected. That might include passers by, participants' families, others in your department, or those likely to be in the area once you have finished your work.

Risk assessments

- Use guidelines provided by your department.
- Find out about the obvious and more subtle health and safety risks related to your research.
- Identify the risks that could arise for others from your research.
- Evaluate the likelihood and the level of harm that could result.
- State how you will mitigate such risks through good planning and management.

It is unlikely that you can eliminate all risk. Unexpected accidents and outcomes arise, and if these did occur, you would be asked to account for how carefully you had thought through the safety of your participants. This is true for all participants although, depending on the risks, you may need to pay special attention to certain participants such as:

- children of different ages
- people with different disabilities
- people with various learning difficulties
- pregnant (or breast-feeding) women
- people who are ill, or who could be
- anyone vulnerable in that context.

Keeping yourself safe

The importance of maintaining your personal safety may seem obvious but you do need to show that you have thought this through in a detailed and systematic way.

- Draw up a separate risk assessment for you as the researcher and for each location in which the research takes place.
- When interviewing, do so where other people would be passing by.
- When researching in the field, choose safe locations; maintain phone contact.
- Always let others know when and where you are going, by which route, and when you will return. Provide contact details. Let them know when you return.
- Don't give out your personal address; use your department's phone number and address.

Set boundaries

Set out everything clearly from the very beginning, so that you eliminate the possibility of creating false expectations of any kind. This helps avoid awkward situations, misunderstandings, disappointments, unwanted behaviours, complaints and litigation. Some ways of setting boundaries are listed below.

- Select participants wisely; clarify who might be problematic within the context of the research.
- Maintain a professional manner at all times, so that your motives can't be misinterpreted.
- Focus on the project, the participant and neutral topics. Don't talk about yourself.
- Communicate project expectations clearly, stating what will happen, when, how and why.
- Ask prospective participants to sign to say they understand the purpose of the research and what they are being asked to do.
- Stick exactly to what was agreed.
- Don't linger for chats with participants.

Ethical implications

Keeping your participants and others safe from harm is an ethical consideration that you may be asked to address through your department's ethics committee. See page 107.

Find out: insurance arrangements

It is likely that your institution has insurance that covers student research. Find out what the arrangements are for yourself and for participants. What would be covered and what would not?

Communicating with participants

Informing participants

It is generally a good idea to inform participants both through written information and talking them through the details in person.

- Telling them yourself means that you know they have not skipped important information when reading and that all the key points have been conveyed. If you notice any confusion, you can go back over the point, explaining it.

- Using written information provides evidence that you provided the correct information. It is advisable to include a section for their signed consent (page 108).

Writing information for participants

This generally takes a great deal of thought as you need to provide information that meets several different sets of requirements:

- to reassure the ethics committee
- to convey your methodology to participants
- to inform and support participants
- to meet potential participants' needs.

Brief and succinct: people do not usually have the time or patience to read more than a few lines.

Clear: there should be no ambiguities or content which participants might misinterpret.

Reassuring: your information should be written in such a way that participants are left feeling comfortable about what they are being asked to do and why, that they will be safe and treated with dignity and respect throughout, and that you can guarantee confidentiality.

Informative: participants need to understand fully what is involved. If they are not sure what they will have to do, then they are less likely to take part. Too much information can mask the key information.

Comprehensive: the information provided needs to cover the aims of the project, what participants have to do, what happens to the information, and who gets to see the report.

Putting the participant first

You have responsibilities towards participants. Even if you are working with student participants that you know already, you must treat them as any researcher should treat the public.

It is also in your interest to look after your participants. If you put them at their ease, they will continue to participate and will ask for clarification if needed. Otherwise, they may not take part, or may provide just the answers that they think you want, resulting in inaccurate data.

Checklist: putting the participant first

Reflect on the issues related to each of the following questions.

Check off ☑ each of the following once you have considered it fully and addressed it in your materials for participants.

- ☐ What concerns might potential participants have about taking part in any research project?

- ☐ What might be their concerns about this particular project?

- ☐ What would make them feel comfortable to ask me about such concerns?

- ☐ How long is it reasonable to ask the participants to engage with the interview/ survey/observation/case study?

- ☐ What might 'no harm' mean to potential participants in the context of this research?

- ☐ What risks or challenges might individuals be taking through participating in the research?

- ☐ What other barriers might there be that would prevent good participants from taking part?

What do participants need to know?

Participants generally need to be reassured about becoming involved in research. Bear in mind that they may have more questions, or be more anxious or pressed for time, than they like to communicate. Plan your answers to questions such as these, addressing potential concerns, spoken or not. Don't wait to be asked. Think how you can present your project, so that potential participants feel reassured in advance of asking.

Children and vulnerable people as participants

Supervised or accompanied throughout

It is advisable to select projects where you would not be unsupervised or alone with children or other vulnerable participants. This is for the safety and peace of mind of all stakeholders, including you as the researcher.

Nancy expected her research might keep her tied up for a while

Clearances needed

If you will be working on a sustained basis with vulnerable participants, you may need to undergo specific checks. In Britain you would need:

- a criminal records check from the Disclosure and Barring Service (DBS); there may be a charge and it takes time to arrange
- *and*, if applicable, signed consent from the organisation (school, youth centre, agency) working with the children
- *and* signed consent of parents or carers
- *and* the agreement of the child or vulnerable adult if they are able to give it
- *and*, normally, the approval of your institution's ethics committee or panel.

Preparation for consents and approvals

As part of gaining informed consent, provide:

- clear, succinct information for the parents/carers/organisations to help them decide if it is right for the dependant to be involved
- a clearly worded form that expresses, unequivocally, what they are consenting to.

Protecting vulnerable participants

Before consents and approvals are given, those concerned want to know that you have thought through everything from the perspective of the child or vulnerable person. They need clear information about such issues as:

- what is involved
- how you will explain to the child or vulnerable person what is happening
- how you will keep participants safe from all kinds of harm; they may ask to see your risk assessment and risk management plans
- how all due care would be taken in matters such as dignity, health and self-esteem
- how you will maintain participant anonymity, especially if photographs or audio-visual material will be generated
- what use will be made of material or data – and that usage would not be against the interests of the participants in any way
- what the process would be for complaints
- details of a contact person at the college or university, for complaints.

To parents, schools, care homes, hospitals/organisations, provide details such as:

- dates, times, durations and locations of activity undertaken with participants
- whether the education or care of others would be disrupted, such as through noise, blocked exits, equipment, trailing wires, etc.

Practical issues

Working with children and vulnerable people does require a high level of forethought. Consider:

Complexity of tasks: Abilities vary a great deal.

Use of language, tone, body language and non-verbal cues: How will you ensure that participants understand fully what is required and could not misinterpret your intentions or requirements?

Duration: How long would participants be able to take part before becoming tired?

Controlled conditions: Are these possible and/or desirable with your participants? See pages 139–40. If you needed to, how would you manage these?

Working with participants in the workplace

Many student research projects are conducted in a workplace, typically in a student's current place of employment, or as a work placement, or as a specific project for an employer-as-client.

Permissions from employers

There are some kinds of covert research that may be permissible without employer agreement, such as those that are based only on data that is in the public domain. Such information might include annual financial reports, material available through public facing company websites, or available on other public websites such as that of the Charity Commission.

If you are not considering gaining permission, it is advisable to talk this through with your supervisor first, and to have a good rationale.

The kinds of permissions that you need to seek from employers, including your own, are:

- to conduct research in your work time
- to conduct research on your work premises, even if on an unrelated topic
- to use company information that is not in the public domain
- to gather material for your research from interviews, observations or other means in the workplace itself
- to present research that you are conducting for an employer as a student assignment.

Employers are more likely to give permission if:

- your research would be of practical benefit to their business
- you can demonstrate an understanding of their business and business needs
- you can ensure that confidentiality and anonymity will be maintained
- no reference will be made to the company in your research, OR that full recognition will be given (whichever is relevant)
- you can address their concerns in a satisfactory way.

Sometimes, company personnel will have reasons for not giving permission but which they are not at liberty to explain. If so, that is their prerogative.

Typical employer concerns to address

You need to put yourself in the employer's shoes. They have liabilities, responsibilities, costs and many stakeholder interests to consider. They may not have much time at their disposal for talking through issues that arise from student projects. If you want permission, it is best to demonstrate that you have thought these through already for yourself. Look to reassure employers …

- that you will not generate any unwanted legal issues or financial costs for them
- that your research will not have an adverse impact on their reputation
- that health, safety, security, data control and other risks have been identified and that your risk assessment and risk management plans look realistic
- that you will respect confidential information such as employee or client data
- that you will not leak any information that might have an adverse impact on their business, or give competitors an advantage
- that no damage will be done to the property or environment
- that you and your research are covered by your institution's insurance, or other insurance, and that your research will not have an impact on their insurance
- that you will avoid getting in the way or disrupting everyday business in any way
- that you are not going to annoy their employees.

Working with participants

Check off ☑ each of the following once you have addressed it in full. Put a line through any items that do not apply. Address any aspects that require further attention.

Presentation and responsibilities

- ☐ I have thought through how best to manage participant perceptions of the research.
- ☐ I have given thought to how I will dress so that I 'look the part'.
- ☐ I have given thought to how to act in an 'ambassadorial role' (page 130).
- ☐ I have considered the ethical considerations outlined in Chapter 12.
- ☐ I have conducted risk assessments relevant to my research (see pages 39–42 and 131).
- ☐ I have worked out how to maintain suitable boundaries, in line with page 131 above.
- ☐ I understand how to keep my project within the university or college insurance arrangements.

Communication with potential participants

- ☐ I have worked out the time it will take to talk through the project with potential participants.
- ☐ I have taken on board potential participants' needs and motivations.
- ☐ I have prepared a list of items to cover when speaking to potential participants.
- ☐ I have prepared answers to questions they might have.
- ☐ I have a strategy for keeping to time.

Communication with participants

- ☐ I have produced a handout for participants, in line with the guidance on pages 130 and 132.
- ☐ My handout clarifies expected time commitments.
- ☐ It clarifies what participants will have to do.
- ☐ It includes details of who to contact at the university/college in case of a complaint.
- ☐ I have prepared a schedule to structure my time with participants.

Authorisations and consent

- ☐ I have clarified to participants how their personal data will be stored, used and protected.
- ☐ I will be able to ensure the level of confidentiality and anonymity participants expect.
- ☐ I have designed clear consent forms.
- ☐ I have received signed consents from all participants.
- ☐ If relevant, I have received agreements from employers or organisations for me to use their data.
- ☐ I provided suitable background to ensure that all those signing consent were appropriately informed.

Working with children/vulnerable groups

- ☐ I have designed the research in ways that maintain participants' dignity, self-esteem and safety at all times.
- ☐ Tasks are within their capability/understanding.
- ☐ All material, explanations and instructions have been made accessible and age appropriate.
- ☐ I have the signed consent of parents/carers.
- ☐ I have kept relevant third parties well informed (such as schools, care homes, hospitals).
- ☐ If working unaccompanied, I have clearance from the DBS (see page 134).

Use of data

- ☐ I have checked my draft report to ensure that anonymity has been maintained.
- ☐ I checked that anonymity and confidentiality are maintained in appendices/acknowledgements.

Chapter 16
Experiments

Experiments are the main method of research in many sciences. They are common within the social sciences and can be used in any subject discipline if the topic lends itself to the method.

Characteristics

Many of the premises and approaches that underlie experimental work have been addressed in previous chapters. Specific characteristics to note are:

- use of science/positivist paradigms
- empiricism (page 100)
- objectivity (page 92)
- quantitative methods (page 93)
- testing hypotheses (pages 100 and 116)
- controlled conditions (pages 139–40)
- selecting samples (page 125).

Useful for …

- investigating cause and effect, when the variables can be tightly controlled
- testing theory in controlled conditions, demonstrating that results are consistent with a theory or hypothesis; experiments cannot fully disprove a theory (as a further experiment might have different results).

Advantages

- There are many long-established, well-documented methods to draw upon.
- Experiments can be relatively easy to manage for scale, scope, costs, time constraints, and other risks, as you have more control over the conditions.
- They enable accurate data collection.
- Findings can contribute to a broader database of results, which helps to establish the likelihood of a theory being sound, and with drawing generalisations.

Disadvantages

- Ecological validity: your findings may not be applicable outside the controlled conditions of the experiment. It may still be useful to conduct the research, if it throws new light on the topic.
- There may be resource constraints in accessing labs and equipment, or in the costs of materials and technicians.
- Experiments often do not go to plan.
- It can require much patience, waiting for an experiment to run its course.
- When participants are involved, it is harder to control the conditions (see page 140).

The design challenge

Although many opportunities for carrying out experiments may be provided at earlier levels of study, these may have been presented in a formulaic way, rather like 'recipes' to be followed. Even if students were told to draw out general observations about method, they may not have grasped sufficiently how to formulate hypotheses and design experiments for themselves. Many find it difficult to do so, at least at first.

If you are finding that this is true in your own case, plan to put some time aside to:

- look again carefully at the design details of experiments that you have undertaken as part of your coursework
- read the methods sections of journal articles relevant to your discipline
- consider which methods you might be able to adapt for your own research.

Experiments: planning your experiments

Considerations

The checklist on page 142 leads you through the key steps in planning and conducting an experiment. Bear in mind the broader issues covered in earlier sections, such as:

- choosing a good, feasible topic (Chapter 8)
- good research principles such as reliability and validity (Chapter 10)
- project planning (Chapter 3)
- ethics, health and safety, and the needs of participants (Chapters 12 and 15).

Focus and precision

Your planning should be meticulous. Experiments are characterised by precision in:

- thinking through the concept: each step should follow logically from the hypothesis
- terminology and use of language
- observation, measurement and recording.

What are you really measuring?

You need to be clear that what you measure is, in practice, what you purport to measure:

- that doing X causes Y…
- to the extent that you say it does …
- and that nothing else caused Y.

This means setting up the experiment in such a way that you can rule out the possibility that your results were simply the effect of:

- other factors, or variables, that were not intended to be part of the experiment
- random chance – or accident
- normal developmental or change processes, such as aging, growth over time, or natural erosion.

Plan for recording your findings

Decide how you will record your observations and results, such as through record sheets, observation notebooks, Blog, digital recording or relevant software and tools.

Check carefully for all potential variables …

Plan a trial run (pilot)

Pilot your methods, including how you will record results, to check for any unforeseen hitches in design. Fine-tune your methods until you are confident that they have a reasonable chance of providing the kind of data that you want.

Experiments: controlling the conditions

Controlled conditions

Your aim is to set up conditions for your experiments that make it as easy as possible to interpret accurately what your results are telling you. This means eliminating any factors that might:

- have unwanted effects on the experiment
- muddy the waters about what your results mean

Your aim is to create conditions that enable you to measure the impact of one thing, or 'variable', on another – to see whether X does cause Y. That means removing other 'variables' that might affect the result. Broadly speaking, this means setting up two (or more) experimental conditions which are exactly alike in every way except for the one factor that you are varying.

The way that you control for variables will depend on your experiment. Setting up conditions that are 'exactly alike' means something different for each experiment. It might mean setting up identical sterile conditions for testing a medical procedure – or matching two groups of participants according to age and gender to test reaction times to visual stimuli.

Some differences are highly unlikely to have an impact on the particular aspect that you are measuring, and others would make a great difference. You need to make a judgement about what is likely to be relevant or irrelevant.

Experimental conditions

You may wish to compare the impact of manipulating a variable in several different ways. Each distinct way of doing so is referred to as a 'condition'. So, if you wanted to test the impact of changing:

(1) temperature alone, *OR*
(2) pressure alone, *OR*
(3) a combination of temperature and pressure

… you would set up at least 3 conditions.

'Controls'

You would normally also include a 'control' of some kind so that you have a point of comparison for measuring your results. The control indicates what would have happened in ordinary circumstances, if you hadn't altered, or manipulated, any independent variables. In the instance above, this would mean setting up a fourth condition in which you didn't change the temperature or pressure.

Condition 1 (Control): No manipulation of the independent variables

Condition 2: Manipulation of the independent variable, temperature

Condition 3: Manipulation of the independent variable, pressure

Condition 4: Manipulating independent variables of both temperature and pressure

Experiments: controlling the conditions continued

Control groups

Similarly, if an experiment were to test whether an energy drink improved student performance, then in one condition, a 'control group' would not be given the energy drink.

However, when participants are involved and consent is gained for taking part, their behaviour might vary just by knowing that they have been given an energy drink. This psychological response is a variable that you need to control too. You might choose to control for this by: giving the experimental and the control groups a drink that appears identical but where the control group's drink is an energy-neutral alternative. Neither group should know which drink they have received.

Double blind experiments

Researchers' behaviour can also be affected if they know which is the control group and which is the experimental condition.

To control for researcher behaviour as a variable in its own right, many experiments are designed as 'double blind'. This means that no-one involved in the observation, measurement or recording of the experiment has access to information that could affect their own behaviour, such as influencing to which group each participant is assigned.

Clarify the independent variable

The independent variable is one item or aspect you are changing or manipulating so that you can test its impact on one other isolated, measurable variable (the 'dependent variable'). The independent variable might be: increasing the temperature; changing the font size; refreshments provided at meetings, etc.

Clarify the dependent variable

The dependent variable is the one that you are investigating to measure what occurs when it is put under changed conditions – that is, when you manipulate the independent variable. This might be the rate at which ice melts when the temperature is varied; the time that people spend on a portable device if font size is varied; the number of people attending a meeting if refreshments are provided.

Decide:

- What does 'controlled conditions' mean in the context of your experiment?
- Which variables will you be measuring? (See 'Clarify the dependent variable'.)
- Which variables will you be manipulating? (See 'Clarify the independent variable'.)
- How will you isolate these, and eliminate or reduce the impact of other variables that might contaminate your results?
- Will you use one or more controls (or control groups if working with participants)?
- Will you use double blind conditions?

Jermaine had no idea which participant had selected the energy drink

Experiments: locations

Although the typical image of an experiment is of a lab-based experiment conducted by people in white coats, experiments can be conducted in a variety of settings.

In a specially designed laboratory

In subjects where experimental work is typical, it is probable that specialist laboratory space and equipment will be available. You would need to check what kinds of resources were open to you and for how long. There may, for example, be allocated lab space, or budgets for each student for lab space, technicians and materials.

Laboratory-based experiments tend to confer advantages in enabling tight control over the variables that are being manipulated and the general conduct of the research. Lab-based observations for people-based experiments are covered in Chapter 17.

In the field

Experiments can be conducted outside of laboratories, in the 'field'. The field might actually be a field, such as for earth and environmental scientists, agriculture or land-surveying, but the 'field' might be any setting outside of the lab and relevant to the experiment: in a classroom, hospital, supermarket, underwater, etc.

Where field experiments involve human participants, the usual issues of consent would normally apply. You could design experiments where consent isn't needed, such as providing refreshments at meetings and taking quantitative data on whether attendance increased as a result.

Web-based

Depending on their focus, experiments can be conducted using the internet. The internet opens up ever new and interesting possibilities for experiments, especially in people-based subjects such as social sciences, media and performance arts, humanities, healthcare and business, or in technology and design-based areas. As long as you can, ethically, manipulate variables online, you can use online tools to observe online behaviours or their effects. These could be global results, involving large amounts of data.

Alan classified pillows as 'essential equipment' when it came to his online research project

Google tools enable you to track collective behaviours, trends and changes, and to compare these according to many kinds of variable – such as region, timing, length of visits, etc. You could also design experiments where participants provide consent for personal data to be used, such as their age or ethnicity.

The ethical considerations are significant. You would need to demonstrate that your online research would not be used in ways that:

● invade individuals' privacy or risk the security of their data

● could be used to manipulate or deceive the public.

Experiments

Check off ☑ each of the following once you have addressed it in full. Cross out any that do not apply. Address any aspects that require more work.

Before you start

- ☐ Formulate the hypothesis (page 116).
- ☐ Clarify how you will gather data to test your hypothesis.
- ☐ Consider what 'controlled conditions' means in the context of your experiments.
- ☐ Clarify the independent variable(s).
- ☐ Clarify the dependent variable(s).
- ☐ How, and to what extent, will you vary these?
- ☐ Decide the number and type of experimental conditions.
- ☐ Decide on the controls/control group(s).
- ☐ Decide how to ensure participants will not know which group they are in.
- ☐ Set up double-blind conditions, if needed.
- ☐ Decide how to measure any changes that occur when you manipulate the variables.
- ☐ Decide time intervals for recording measurements and observations.
- ☐ Decide how to note or record findings.
- ☐ Design, purchase or adapt material or tools for recording findings.
- ☐ Check that resources are definitely available.
- ☐ Weigh up the ethical considerations.
- ☐ Address health, safety and security.
- ☐ Plan out your methods in fine detail.
- ☐ Write up your planned methods.
- ☐ Create (or purchase) any materials needed for the experiment.
- ☐ Create any materials needed for informing participants (page 132).
- ☐ Select your sample (page 125).
- ☐ Ensure that you have all consents and permissions before starting.

Pilot

- ☐ Set up the controlled conditions as planned.
- ☐ If you change anything in the course of setting up the experiment, rewrite your methods. Check this with your supervisor.
- ☐ Pilot the methods, noting areas for improvement.
- ☐ Fine-tune the methods, and then rewrite the methods section of your report.
- ☐ Pilot and fine-tune again if necessary.
- ☐ Write up the pilot in the methods section of your dissertation or report.
- ☐ Include copies of the materials you used for the pilot in your appendices.

During

- ☐ Once you start the experiment, follow your method exactly as planned – as a 'recipe'.
- ☐ If later stages must be redesigned in the light of what actually occurs, discuss first with your supervisor. Rewrite your Methods section. Address this in the Discussion section of your report.
- ☐ Make accurate records, using the tools you devised.
- ☐ Store records carefully during the experiment.

After

- ☐ Collate your results.
- ☐ Select a format for presenting them clearly, such as graphs, charts, etc.
- ☐ Clarify whether the research hypothesis was supported or not.
- ☐ Clarify the level of significance.

Chapter 17
Observations

Observational methods are common to both science and social science subjects.

Useful for ...

- in-depth analyses of behaviours in adults, children, animals, events or phenomena
- testing theory or products in real-life or simulated settings

Advantages

- They can yield rich information.
- You gain a more immediate sense of the subject, context, and how multiple variables interact.
- You gain insights into aspects that you might not anticipate when designing the project.

Disadvantages

- They can be time consuming.
- It can be difficult to find willing participants.
- It can be hard to generate useful information.
- There are complex ethical issues.
- The findings can be highly subjective and difficult to generalise from.

Organising your observations

Observations tend to lack natural structure, so be especially rigorous in deciding their parameters before commencing. Otherwise, it can be hard to decide which material is relevant. Be clear on your purpose – what do you want to understand better? How will the style of observation or the range of participants that you have selected help you to achieve that?

Set clear parameters

- How many observations?
- Of whom or what? For how long?

Focus

If it fits your research design, decide in advance exactly which aspects you will focus on and what you will record – and what kinds of things you will choose to ignore. Check to see that you have a manageable number of items to record as part of your observation. If your research methodology requires open-ended observation without note-taking during the observation, consider when and how you will take notes following the observation.

Recording your observations

Decide how you will keep records during the observation. For example, will you:

- design tally sheets (page 146)?
- jot down notes at the time (pages 148–9)?
- write up notes afterwards (page 148)?
- make a digital recording?

Pilot it

Test out your methods in one or more trial runs. Note the challenges and difficulties that arise and address these before conducting those observations that will count towards your data.

What kind of observation?

This is a key question for observations as your location and/or participation as an observer may have an impact on the kinds of results you receive. Different kinds of ethical and safety issues may also apply.

My observation method will be ...

- [ ] Direct observations in laboratory conditions
- [ ] Direct observations in everyday settings
- [ ] Open participant observations
- [ ] Hidden participant observations
- [ ] Structured observation
- [ ] Unstructured observation

Observations: direct or participant

Direct observations

In a specially designed laboratory on campus

These allow unobtrusive observations from behind tinted glass, using two-way mirrors or through camera links. The advantages are that your personal presence would not have a direct impact on the participants' behaviours. It is also possible to record the session and look back over the details later to corroborate the findings of your observation, or to test the accuracy of your observations. There are usually benefits in terms of safety, ease of arrangement, and technical support. These provide useful settings for both structured and unstructured observation.

The disadvantages are that there may be restricted time available for using the resource, and technology can go wrong. The setting is generally rather unnatural, even when made user friendly, and it may not be clear how far that affects your results.

You would normally inform adults, parents and older children that they were being observed, which might affect their behaviours and responses, especially for shorter sessions. Children might not be aware they are being observed but tend to be more sensitive to unfamiliar settings so the results might be different from those in everyday life.

In everyday settings

Observing others in their everyday lives is ethically sensitive and would not be appropriate for some kinds of observations – and certainly not for repeated observations of individuals. However, there are some kinds of observation, such as those involving the behaviours of crowds, which are less contentious ethically.

For example, you might observe how the public make use of a pier, beach or café facilities, or changes in behaviours depending on whether ticket gates are left open or closed at a railway station. These wouldn't normally infringe on privacy or interfere with the normal functioning of the location.

Participant observation

In participant observations, you are a participant in the context that you are researching, as in ethnographic research. These lend themselves more easily to broadly based, qualitative findings, such as about attitudes, behaviours, changes or events.

There is a spectrum of types of participant observation, depending on how far you would have been engaged in the particular context even if you had not been researching it (such as through your employment, community or leisure activities) through to participating in a context primarily to research it (Burgess, 1984).

Open observations

This means that you let people know that you are observing them. This has the advantage of addressing potential ethical concerns about the observation and ensures that your participants are willing and informed. However, knowing that they are being observed may alter how participants behave. Additionally, even if you play no active role in the observation, characteristics such as your age, gender, ethnicity or even body language may have an impact on participants' behaviour and responses.

Hidden observations

Those being observed would not be aware that you are observing them. This has the advantage of not inhibiting participants' 'normal' responses during the observation. However, there are significant ethical considerations. Hidden observations may be acceptable for short-term studies, conducted in public places. Hidden participant observations are not recommended for student projects.

Structured observations

Structured observations: process

For these, you decide in advance which specific facets of the situation or which types of phenomena you will record in each observation. Structured observations don't tend to lend themselves well to participant research.

Purpose

Decide what you want to find out through the observation – and why.

Focus

Isolate which particular behaviours you will focus on for your observation. This might be identifying how customers respond to in-store displays or tasting sessions; how often a teacher offers praise and for what, or how participants behave during the first 20 minutes of sleep.

Definitions

One of the challenges for conducting observations is deciding 'what counts' as an example of the behaviour being observed. 'Praise', for example, might seem an easy thing to count but this can be offered in distinct ways. You would need to define exactly what would constitute praise for the purpose of your research: A nod and a smile? Or use of particular words? Would a distracted repetition of the word 'excellent' count as praise? Does it matter if the intended recipient hears or acknowledges the praise? Should different kinds of praise be counted separately?

> ### Reflection: Defining terms exactly
>
> - For your research: what 'grey areas' might arise about what to include or omit?
> - How will you decide what should count and what will not, so that you are sure that you record occurrences consistently?

Feasibility

Consider how feasible it will be to capture what you aim to record. Will you be able to see and hear each occurrence? Would you be able to record one occurrence without missing others? How many phenomena can you keep track of during a single session?

Participants

- How will you select participants?
- Is a particular sample needed (page 125)?
- What permissions are needed (pages 134–5)?

Measurement

Decide on a realistic method for measuring the phenomena. Will this be:

- a frequency count: how many times does something occur during the observation?
- a duration count: for how long does it last? For what % or proportion of the total time that the observation took place?

Significance

Identify how many participants, observations, and/or how much time spent in observation you would need in order to collect sufficient data to achieve significant results. Depending on your data, this might mean statistical significance using a method agreed within your discipline or, more informally, a 'reasonable amount' of observation(s) to ensure the identification of recognisable trends or patterns.

Recording a structured observation

Decide how you will keep records during the observation. The most typical way of recording information in structured observations is through a tally sheet.

Designing a tally sheet

Use tally sheets to keep track of the specific items that you have selected for recording during each observation. These should be easy to use at speed.

A single side generally works best for paper-based tally sheets.

No scroll: A table or chart that can be completed without scrolling works best if you are using a laptop or tablet.

Number of items: Decide on a manageable number of items for recording whilst conducting the observation, and which would not distract you from it.

Tracking method: Decide on the easiest way of keeping track of the items that you decide to record – such as making a single stroke for each occurrence, or using a '5 bar gate' if you consider there would be time for this.

Clear sections: Divide the sheet or screen into sections, one for each category of information that you will record. Set out the tally sheet (or screen) in sections that are the most intuitive for you to use.

Practice completing the sheet without looking at it for more than a glance.

Example 1: Observation Recording Form

Target behaviour: A sparrow lands on the bird table and successfully accesses seed from the bird feeder.
Observation Time = 1 hour

Date	Start Time	Incidences of target behaviour	Total
26/8/13	07.00	HHH HHH II	12
26/8/13	11.00	IIII	4
26/8/13	15.00	HHH I	6
26/8/13	19.00	HHH HHH III	13

Example 2: Behavioural Observation Form

Date	Time	Gets up from desk without permission	Flaps hands in front of face	Taps pencil on desk	Rocks back and forth in seat
02/09/13	9.30–10.00	III	HHH HHH I	HHH I	HHH HHH
02/09/13	2.00–2.30	HHH	HHH III	II	HHH IIII
03/09/13	09.30–10.00		III	I	IIII
03/09/13	2.30–3.00	II	HHH HHH III	III	HHH HHH I

Unstructured observations

Unstructured observations: process

These generally lend themselves well to participant research and are popular with research students.

The lack of structure can be appealing, initially, but can also be a 'false friend' if the research ends up as unfocused. Such observations require a different kind of mental discipline, especially in analysing the results and identifying what is significant within these.

Select the context for research

Choose one that, in the time available, you can get to know sufficiently well to understand its complex nuances.

Identify your role

Will you participate? If so, how? How will you balance 'joining in' with the research itself?

Objectivity

Select contexts, roles and themes which allow you to hold an objective perspective.

Justify your choices

You cannot focus on, nor note down, everything that takes place. Of necessity, you will have to choose, or acknowledge that there will be gaps in your recording. Consider carefully in advance how you will make such choices once you are conducting the observation. What kinds of behaviours or situations might arise for you to note? How would you choose between these?

For example, will you select one or more people (or animals) to track throughout the observation? Will you decide these in advance, on arrival, or at the start of the observation? Or will you select specific events to note in detail, if and when these occur?

Recording your observations

Decide how you will keep records during the observation. For example, will you:

- [ ] jot down detailed notes of what arises at the time, selecting relevant aspects later for analysis?
- [ ] make focused notes on selected themes whilst you observe?
- [ ] observe without making notes, and then write up observations immediately afterwards?
- [ ] make a recording to use alongside the observation?
- [ ] combine several methods?

See pages 148–9.

Making sense of your observations

For unstructured observations, it is especially important to draw out the meaning or significance of what you have observed. This may mean returning to your original reading or undertaking further reading to make sense of your observations within the broader context of your discipline. For some courses, you might be invited to discuss your observations with your fellow students in seminars.

Generally this means relating your observations:

- *either*: back to theory and/or previous research in a meaningful way
- *and/or*: to conclusions and recommendations that arise from your research.

Recording unstructured observations

The following section follows two students who are both conducting unstructured observations, and shows the steps that they took in recording and making sense of their observations.

Observation notes and analysis 1

Marcia is a third-year social work student conducting research into the development of pro-social behaviours in young children. She is using the 'child observation' method, which involves visiting the same young child each week for an hour over a period of at least a few months. This method encourages students not to interact with the child that they are observing and not to make notes during their observations.

Before the observation

'As I walk to the nursery where I will observe Billy I try to focus my attention and clear other thoughts from my mind. I know I will have to concentrate hard for the hour I am there and I don't want to be distracted by other things. I mentally rehearse how I will respond when Billy tries to interact with me – I find it hard not being able to play with him. Before I started the observations, I made sure that the nursery staff knew what I was doing and why, and now they know not to chat to me during my visits.'

During the observation

'I watch everything that Billy does for the hour I am with him. I sit on a chair at the corner of the room. I don't take any notes whilst I am in the room – I try to mentally note everything that Billy says and does. If other children try to talk to me I smile but try not to get involved.'

After the observation

'After I leave, I need to quickly find somewhere quiet to sit and write up my notes. I go to a nearby cafe. I write out everything I can remember about what I observed. I couldn't remember that much for the first few sessions but now I can get about 3 pages of notes from each visit.'

An example of observation notes

'Billy sees Abbie pick up the fire engine and rushes towards her shouting "mine!" She frowns and pulls away from him and he throws himself against her, trying to get the toy out of her hands, making a low moaning noise as he does this. Julie, the nursery nurse, shouts across the room at him "C'mon Billy, share nicely", which Billy seems to ignore completely. He continues to try to pull the toy from Abbie's hands. After about two minutes, Julie moves towards him and moves him away from Abbie saying "any more of that and you will have to go in the naughty corner". Billy throws himself on the floor and starts crying, drumming his heels against the floor and turning red in the face. After 30 seconds, he pauses for breath and appears to look round the room to see if anyone is watching him. He makes eye contact with me, holds it for about 5 seconds then throws his head back towards the floor and screams again. At that moment, Xander, another child, brings a picture to show me. Billy lifts his head from the floor and looks at us before shouting out, "No – mine!"'

Making sense of the observation

'I have a weekly seminar where a group of 9 of us take turns in discussing our notes. This really helps me think about emerging themes in my observation such as a child's sense of possessions and the development of sharing behaviours. It also helps me link what I see with theories of child development. I am starting to realise that Billy is at a developmental stage where he believes that everything – objects and people – belongs to him. He does not yet understand the concept of sharing.'

Recording unstructured observations

Observation notes and analysis 2

Jake is studying for an MSc in Town Planning. His research is considering the usage of urban open public spaces. Within this, he has been carrying out unstructured observations in open public spaces to gain data about how those spaces are currently used.

Before the observation

'Most people have a sense of how public spaces are used – meeting people, eating lunch and so on. For my observation, it is important that I am really looking at what is happening rather than confirming something I am expecting to see. Before I start my observation, I like to sit for a couple of minutes in the space where I will observe and just quietly take it in.'

During the observation

'I observe over a 30-minute period and visit each location at three different times of day. I try to find a bench or somewhere to sit with a good view of the whole area I am looking at. For those 30 minutes, I try to take in everything going on in the area. I note down on my tablet all of the different activities going on in the area, trying to just describe exactly what I see, rather than interpreting what I think is happening. I only note down people who have stayed in the space for more than 2 minutes, so I don't take note of people just passing through. It can be a challenge at times – especially if someone asks me what I am doing! They are usually interested when I tell them about my research but that can mean quite a bit of lost observation time.'

After the observation

'At home I save my notes onto my main computer – making a separate folder for each location. Until I have finished all the observations in an area, I try to resist analysing my data and making conclusions as I find this stops me from observing with an open mind during my next visit.'

Example of observation notes

10.31 – 6 people in Jubilee Square: mother with young child, playing catch on grassy area; young woman with smart phone sitting on bench, typing; 3 men in casual clothing standing near fountain talking and laughing.

10.33 – man in suit comes to join woman on bench and takes out tablet computer. Holds it up in air – trying to get internet signal? Looks annoyed.

10.35 – man and woman leave square

10.37 – young man joins group in front of fountain and they leave the square

10.40 – Older woman comes into the square and sits on a bench. Takes out a book from her bag and starts reading.

Making sense of the observation

'After I have completed my observations at a location, I look over my notes and start to draw out themes and trends. Sometimes things surprise me, like how often people appear to hold business meetings in public spaces and how the poor internet access in some of those areas seems to put people off. I expected the spaces to be used for leisure activities, such as reading or eating lunch, but I hadn't really thought about them as potential work-spaces.'

'Sometimes, I share my observations with other students on my course via our Facebook page. Some of their comments have really helped me think differently about my research or direct me to helpful reading.'

Evaluate your observational method

Check off ☑ each of the following once you have addressed it in full. Cross out any that do not apply. Address any aspects that require more work.

Before you start ...

☐ Clarify the phenomena or behaviour you will observe.

☐ Decide how you will select your observation participants/sample.

☐ Decide whether direct or participant observation fits your project best.

☐ Decide whether structured or unstructured observation fits your project best.

☐ Determine the best recording method for your observation, e.g. interval recording.

☐ Decide where you will carry out your observations.

☐ Decide how many observations you will carry out.

☐ Decide how long you will spend on each observation.

☐ For a structured observation: design and pilot a recording form.

☐ For an unstructured observation: decide whether you will take notes during or after your observation.

☐ Decide whether you need the informed consent of your observation subject(s).

☐ Ensure you have considered the potential ethical implications of your observation and that these are acceptable within the ethical guidelines for your course.

☐ Decide what role you will take in the observation and whether you will interact with your subjects or not.

During the observation ...

☐ Ensure you locate yourself somewhere where you have a good view of your subjects.

☐ Plan how you will maintain your focus during your observation in the face of possible distractions.

☐ Ensure that you can note all occurrences of your target behaviour or phenomena.

☐ Ensure consistency of recording behaviours between each observation session.

After the observation

☐ If you are not taking notes during the observation, identify where and when you will write up your notes.

☐ If you have written notes during the observation, how will you make sense of these, e.g. identifying themes?

☐ Identify themes and trends from your observation data.

☐ Identify how you can make use of fellow students and tutors in discussing and making sense of your observations.

Chapter 18
Surveys and questionnaires

Questionnaires and surveys are popular methods for gathering evidence for projects, especially for student assignments.

Useful for ...

- gaining opinions, attitudes, preferences, evaluations, understandings
- gathering quantitative data that can be collated systematically, including electronically (page 155)
- gathering qualitative data – you can include opportunities for open-ended responses
- gathering a combination of quantitative and qualitative data.

Nariko only had a few questions left ...

Advantages

- You can use them to collect and sort large amounts of data at speed, especially if you use tools designed for that purpose.
- If questions are designed well, a survey or questionnaire can be relatively easy to use.
- Very flexible: they can be of varied lengths, include different kinds of questions on all kinds of topics and using many different techniques for gathering responses.
- You can replicate previous research easily with new participants or target groups, to see if results hold true.

Disadvantages

- Response levels can be low.
- Participants may misread or misinterpret the questions.
- Participants may misunderstand rating scales or the method of response.
- Participants tend to provide the answers that they believe researchers are looking for.
- Setting questions that are easy to answer can sometimes lead to irrelevant data.
- Poorly designed questions or rating scales compound these problems, yielding unreliable results.

Designing for sound data

Reliability and validity

Design your questionnaire and word your questions in such ways that you maximise the likelihood of gaining clear, incontrovertible, accurate data that measure what you set out to measure. This means taking care of basics, such as that participants:

- understand the questions
- understand how to answer
- understand the response options
- understand the rating scales used
- cannot guess which response you prefer
- are not presented with 'leading questions' that prompt a particular answer
- feel able and comfortable to provide a true response
- can provide accurate responses through the choice of options that you provided.

Provide sufficient alternatives

It is irritating for participants if they wish to make a response for which no option is provided. In particular, consider whether your participants will need to have the following options:

- ☐ 'Don't know'
- ☐ 'No preference'
- ☐ 'All of the above'
- ☐ 'Not applicable'
- ☐ 'Other' (please specify)
- ☐ A choice of more than one response

Checking for sound data

To help achieve sound data, consider your survey or questionnaire for each of the following.

Comprehension

- ☐ Ensure instructions are both clear and brief.
- ☐ Present questions in a logical order.
- ☐ Use straightforward phrasing and language that will be understood by participants.
- ☐ Check for ambiguous phrasing: might the question be open to several interpretations?
- ☐ Explain any unfamiliar terms; aim to avoid specialist terminology and jargon.

Consistency of response

- ☐ Consider setting several questions on the same issue, using different wording, to help check for consistency.

Ease and accuracy of response

- ☐ Avoid personal questions that might embarrass or distress the respondent.
- ☐ Ensure that each item is a single question. (Avoid 'two questions in one'.)
- ☐ If appropriate to the methodology, use closed questions that elicit 'yes/no' answers or responses that are easy to record and count. Page 146.
- ☐ Where a participant might agree with only part of a draft question or statement, such as 'The hotel was warm and friendly', separate these out: 'The hotel was warm' and 'The hotel was friendly'.

Neutrality

- ☐ The information provided to participants does not hint at any preferred response to questions.
- ☐ Participants would not be able to guess the researcher's position from the way questions are phrased.
- ☐ Questions/statements, and responses, are phrased carefully so as to avoid in-built bias.
- ☐ None of the questions are 'leading questions' (prompting a particular response).

Managing the process

Apply good research principles

- Be clear which methodology informs your research. Choose methods of designing and conducting your questionnaire that are consistent with that methodology. Pages 91 and 97–106.
- Select a representative sample, appropriate to the project brief. See page 125.
- Use controlled conditions, if appropriate, so you know exactly how the questions were delivered and who answered them.

Keep participants in mind

When collecting this kind of data, you are highly dependent on your participants. You have to design your research, word questions and conduct the process so that you maximise the probabilities of the right participants:

- taking part
- completing all questions
- providing reliable responses.

At each stage of the process, consider, in detail, the characteristics of intended participants and how they are likely to interpret the approach, instructions and questions.

Provide accurate information about …

- the purpose of the questionnaire
- how long it will take to complete
- how many questions there are in total.

Provide clear instructions on how to:

- use the questionnaire or survey
- use any rating scales provided
- navigate and submit electronic surveys.

Keep participants in mind

Check off ☑ each point below once you have considered it and made your decisions.

- ☐ Who do you want to complete your questionnaire? (Who would you be targeting?)
- ☐ Where will you find such participants?
- ☐ What kind of questionnaire would such participants find off-putting (and not complete)?
- ☐ What would encourage them to engage?
- ☐ How long are they likely to spend on answering questions before wanting to stop?
- ☐ How many questions could they answer in that time, realistically?
- ☐ How many questions would they be willing to answer in total, even if questions were short?
- ☐ Which kinds of rating scale would they find easiest to use?

Administering the questionnaire/survey

Decide whether, to gain the best results, your questionnaire will be:

- ☐ paper-based, completed by participants
- ☐ paper-based, completed by an interviewer
- ☐ phone-based, completed by the interviewer
- ☐ completed electronically/online
- ☐ hand-held voting sets in response to questions asked of a room of participants?

Conducting surveys face to face …

- Make the whole process quick and easy.
- Introduce yourself, provide a short flier with background information and contact details at your institution.
- Avoid giving lengthy background information – participants don't usually want to hear it or read it.
- Ask closed questions or those that elicit short answers that are easy to record.
- Set the minimum number of questions possible for gaining the information that you require.
- Assume people want to make a quick get-away and may not answer more than 3–5 short questions.
- Use a professional approach. Page 130.

Ways of eliciting responses

Types of response

To closed questions

Participants are most likely to respond if they can give a quick response such as by:

- choosing 'yes' or 'no'
- selecting from up to 5 short options
- using a clear rating scale.

To open questions

Many questionnaires include open questions for participants to provide longer responses. However, these require more time and effort on the part of the participants, so may not elicit many responses. If you do use open questions, beware of giving undue weight to a small percentage of respondents who offer comments.

Select from response options

Participants tend to engage with these relatively well, as they are easy to use. Make it clear whether more than one option is permissible.

Example: selecting from choices

What was your experience of the service you received today? For each question below, select the ONE response that best applies.

How long did you have to wait to get served?

- ☐ (a) Under 10 minutes.
- ☐ (b) 10–30 minutes.
- ☐ (c) More than 30 minutes.
- ☐ (d) Don't know.

Using rating scales

Participants tend to respond well to rating scales that are:

- easy to navigate and intuitive to use
- consistent in the way the scale is used.

For example, if a high rating indicates the most positive response in the first question, then continue to use a high rating to indicate positive responses throughout the survey.

Example: rating using a Likert scale

Rate the service you received here today on a scale of 1–5 (1 = excellent; 5 = poor). Circle the rating that best applies

e.g. *The availability of staff*	1	2	3	④	5
The welcome you received	1	2	3	4	5
How quickly you were served	1	2	3	4	5
Professional attitude of staff	1	2	3	4	5
Value for money	1	2	3	4	5

Agree/disagree

One way of collecting data is by giving participants a list of statements to which they indicate agreement. These can be designed so that it is easy for participants to respond.

Example: agree/disagree

For each of the following statements, select ☑ the ONE response that best matches your experience.

I received a professional service here today.

- ☐ Strongly agree
- ☐ Agree
- ☐ Neither agree nor disagree
- ☐ Disagree
- ☐ Strongly disagree

My questionnaire/survey will use:

- ☐ yes/no responses
- ☐ selecting responses from a short list of options
- ☐ selecting a numerical rating
- ☐ a verbal rating scale (e.g. good/OK/poor)
- ☐ open questions to encourage comments
- ☐ other kinds of response.

Conducting the survey electronically

Electronic tools

It is worth considering conducting your survey or questionnaire electronically. This confers advantages in:

- inbuilt design features and guidance
- speed and ease of distribution
- being intuitive to use when designing your own questionnaires
- professional appearance of survey
- speed and ease in collating responses
- speed and ease in presenting data.

Survey monkey

- An online survey generator that makes it easy to set up basic surveys
- Free for surveys of 10 questions or fewer
- Easy for participants to access and complete online
- Records responses automatically and gives you an overview of these.

Bristol online survey (BOS)

An online survey generator which makes it easy to set up both basic and more advanced surveys.

- It requires a subscription to use. However, most UK educational institutions subscribe and their students are covered by their institution's licence.
- It is easy for participants to access via an internet link and complete online
- It records responses automatically and gives you both an overview and more detailed analysis of these.

Conducting surveys through Facebook

If you create a Facebook page for your project, you can gather information in 2 main ways.

(1) You can post a general question on your page and allow people to respond with comments. This gives you qualitative data from a self-selecting sample.

(2) You can also use the in-built 'question' option. However, this will only be sent to people who are 'fans' of your Facebook page. This will require you to have pre-selected potential respondents by asking them to become fans of your page.

Facebook can also be a good method of distributing an online survey created using another tool. Post a link to the survey on your page.

Communicating with participants

If you use electronic tools such as these, contact the intended recipients in advance to tell them about your research and ask if they would be willing to participate. Sending these out without warning tends to mean they are ignored. Otherwise, send a brief accompanying letter or email with the survey or questionnaire.

- Introduce yourself.
- Invite the person to take part.
- Explain the reason for the survey.
- State accurately how long it takes to complete.
- State clearly the final date for submission.
- Clarify what will happen to the results.
- Provide your institution's contact details.

Trial it first

Test your questions out on other people to see whether they could be interpreted other than as intended. As a general rule, you should aim to trial these with at least 10% of your intended number of respondents.

CHECKLIST

Evaluating your questionnaire

Check off ☑ each of the following once you have addressed it in full. Cross out any that do not apply. Address any aspects that require more work.

Will my questionnaire ...

... encourage participation?

☐ It looks professional.
☐ It looks non-threatening.
☐ It appears to be worthwhile.
☐ It looks easy to complete.
☐ It is easy to navigate.
☐ It doesn't look too long.
☐ It is set out clearly.

... be quick to complete?

☐ The total number of questions is not off-putting for the intended recipients.
☐ Every question is necessary.
☐ Each can be answered quickly.
☐ The time required for completing the questionnaire is spelt out clearly.
☐ The timescale indicated is accurate.

... yield the kind of material I need?

☐ I am clear what kind of sample I need.
☐ I will be able to find such a sample.
☐ I use closed questions to elicit precise answers when needed.
☐ I use open questions to gain qualitative data, if needed.
☐ I provide sufficient options to enable people to make accurate responses.
☐ I provide follow-up questions needed in order to clarify responses.
☐ I have avoided leading questions.
☐ I have set up the questionnaire in such a way that participants are reminded or encouraged to respond to any questions they have missed.
☐ I can cross-reference responses if needed.

... be clear to participants?

☐ The purpose is explained briefly.
☐ Instructions are succinct.
☐ Instructions are clear.
☐ Good examples are provided.
☐ Practice examples are provided.
☐ Rating scales are used consistently.
☐ Participants can return to previous responses and change these if they wish.
☐ It is clear how to submit the survey, if online.

... be easy to answer?

☐ Questions are reasonably short.
☐ Questions are carefully worded to avoid ambiguity.
☐ Each item consists of only one question.
☐ For closed questions, a range of options is provided as responses to choose from.

... be manageable for me to use?

☐ It will be easy for me to record participants' responses in the field (if relevant).
☐ It will be easy for me to collate responses.
☐ It will be easy to present the results.
☐ I have addressed all the issues that arose during the pilots.

Chapter 19
Interviews

Interviews are used in a range of disciplines, from healthcare and social sciences to business, media, arts and communications, and in the humanities for research such as oral history. They may be used as the sole method of gathering data or alongside others.

Useful for ...

- gaining rich, qualitative information about individuals' experiences, attitudes or perspectives
- being able to follow up immediately on responses for clarification or further detail
- developing a working relationship with the interviewees that can lead to them feeling more comfortable talking to you and providing the material you need.

Advantages

- They can be used flexibly in combination with other methods in order to elicit different kinds of information.
- You have more opportunity to set the agenda and direction of travel in order to gain the material you need (compared with observations, for example).
- If you don't receive the material you need, you can ask again.
- You can combine closed and open questions effectively.
- You can sound out whether participants understand what they are being asked.
- If you are skilled at interviewing, you may gain insights difficult to achieve through other methods.

Disadvantages

- They are time-intensive.
- Few can be undertaken.
- Results are not open to generalisation.
- It can be difficult to find willing, appropriate participants.
- Much depends on how well an interviewee reacts to the interviewer.
- Except for the most structured interviews, they generate a great deal of material, much of which may be irrelevant.
- The interpretation of the data can be highly subjective.

Planning for interviews

As interviews are time-consuming, they take significant effort to plan, conduct, collate or sift, and interpret. This includes planning, carefully:

- how you select interviewees, to ensure they are engaged, understand the process and will provide relevant material
- how you will run the interviews, so that you don't waste participants' time
- how to conduct the interview and use equipment so that you don't waste your own time.

Consistency

If you are interviewing more than one person, carry out the interviews in near-identical conditions so as to ensure consistency.

- Devise your questions prior to the interview, along with possible prompts.
- Practise in advance so that you phrase questions and record responses consistently.
- Conduct the interview just as you practised it, so that you interview each person in the same way.

Interviews: how much structure?

Structure and pre-planning

You can choose how far you wish to structure the interviews, whether highly structured, completely unstructured, partially structured or a combination of these. The 'right' way depends on your research philosophy and on the kind of material you need.

Highly structured interviews

- These are based around closed questions, with a limited choice of responses.
- The interviewer can circle, highlight, or mark down responses easily.
- Questions are all designed in advance.
- They tend to be one-off with each participant and relatively short.

Advantages

- You have more control over use of time.
- You can ensure you cover the material.
- You can conduct more of these, so may gain results that can be generalised.

Disadvantages

- They can feel rather 'routine'.
- Participants may focus more on providing an answer than on the quality of their answer.

Unstructured interviews

At the other extreme, you may want the richer kinds of data that can emerge from building a rapport with interviewees over a long time, allowing different themes to emerge. You may continue with this approach, or become more directive over time in order to follow up on useful themes and/or to fill in gaps in the material.

Advantages

- You can gain a rich understanding of a few individual cases.

Disadvantages

- You can conduct fewer of them.
- Without any direction or structure, you may not gain much of the material that you need.
- It can be hard to maintain the interest and consent of the interviewee.
- If the interviewee decides to stop the interviews, it takes a long time to cover that ground with a new interviewee.

Mixed approaches

It can be useful to combine aspects of both approaches, so that you have information that is easy to compare across several interviews, as well as the richer information that can emerge from unstructured approaches.

The more structured the approach, the less the participant may feel comfortable in taking the initiative or volunteering useful information.

Semi-structured interviews

For time-limited research based on interviews, it isn't usually feasible to take fully open-ended, unstructured approaches. To gain the material that you need, consider:

- organising interviews around a series of themes, to which you can encourage the interviewee to return
- open-ended questions on those themes
- some closed questions to elicit particular details that you need, if these cannot be gained in other ways.

Interviews: questioning techniques

Prepare for the interview

Good preparation helps you to maintain control of the interview, improving the likelihood of gaining the material that you need whilst keeping to time.

- Ensure that you have all consents (pages 134–5).
- Prepare and trial everything in advance, taking ethical considerations on board (pages 107–12).
- Consider what kind of first impression you will make (page 130).
- Introduce yourself clearly. Ensure that the interviewee is aware this is a student project.
- Remind interviewees of the process, even if explained previously.
- Reassure interviewees about confidentiality.
- If you are using equipment, clarify how long this will take to set up.
- Decide how you will close the interview.

Ground rules and boundaries

Take steps to maintain a friendly but professional distance that is safe for you and the interviewee.

- Set the right tone – polite but not overfriendly.
- Avoid sharing any personal information (this can distort the responses you receive).
- Explain the process clearly – and then stick to it.
- Don't accept gifts or more than basic hospitality as this could be misinterpreted.
- Specify your requirements for interview space or privacy. Negotiate acceptable alternatives. If there are any risks to you, do not proceed.

Conducting the interview

- Be confident, polite and friendly.
- Sit at right angles to the interviewee.
- Be clear when the interview is starting.
- Maintain eye contact; smile and be reassuring between questions.
- Know your questions: sound conversational, not as if you are reading them out.
- Keep it short: don't impose on people's time.
- Thank people for participating.

For structured interviews

Design questions much as you would for conducting face-to-face surveys (see page 153). As interviews generally take longer, you would also:

- organise questions into logical sections
- pause between sections so as to break up the time, such as by introducing the next batch of questions
- pace questions steadily: avoid racing through questions or including so many that the interviewee is exhausted.

For unstructured interviews

Open questions: a few well-designed interview questions can generate a great deal of rich material. Avoid questions that encourage 'yes/no' or single-word responses.

Use prompts and non-verbal cues: express interest, sit forward and ask follow-up questions to encourage the interviewee to open up.

Invite interviewees to consider an issue from different angles. For example, 'Were you glad that you took part in the event/treatment/etc.?' 'Did you ever regret taking part: were there any downsides?'

Avoid leading questions/prompts (that guide the interviewee towards a particular answer): 'It must have been good to take part?' 'Did you love it?' 'I assume you are pleased with the results'? 'That must have been annoying?'

Prepare prompts to refocus the interview, to encourage the interviewee to return to the point:
- *You raised an interesting point earlier about …*
- *That's very helpful. Thank you. I'd also like to ask you about …*

Interviews: face to face and at a distance

Face-to-face interviews

Advantages

- can be easier to establish rapport
- allow you to use non-verbal cues to elicit further responses
- allow you to see non-verbal communication.

Typical issues to plan for

☐ Many participants find face-to-face interviews more demanding than phone-based, especially if the topic is of a sensitive nature.

☐ You can be seen and judged by your attire, posture, the location selected – which could have an impact on the responses you receive.

☐ You need to ensure that your facial expressions and body language do not reveal your position on the issues at all. Beware of nodding to reassure interviewees as they speak. They may interpret that as a sign that you prefer a particular response.

Phone interviews

- These are relatively easy to arrange.
- You save on travelling time.
- As interviewees can't be seen, they can be relatively at their ease, jot down questions and prompts, make notes, pull faces, sip coffee or whatever they like.

Typical issues to plan for

☐ Some participants don't like interviews where they can't see the interviewer.

☐ Although there are ways of recording phone interviews, this can be complicated to arrange.

☐ As an interviewer, you won't know who else might be listening in or prompting answers, which could make some responses invalid.

☐ The interviewee can end the call at any time.

By webcams/video link

These are a useful way of conducting an interview when interviewees are at a distance, time-constrained or have difficulties with travel. They work best where interviewees are well-used to the medium, such as being familiar with Skype, webcams or video conferencing.

Typical issues to plan for

☐ Interviewees may find it unexpectedly difficult to work with the screen or camera, or refuse to do so on the day.

☐ Interviewees may not have the right equipment or connections at the time planned.

☐ You may not be able to make, or sustain, a good connection on the day.

☐ Interviewees may be at locations where they are prone to interruptions.

☐ As with face-to-face interviews, your attire, body language and surroundings can all be observed and may affect the responses you receive.

Mistakenly, Nareen prided herself that her interview techniques never betrayed her own views on the matter

Interviews: recording the information

Your record of your interviews will form the raw material that you analyse for your report. There are various ways of making such records, all of which have both benefits and drawbacks. You need to balance the needs of the research with the preferences of the interviewees.

Form-filling

- Used for highly structured interviews
- work best for short interviews, as it can become tedious for the interviewee
- quick and easy for you to complete (ticking boxes, short answers, circling responses)
- can be easy to collate, present and analyse
- allows easy comparison between interviews.

Considerations

However, these can feel rather mechanistic or 'cold' to interviewees so it helps to develop a good rapport with them. Use explanations, body language, eye contact and other non-verbal communication to indicate that you are interested in interviewees and their views, without signalling agreement or disagreement.

Making notes

- In making notes, you are already starting to distil information, which can be useful when you come to collate and analyse it later.
- You can train yourself to take notes whilst maintaining good eye contact.

Considerations

- How will you make notes whilst maintaining eye contact and without interrupting the flow or keeping the interviewee waiting?
- Some interviewees feel distanced by interviewers who type responses.
- How will you note non-verbal communication (if at all)?

Audio

- Can free you to focus on the interviewee and maintain eye contact
- can provide a fuller record than notes – and complement notes well
- can provide useful material to quote.

Audio-visual

- Can free you to focus on the interviewee
- provides a full and permanent record
- captures non-verbal communication
- can be easier to transcribe than audio
- flip cameras are cheap, and easy to use.

Considerations for audio and audio-visual

- Become expert in the equipment before using it for the interviews.
- Many people can be reluctant to be recorded, especially on the day itself.
- Interviewees may censor their responses.
- Material can take a long time to analyse.

Recording Skype-based interviews

Gain signed consent from interviewees in advance. There isn't a facility within Skype to record interviews directly. There are apps you can purchase that would allow you to do this:

Audio recording: SkyRecorder; QuickVoice

Audio-visual: Pamela (free for interviews of under 15 minutes); Evae.

Decisions

Decide how you will record your observations:

- ☐ writing notes on paper
- ☐ using a portable device
- ☐ as an audio recording only
- ☐ as an audio-visual recording
- ☐ other?

Interviews

Check off ☑ each of the following once you have addressed it in full. Cross out any that do not apply. Address any aspects that require more work.

Before the interview(s)

- ☐ Decide on an interview method (pages 158–60).
- ☐ Organise any audio-visual equipment.
- ☐ Organise the venue if needed.
- ☐ Decide criteria for selecting interviewees.
- ☐ Prepare my explanation of the research for interviewees (see page 132).
- ☐ Consider answers to questions that potential interviewees might have.
- ☐ Prepare consent materials for interviewees.
- ☐ Locate appropriate interviewees.
- ☐ Contact appropriate interviewees to talk through the process; address concerns.
- ☐ If using equipment, check that potential interviewees are comfortable using it.
- ☐ Select potential interviewees, and good back-ups in case any fall through.
- ☐ Gain the consent or agreement of a suitable number of relevant interviewees.
- ☐ Store consents carefully.
- ☐ Organise times and locations suitable to both parties.
- ☐ Provide maps/directions to venues.
- ☐ Send written reminders of the details, especially the date, time and venue.
- ☐ If interviewing at a distance, such as through Skype, ensure interviewees have the right connections and equipment.
- ☐ Provide easy directions on how to use the equipment.
- ☐ Assume that interviewees may wish to end interviews early – plan accordingly.

The day of the interview

Plan in advance your strategy for dealing with the following points.

- ☐ Have identification with you, to prove you are who you say you are.
- ☐ Contact the interviewee to ensure that they are expecting you/haven't forgotten the day, time or location.
- ☐ Settle the interviewee if they are anxious. Provide a brief reminder of the research and/or of ground covered so far.
- ☐ Start with warm-up questions that will be easy and interesting for the interviewee to answer.
- ☐ Move to the most essential questions as early as possible, so that you don't run out of time.
- ☐ Don't introduce delicate or controversial subjects too early.

After the interviews

- ☐ Note down your immediate thoughts and observations, before you forget them.
- ☐ Label and store notes/recordings carefully.
- ☐ Work through the interview while it is still fresh in your memory: this may help you to make sense of parts that are hard to hear or read.
- ☐ If relevant, make a transcript of recorded interviews, or selected sections.
- ☐ Decide whether to transcribe pauses and non-verbal communication, and how you will do this consistently.

Chapter 20
Case studies

A case study is an in-depth study of an entity or phenomenon. It could focus on almost anything, such as an organisation, event, person, business, programme, utterance, text or locality. A case study can draw on any one method or combine many.

Characteristics of case studies

- Tend to be drawn from 'real life' although could be based on models or simulations
- usually generate rich data for qualitative analysis, though can be designed to generate measurable data
- are investigated with reference to existing research and relevant theory
- involve detailed critical analysis – they are not simply descriptions of observations or summaries of interviews
- can provide rich insights into aspects of a phenomenon, bringing out details or issues that may be less apparent in everyday life
- often lead to recommendations, such as for a business or an organisation.

Useful for …

- building a base line for future comparisons
- gaining insights into the complex interactions of many variables
- meeting the particular needs of an organisation
- investigating phenomena or instances that are unique or which have unique aspects.

Advantages of case studies

- They can have real-life applications, making them feel very worthwhile.
- They allow you to examine the complex inter-relationships of many variables.
- Case studies can reveal unexpected insights into complex systems or issues.
- Different results can emerge than might under controlled conditions such as experiments.
- They enable you to investigate fine details that throw new light upon how something really works in practice.
- Detailed case studies can throw different light on theory or practice, helping to advance the theoretical framework.
- They can indicate a direction for how existing theory or workplace practice could be adapted to meet the needs of special cases.
- You can scale them to suit the size of the student project.
- They can draw out examples of good or bad practice in the workplace.

Disadvantages and risks

- As they are studies of individual instances, they may not be representative of what happens in general, and may be misleading.
- The findings may not be relevant to any other context.
- It is risky to draw generalisations from a single example or small sample.
- Any one case study is time-consuming, so only a few can be undertaken; that limits the feasibility of the method.
- They can generate large amounts of information, which can be difficult to manage.
- It may be difficult to isolate the truly significant from the ephemeral or anecdotal.
- Judgements about what is significant are subjective and open to challenge.

Research strategy for your case study

The research strategy for a case study is, in many ways, typical of any research project, but varies in that you are looking at the 'particular'. This can raise methodological challenges as there may be little published that appears similar to your own case.

Your research strategy

Your strategy will vary to some extent depending on the topic. Typically, you will need to cover the following stages.

1 Read around the subject (see Chapter 9, 'Literature search and review')
2 Decide on your purpose
3 Select your case study
4 Investigate the background to the case
5 Decide on your methodology
6 Set the parameters
7 Decide on your sources
8 Decide on your methods
9 Gather your data/ information
10 Corroborate the 'evidence'
11 Analyse your findings
12 Contextualise your findings with reference to the literature.

1 Read around the subject

As for any long assignment, you begin by researching your field, first broadening out and then narrowing down on a particular topic. For case study research, you will need to balance more generic research relevant to your topic with background reading that is more specific to the case study. There won't always be a sharp division between where generic background research ends and the case study begins.

2 Decide your purpose

As with any other kind of research, you need to clarify the purpose of your study. What exactly do you want to discover through the case study?

- Is it your aim to use the case study to examine a pre-selected issue? *OR* is your aim to use the case study to see what kind of issues emerge?
- Are you working with particular individuals, events or contexts in order to understand what is unique to them – *OR* to investigate these as individual examples of a more general 'type'?

3 Select your case study

Possible avenues for student research

- To help an organisation to investigate a particular problem and arrive at a solution or recommendations
- to understand the lived experience of an individual, community or organisation, such as how their particular conditions affect their perceptions of an issue, their use of technology, their responses to change, etc.
- to investigate whether a theory covered on your course applies in a particular instance, such as in a local community, business, school or geographical location investigated on a field trip.

How many cases studies to include

Case studies take time to conduct, so research tends to focus on just one example, or a very small number of case studies for comparison. The right number depends upon the scale of the assignment (word limit, level and timescales) balanced against the amount of detailed investigation undertaken for each case study. You could choose to undertake one focused case study or compare two or more case studies in less detail.

It may be appropriate to include a larger number of less detailed case studies to exemplify diverse approaches, responses, solutions or impacts. In such cases, the case studies need to be selected carefully to illustrate different points whilst still reinforcing a coherent overall argument.

Research strategy for your case study

4 Investigate the background

Before starting to investigate the case, gather as much information as you can about it. Read about the history of the organisation or the background of the person(s) or issue until you know the case thoroughly. This will mean that you will be able to make sense, more readily, of new information about the case as it emerges in your research. This can also mean that you can take rapid action to refocus the direction of the project, or individual interviews if appropriate, to achieve the key purpose of the research.

5 Decide on your methodology

Decide which methodology or philosophical approach you want to bring to your research (see Chapter 11). How will this affect the kind of information that you are able to gather? Is your intended research question suitable for this kind of approach and the evidence base that can be generated using it?

Decide whether it is your intention to:

- limit your own intervention, so as to see what emerges from using open-ended methods? If so, then select a narrowly defined project.

- *OR* to manage more closely the kind of data you will gather in order to gather specific kinds of information or to answer prescribed questions? If so, set precisely worded questions in advance and pilot these to test out the kind of information that you are likely to generate.

6 Set the parameters

Case studies rarely come with clearly pre-set boundaries, even if they might appear to do so. They are especially prone to 'sprawl' effects, branching off in unintended directions, generating a great deal of tangential information. This can create additional work and slow down the research. This is especially so if you are using open-ended techniques.

Be prepared to make many and frequent decisions about what to include. Consider:

- What information do I need in order to make this case study meaningful?
- At what level of depth do I need to investigate this particular aspect?

Be alert to the information that is accumulating. Take action at regular intervals to sift out what is not needed and to refocus on what is most relevant.

Sprawl effects can be made more manageable, such as through exercising care in your choice of a narrow strand of the issue upon which to focus. Set relatively narrow parameters for the research if the investigation is likely to yield copious rich data.

7 Decide on your sources

Published material: read broadly around the range of issues that emerge as you conduct your research. This might be anything from general textbooks, research articles, other case studies, and information in the public domain such as government papers, company financial reports, official data, architectural plans, etc.

Personal materials: you may be permitted access to material such as medical notes, letters, diaries, and personal documentation; these should be treated with respect for individual confidentiality. Always check whether the person can be named (such as in thanks and acknowledgements) or whether their information needs to be carefully edited to remain anonymous.

Other confidential information: you may be provided with company records. You would normally be asked to sign a confidentiality agreement and there may be restrictions on how you are able to use or cite these sources.

Research strategy for your case study

8 Decide on methods

Case studies lend themselves to a number of research methods or techniques, such as:

- structured or unstructured observations
- survey(s) of communities or organisations
- long interviews, structured or unstructured
- close critical analysis of a single text
- analysis of a range of documentation and/ or data on one aspect of a business, historical event, outbreak of disease, etc.
- analysis of data that you collect yourself or that is already in the public domain
- piecing together a picture from multiple sources.

Observation and questioning

Typically, for a case study, you would:

- take an open-ended approach at the start, to help shape your research design
- become increasingly focused in your observations or questions as you proceed, so as to home in on specific themes, or to address gaps in your information.

Once you have decided on which kinds of methods to use, then plan through in detail exactly how you will structure your approach to gathering, recording and analysing your data.

Writing a first draft of your methods

Write an initial draft of your proposed methods. This helps to flag potential gaps and oversights that you can address before starting on your case study. In writing your draft, consider how you would justify your choice of methods to your supervisor or client, especially if asked:

- Why these methods and not others?
- What kinds/amounts of data will be generated?
- Whose permission or involvement is needed, and how will you obtain this?
- What potential problems have you considered and how will you address these?
- Will these methods really yield the information you need to answer the questions you are setting out to answer?

9 Gather your data/information

Once you decide on your methods, prepare tools or materials to help gather, record and store the information. Be aware that it isn't always possible to run a pilot for case studies using a small number of participants.

10 Corroborate the 'evidence'

Where possible, look for ways of cross-referencing information gained from the participating individuals or organisations to other sources. Depending on your project, this might mean comparing their understandings or memory with official data, generic theory or other stakeholders. For example, a company's view of its marketing could be checked against the opinions of focus groups from target markets. Historical or official records might offer a different picture from that provided by an individual or organisation – you may have to consider which is likely to be the most accurate.

11 Analyse your findings

By the end of a case study, you would be looking to make sense of the 'whole' – how the different pieces contribute to an overall understanding of the issue. Analyse early data for emerging themes. Use these to help guide later stages of your research.

12 Contextualise your findings

Identify relevant theory, examples of previous research, recently published government data, or other well known cases that enable you to draw parallels between your own case study and a wider context. Where possible, cite evidence from outside of your own case study that helps to support or, if it is the case, challenges your own findings.

Writing up your case study

Which style?

There isn't a single structure or style for a case study. As case studies are very varied, the style and structure needs to reflect its particular aims and objectives as well as conventions of the discipline.

The importance of structure

Because a case study is unique, there can be a temptation to let that over-influence the structure of the report, either deviating too far from similar case studies in the subject or lacking structure altogether. Swetnam and Swetnam (2010) commented that '… poor case studies often degenerate into unstructured descriptions of randomly chosen features'. This is something to guard against. A broad outline for structuring your case study is provided below.

Introduction

Purpose: State this briefly. If the case study was commissioned by a client, what gave rise to the commission and what are the client's objectives? What kinds of answers is the case study setting out to discover? If it is not commissioned, what prompted you to select this case study? State clearly the problem, issue or focus.

Context: Provide a succinct, selective, but detailed background to help the reader understand the project's purpose, methods and outcomes. For a commissioned report, provide background of the client, taking care to anonymise this if needed.

Literature Review

Include a literature review (Chapter 9), indicating the theoretical and research background. Refer to what can be learnt from similar kinds of case study and how these influenced your approach, methods, analysis or recommendations.

Sections/chapters

Depending on the case study, some or all of the following sections may be required.

- Methodology (Chapter 11)
- Methods used
- Previous actions or interventions, if any, and their outcomes
- Current action or intervention
- Client responses to any action or intervention
- Feedback from stakeholders
- A critical evaluation of the intervention or action
- Any outstanding issues or problems
- Probable causes of any outstanding problems
- Evaluation of potential solutions
- Conclusions/Recommendations for action.

Analysis

Look for themes and relevant examples of probable cause and effect, or links between different issues. How far does this case study illustrate or contradict previous research and existing theory? How typical is it of other cases? What does your case study add to the understanding of broader issues as well as of the particular case?

Making recommendations

If required, provide these as a numbered list. Good recommendations are:

- **relevant** – they are based on real needs as identified by your research

- **reasoned** – your report should provide a good case for each recommendation, based on the evidence; your report should have indicated what kinds of outcomes could be expected if such action were to be taken

- **suitable** – they fit the culture of the organisation or the situation of the individual

- **pragmatic** – they would be affordable and feasible within the relevant timescales and with the expertise available

- **specific** – it is clear exactly what must be done, by whom and when.

Case study

Check off ☑ each of the following once you have addressed it in full. Cross out any that do not apply. Address any aspects that require more work.

Before

1 ☐ I am clear what I aim to achieve from this case study.

2 ☐ I have decided what kind of case study/studies to select.

3 ☐ I have decided how many cases to include.

4 ☐ I have read similar kinds of case study to inform my thinking and methods.

5 ☐ I have decided what kind of methodology or approach to use (see Chapter 11).

6 ☐ I have worked out what kind of background information I need, particular to this case study.

7 ☐ I have gathered background information.

8 ☐ I have written a draft of the background.

9 ☐ I have set clear parameters (scale, timeframe, structure, etc.).

10 ☐ I have decided which methods to use.

11 ☐ I have prepared relevant information and materials for participants (see Chapter 15).

12 ☐ I have set up a schedule for meetings, interviews, observations, accessing data, etc.

13 ☐ I have decided on appropriate tools for gathering and recording information.

14 ☐ I have piloted my methods and adapted these as needed (see page 114).

If commissioned by a client

15 ☐ I have met the client commissioning the study/read their written brief (if relevant).

16 ☐ I understand what the client wants to achieve from the case study.

17 ☐ I have clarified any issues of confidentiality and ground rules.

18 ☐ I am keeping in touch with the client, keeping them informed (if relevant).

19 ☐ The client is aware of what I need from them in terms of information and access.

20 ☐ The client has agreed to this access.

21 ☐ I talked through my conclusions, recommendations, evidence base and reasoning with the client.

During/after

22 ☐ I have corroborated my findings against other sources rather than relying only on information provided by the client or participants.

23 ☐ I have analysed my findings in relation to questions and themes, rather than just providing a narrative ('story') of the case.

24 ☐ I have structured my material into themed sections or chapters.

25 ☐ I have drawn reasoned conclusions and recommendations based on the evidence.

26 ☐ I have contextualised my findings with reference to relevant theory and research.

27 ☐ I have provided a succinct, numbered list of recommendations.

28 ☐ I have considered the broader issues that can be learnt from this case study, such as new understandings about the wider population or a specific issue.

Chapter 21
Interpreting your findings

The interpretation of your data is a combination of three approaches:

1 highly specialised methods that will have formed the larger part of your course, such as statistical methods or discourse analysis

2 application of generic critical thinking skills, such as those covered at earlier levels of study. For more detail, see Cottrell (2011)

3 generic high-level approaches to analysis, such as are covered in this chapter.

The thinking stage

For many students, this is the most interesting and compelling part of a research project. If your preparation has been solid, then it is very exciting to see your results coming in. For a project at this level, it is likely that there will be unexpected outcomes and challenges. This means giving a great deal of thought to your evidence base in order to make sense of what it is really telling you.

'So what?'

One of the most important questions that your reporting will need to address is 'so what?' In other words, you have collected information, but:

● What does it mean?

● What does it add to what we already know?

● For quantitative research, is it statistically significant?

● What difference might it make, and to whom?

Looking for answers

For larger-scale research projects at this level of study, it isn't likely that there will be a short and straightforward answer such as 'yes' or 'no' or '42%'. Your examiners are looking for how you make sense of the material and interpret this within the broader context of your discipline.

Keep an ideas book or file to hand. Jot down any emerging thoughts about how subtle changes to your method or sample might generate different results. Continue to read around the topic for inspiration or new angles on your findings. See 'Thinking through writing' (page 170).

Be organised

Check whether your methods of organising your material are really helpful to you in making sense of your findings. See pages 172–3.

For quantitative research

For research with a number-based evidence base, the bulk of the interpretation takes place once the full dataset has been collected. It is natural to want to start looking for meaning as soon as any results are in – and sometimes this is worthwhile to do. At other times, the incoming results are liable to swings, so that taking interim snapshots is not a good use of time. Weigh up the best time to start analysis of your data (pages 170–1).

For qualitative research

For qualitative research, the process of making sense of the material tends to be intrinsic to each stage of the research. It is rarely a good idea, or even possible, to collect all the material first and then to start interpreting it (see page 171).

Interpreting 'as you go'

Start early

Do not leave the analysis and interpretation of your results until the later stages of the project. As you gather your material, be proactive in working with it in an engaged way as early as possible. See 'Making sense of your findings' (page 171).

Look for emergent themes

- **Examine your findings from many angles**
  Look for patterns and trends: What messages seem to be emerging from the data? Are these what you had expected?

- **Focus** As early as possible, start to consider how you will make use of the information you gather. Consider how you can reduce down the data/material. What can be eliminated at each step?

It is likely that you will start to see, early on, whether the information is leading in the direction that you had hypothesised or surmised. If you hadn't formed any prior judgements, then you will start to identify a direction of travel and potential, and/or probable, outcomes will start to emerge. If not, and if appropriate to your methodology, start to search for these in an active way, so that you can begin to organise, and reduce down, your material accordingly.

Dealing with emerging results

- Don't ever alter your findings to fit the answer that you prefer, or to support your hypotheses.

- Don't assume that your work is meaningless if it doesn't support your research hypotheses. Your role as the researcher is to test the hypotheses, not to bring about a particular outcome. If the hypotheses are not supported, that can, in itself, contribute to our understanding, provided your evidence base and methods were appropriate.

- Maintain the integrity of your research, even if you think that your tutor, client or employer was hoping for a different set of outcomes.

Think in writing

Elaborate your thoughts through writing down your interim interpretations as 'notes to yourself'. This helps your brain to sift through the mass of information, play with ideas, formulate hypotheses about what the material is telling you and where it seems to be leading, bring critical analysis to your own thinking, and test emerging conclusions.

Getting thoughts written down in this way is an important part of the interpretative process. Although some people prefer to do their thinking entirely in their heads, this can mean that good ideas are forgotten. Usually, it is essential to:

- read through your own thoughts after a day's break, considering how these strike you; often the flaws or gaps are apparent

- keep returning to your notes or, at least, sections of them, and re-examining your earlier interpretations of the material in the light of further data, reading and thinking.

Maintain consistency

If results appear to be going the wrong way, it can be tempting for researchers to make subtle changes to their methods, sometimes without realising that they are doing so. Take care to continue the research as it was started, through maintaining a systematic approach. Be mindful of the potential impact of even apparently minor changes, such as in tone, emphasis, pacing or phrasing of questions or choice of examples.

What if I realise the design is flawed?

If you find that your research design is flawed:

- don't panic: this does happen
- discuss with your supervisor straightaway
- amend the design and start again with a new sample or fresh set of participants/sample
- *OR* continue as you started, and critique your design as part of your analysis of the research.

Making sense of your findings

An iterative process

For arts and humanities subjects and for many other projects where you work with qualitative data, you wouldn't usually wait until you had gathered all of your material before you started to analyse it. Analysis is, rather, intrinsic to the process of generating information. Themes, questions or new hypotheses are likely to arise from the material itself, and some of these would have been hard to anticipate before the research began. That is often the case for some number-based research too.

For your research, the process may be an iterative one: that is, the ideas generated by the first material that you consider give rise to questions that then lead you to the next material. You may find that you move seamlessly between consideration of primary and secondary sources, reading specialist research, monographs or criticism, which stimulates ideas about how to analyse your material from new angles, and directs you to further material.

This presents its own challenges, as the material you gather helps to define or extend your research questions. It is easy to keep generating new questions, finding new leads, following new avenues and tangents, and amassing more material. That means that it is essential to keep standing back and reflecting how the process is working, so as to keep the project manageable.

Segmenting

It is likely that, unless you are active in organising your material and your own thoughts, these will pile up as an amorphous mass of detail. Set aside time for considering how best to segment this.

Ideally, you should aim to do this in ways that help you to identify the probable set of chapters that will make up the body of your dissertation. In practice, it can be hard to establish until late on whether the material will break down best into six chapters or ten. This comes from working with the material and checking for the best arrangement in terms of coherence and for avoiding repetition.

Bring coherence

At frequent intervals, reconsider what appears to be optimal selection and organisation in terms of:

- key themes in your material
- chapters that address these themes in the most logical way
- sections within chapters, so that the material is presented most clearly and flows well
- key points within each section – what are the most important messages to get across?
- illustrative details and examples for each point, drawn from your evidence base, to support your argument.

Disciplined thinking is required to identify:

- the most logical sets of relationships between different aspects of your material
- which items of material fit best together
- what can be covered in depth, and
- which material is becoming tangential to the rest.

Look for the big issues

Bring conscious awareness to those more minor issues that may be interesting in their own right, but which distract you and your reader from the core messages. These can detract from the focus and clarity of your research.

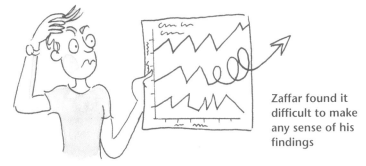

Zaffar found it difficult to make any sense of his findings

Finding the organising principle

Categorising

To help you to segment material as outlined above, it helps to categorise and code it. You would do this so that you could:

- find it easily
- organise in one place all material that you need for a particular purpose
- compare like with like easily
- differentiate your own thoughts and writing from any material that you have drawn from other sources.

'Organising concepts'

A concept is simply a way of thinking about something – an idea or mental model. It helps us to find order in the everyday world and also in any body of information such as that collected for research. Concepts help to categorise information into named sets, types, themes or equivalent.

Finding the right categories

As research is generally at the 'cutting edge', and by its nature looks at aspects that haven't been studied exactly in this way before, it isn't always obvious at the start which organising concepts are most useful, or how your material will ultimately break down into categories. You have to work with the material, sorting it and thinking about the basis upon which you are sorting it, evolving new categories as your research goes on.

Use your reading At the start, use the texts you read for your literature review to help identify useful concepts – or headings and labels – to organise and reorganise material. This is also useful to do as you collect more information.

Start simple Start with as few categories as possible. Divide material under the most obvious headings, aligned as far as possible to the probable layout of your final report. File it under those headings.

Decide on sub-categories Before long, you will find that you have a great deal of information under each heading, or in each file. This will start to feel unwieldy or inefficient. At that point, look immediately for ways of further dividing the material into what are now the most logical sub-categories. Label these in ways that both:

- show their relationship to the chapter/section/larger category or set of related information
- *and* differentiate them from your other material.

Continue this process as you go along. As you gather a lot of information in one area, break it up into logical parts. Label the parts in ways that indicate:

- what they have in common (their features)
- *or* where they will be used within the report (their use).

Filtering

Aim to keep your material manageable by sorting useable information from the rest. At regular intervals:

- summarise longer notes to shorter ones
- eliminate material, or categories of material, that are proving less useful than anticipated
- decide on good examples and illustrative details; plan where to include these within your intended chapters
- categorise and label extraneous but potentially useful material; store in case of future need.

Organising data for analysis

Collating the data

Before launching into an in-depth analysis of your data, give thought to how best to collate, organise and present them so that the messages stand out clearly. Depending on the subject, that may mean:

- entering data into an appropriate database and running them through a statistical package
- presenting information in charts, graphs, tables, maps or other diagrams
- presenting images as photographs or 'plates'
- organising material chronologically so that the sequence of events supports analysis.

For quantitative research, the 'interpretation' stage tends to go hand in hand with presentation of data. It is essential to set out the data appropriately.

- The tables and charts you include represent choices, indicating to your reader what you believe to be most important.
- Including irrelevant data can indicate poor understanding of what is significant in your material.
- The way you name and label diagrams indicates to your reader a particular way of making sense of the data. Whichever scale you choose for these creates a particular visual effect. If your choice of scale is poor, it could appear that you intended to create a false picture of your findings.

For more details on such representation, see Bell (2005) and Denscombe (2007).

Organise your material so that you can compare 'like' with 'like'. This is likely to involve reorganising, or 'cutting', the data in many ways in order to compare different sets of data within your total dataset, or to compare your data with those published elsewhere.

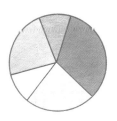

Pie chart

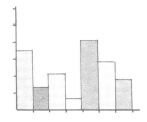

Bar chart

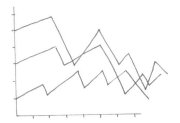

Graph

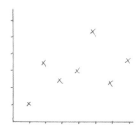

Scatter diagram

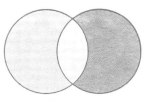

Venn diagram

Country	Capital
England	London
France	Paris
USA	Washington DC

Table

Establishing patterns and relationships

If your data are well presented, this helps you to see patterns in the information. Depending on the subject, that may be:

- relationships between events
- correlations betweens sets of data
- trends over time
- cause and effect
- developmental patterns over time.

Draw relevant headline conclusions

As a starting place, return to your research question and hypotheses.

- How far do your findings provide answers to your research question(s)?
- Does the research support any hypotheses that you had formulated?
- If so, at what level of significance?

Bringing a questioning approach

If it isn't immediately apparent to you what your material or results are telling you, generate a list of questions to help you to work systematically through your research from start to finish. The checklists that you have used for each section in this book may suffice, or can help to prompt you to devise a suitable list.

Questions to help interpret numbers

Thomas (2009) makes the point that, although the approach doesn't appear in many statistical handbooks, it can be invaluable to 'eyeball' your data. This means looking at the numbers in a general way, to see what they look like.

Typical questions would be:

Patterns Are there any patterns in the data? Do they rise or fall in any particular direction? If so, at what particular points do they start to rise or fall, or to do so more sharply? Or do they remain consistent? Or plateau out at any point?

Relationships What are the apparent relationships within the data? Do two or more sets rise or fall in similar ways? Or do some rise at the same points as others fall? Or does each set seem to bear no relation to the others?

Context How do the data relate to context? Do the points where the data start to rise or fall correspond to anything you know from the time, condition or circumstances under which they were gathered? What happened at that point that might explain why the data behaved differently then than previously or later?

Irregularities Are there any data that don't seem to match the rest? Any extreme values or outliers?

Questions to help interpret material

For analysing texts, images and other non-numerical material, typical questions would be:

Authenticity Is this material what it appears to be? What is its provenance (where does it originate and how do we know)?

Value How is this relevant to my research? How would I use it? Is it the most relevant material? How does it complement my other material? Is this the best example I could include to make my point?

Range Is my material sufficiently wide-ranging to represent my position on the issues accurately and fairly?

Conceptual categories Which concepts would help me to identify themes and to segment my information? Which overarching concepts would help me to cluster several different themes or arguments to help me to interpret the material? Have I categorised information in the best way possible to identify the significance of the material?

Relationships How do the different pieces of information fit together? What light do they shed on each other? How does this piece of information help to piece together the overall picture of what is/was happening?

Reference points Which fields of thought, methods of analysis, published research or other background material can help me understand fully what this material might mean?

Argument How does this information advance my own argument? What light does it throw on related arguments within material published on this subject? See page 175.

Contextualise your findings

Relate back to experts in your field

Make sense of your own findings by referring back to research, theory, or established expertise and common practice within the field. Compare your results with what might be expected from previous work within your subject discipline. How do your results compare to/differ from what might have been predicted by previous research or theory?

Whose research findings were closest to your own?

It is useful to look to your literature review to see whose findings were similar to your own. If there do not appear to be any, then look further afield to see if you missed any research or theory that supports your own findings. If the latter is the case, add these into your literature review. If your results build on similar results, then that can add weight to your own findings.

If your research matched exactly what was expected, what was it about the research design that would have made such an outcome likely? In your Discussion or Conclusion, refer to previous research or theory that supports your own findings.

Whose work challenges your findings?

Your aim as a researcher is to be even-handed and thorough. Look for theory or research which appears to contradict what you have found and add this to your literature review, if not already included. Consider what explanations there might be for such discrepancies.

Whose findings are challenged by your research?

Do your research findings challenge those of any previous research? For example, previous research or a specific theory might have made generalisations that were true of their own sample but not of yours. If so, what was distinct about your research that might explain the differences in outcome or in level of significance?

So what?

Give thought to what makes your findings significant, important, worthwhile or of interest, and to how you can best articulate this clearly within your work.

- Broadly speaking, are previous findings, understandings and/or professional practices confirmed or challenged by your findings?
- How do your findings or analyses differ from those previously published, and why?
- How does your research throw further light on what was already known?
- What have your results added to knowledge in the field? What do we know that we didn't know before? How does your research help us to interpret the world, or some aspect of it, differently?
- How could your research lead to a different understanding of the source materials, or the contexts in which they were produced, or their relationships to other materials, or how they have been used or interpreted in the past?
- What further research questions are prompted by your research?

Making sense of the unexpected

It is often the unexpected aspects of the research that provide the greatest insights. Don't be put off if the material seems to be pointing in a direction that doesn't immediately fit previous work in the field. That might be a good thing.

However, do look for specific, probable reasons why this might be the case. It is not usual for previous published research to be incorrect (although it could be). More likely, the reasons would lie in something that was different about your research, especially in the particular nature of your methods or evidence base.

Interpreting your findings

Check off ☑ each of the following once you have addressed it in full. Cross out any that do not apply. Address any aspects that require more attention.

Preparing material for analysis

☐ I have filtered the material/data, eliminating anything that is unnecessary.

☐ I have considered excluding outlier data from either end of the continuum (for numerical data).

☐ I have used the best analytical programmes for interpreting my data (if relevant).

☐ I have identified the most likely key themes for organising my material.

☐ I have sorted material and data against each theme.

☐ Within each theme, I have organised material into the best sequence for analysis.

☐ I have identified the most appropriate statistical analyses for the data.

☐ I have presented numerical data in the best formats to assist my analysis and interpretation (graphs, tables, charts, maps, diagrams, ordered notes, etc.).

Answering the research question

☐ I have used the material to identify whether the research question is answered or not.

☐ I have established whether the findings support the research hypotheses.

☐ If the research hypotheses are supported, I have identified the level(s) of significance.

Establishing patterns and relationships

☐ I have examined my material/data carefully for patterns and trends.

☐ I have looked for reasons for those patterns and trends, both within my own data and in background literature.

☐ I have established the nature of the relationships within my data/material (such as circumstantial; cause and effect; developmental stages; no evident relationship, etc.).

Contextualising the findings

☐ I have selected the most appropriate theoretical basis for interpreting my findings.

☐ I have compared my own findings against those of previous research, theory, or understandings within the discipline.

☐ I am clear where my findings support published research and theory.

☐ I can provide a rationale for where my findings diverge from published research or theory.

☐ I am clear where there might be flaws in my own processes and can specify how these might have had an impact on my findings.

☐ I am clear whether these are serious or minor flaws, in relation to any conclusions or recommendations that could be made.

☐ I am clear about what my findings add to previous knowledge and understanding.

☐ I am clear where my findings might challenge or modify previous theory or understandings.

Critical selection

☐ I understand what is most relevant and important within my findings.

☐ I have worked out which are the most important messages to communicate within my report, essay or dissertation.

☐ I have identified the key points that I want to make under each theme.

☐ I have identified the best examples (if relevant).

Part 4
Writing it up

The importance of the writing stage

However brilliant your research, your thinking is presented to the world, those who commissioned it, and your examiners, through your writing. It is, therefore, imperative that your writing up does justice to all the work that you have undertaken.

The challenge of the writing process

You may find that writing up your research is the most enjoyable aspect of the work. Some students do – and some don't. Whether or not the process is experienced as enjoyable, there are so many aspects to bring together that it can feel like herding cats.

Writing a substantial piece of work is a challenge not just for students but also for professional writers. Even people who love writing can find it difficult to settle down to a writing session or to know where to start on a piece of writing. Most writers struggle at some time with finding the words to express exactly what they want to say – or find that when they read back over their work, it doesn't sound quite as they remembered it.

As you move through the chapters, consider the tips and strategies provided. Check these off if they apply to you.

If you find, at times, that you are less than enthusiastic about writing, it can help to know that you are in good company. Writing up your work is a great test of your personal qualities and of your skills in identifying and applying a good writing strategy.

However you find the writing process, it is likely that, by the time you complete it, you will experience a great sense of achievement.

Contents of Part 4
Key features of the writing stage are followed up in the chapters that follow. These are:

22 Your writing strategy
23 Getting the structure right
24 Fine-tuning your writing
25 Viva exams

Imelda sometimes felt that writing her essay was like herding cats ...

Writing: What students say ...

Loved it ...

I love writing so this was my favourite part of the research. I got behind with the project at the start because I changed my mind about what to do, and my final research idea wasn't very good. I made up for this by writing critically about where my thinking and my methods had gone wrong, and about how I could have done these better. I think this is how I got through with a good mark.

Had to do it ten times ...

I am sure I wrote every word about ten times – maybe more. Every time, I was sure that it all flowed beautifully. Then, the next day I would reread it and find masses of tiny mistakes. Or I'd think of another thing I wanted to add in, and end up rewriting a paragraph or two to save words so that I could fit it in. It took dedication.

Too many words ...

My tutor told me that I had to add in lots more material but also cut down on my words as I was well over the limit. I thought it was impossible, and a waste of time even to look for places to save words. It felt like I was crawling though each paragraph, finding sentences with 20 words and reducing them to 15, just so that I could add in occasional paragraphs to various sections. I did become really good at it though, and eventually I made it a personal challenge to find a saving of at least 50 words every time I rewrote a section. It was painstaking but not that difficult: there's always another way to say something.

Organising the material ...

For me, the hardest thing [about writing] was choosing what to include from the huge mass of information I had in front of me. I spoke to my supervisor and we decided that the problem was mainly that my material was so disorganised. I had to stop writing, sort out my notes and data, and work out which material related to each section. Then I went through it again, deciding what belonged near the beginning or end of each chapter. It was like a huge 'filing' exercise but, at the end of it, I could see what I would include and where.

Sorting my thoughts ...

I pride myself on being a good writer so I was a bit taken aback when my supervisor was critical of my first draft. It wasn't that there was anything wrong with either my research or the accuracy of my writing. It was more about my thinking. My research results were rather ambivalent and I had a lot of ideas about why that might be the case. I was so absorbed by my ideas that I hadn't considered sufficiently whether these were coming across clearly in my writing. I hadn't even noticed that some of my great thoughts contradicted each other and some were rather muddled, to say the least. Once I was clearer in my thinking, the writing fell into place.

The final hurdles ...

I thought when I completed the first draft that I was nearly finished – I would never have dreamed how long it took after that to rewrite the drafts, the references, the abstract. I only just met the deadline.

Chapter 22
Your writing strategy

People are very individual in the way they approach writing tasks. There isn't an absolute 'best time' or 'best way' to write up your research – what works for you in getting each section or chapter written well and on time is the 'best' way.

Your writing strategy

A good writing strategy can help to make the writing process more manageable. It can help to ensure that you:

- Complete on time
- Write to the word limit
- Use time effectively
- Reduce the stress of the task
- Do justice to your research and analysis
- Get your message across.

In working out which writing strategy would be best for you, you can be guided by such factors as:

- Lessons learnt from your previous assignments, especially those you found most difficult to write
- How you consider you will respond to this particular kind of challenge
- Awareness of where, typically, students tend to go wrong and what they wish they had done differently
- Which strategies you consider would be most useful for you – and which you would follow through.

Where do students go wrong?

Overall, students get it right. Most complete their assignments and achieve well. Many might wish they had gained higher marks, but, nonetheless, their writing strategy has been good enough to get the work done and achieve at least a pass, and usually a much higher grade.

The two main areas where students wish they had, in retrospect, approached things differently are:

- that they had put more care into the final product, so as to gain higher marks
- that they had found ways of making the writing process more manageable.

The first of these relates to such factors as writing structure, clarity and style, which are covered in the following chapters.

This chapter focuses on the second of these: making the writing process more manageable – or finding ways of 'getting it done'. In particular, it considers such issues as:

- planning and routine
- when to write
- pacing and timing
- organising your material
- drawing on good examples.

How to get through it ...

- Be kind to yourself during the writing process: give yourself plenty of rewards.
- Intersperse writing with other activities – don't make it an endurance test.
- Be prepared for some productive days, and others where the process may feel painfully slow.
- Organise your material from the perspective of your writing.
- Don't attempt to do it all at once: write as you go.

Writing strategy: planning and routine

Leave enough time

'Longer than you think' ☐ Planned for it.

Bad days ... ☐ Planned for these.

Some days will be less productive than others, throwing out your writing schedule. Leave time to accommodate these.

The effects of length ... ☐ Planned for it.

Because of the length of the work, it is likely it will take much longer to check for such things as repetition, omissions, overall structure and consistency of style. Allow time for looking over your work as a whole. It is probable that some aspects of later drafts will take longer to fine-tune than earlier ones.

The abstract ☐ Planned for it.

The abstract generally takes much longer to write, word for word, than the rest of the report.

Develop a routine

The best way to avoid putting off writing is to develop the habit of writing on a regular and frequent basis. This may not sound very exciting, but it is what is needed in order to develop the discipline required for long pieces of writing.

- Set specific times aside for writing each day or week – and stick to them.
- If you miss a writing session, timetable in another soon after, so that you don't start to feel that you are falling behind.
- Develop a system for starting to write as soon as you sit down for your writing session, so that you know the time will be well used.

☐ I have worked out what routine is likely to work best for me, for each stage of the writing process.

Writing strategy: when to write

Get started on the easier bits

- Write out an initial Contents page, even if only a best guess; update it as relevant.
- Create files for each chapter or section; type out the heading on the first page and save the file in that name. This provides a more tangible sense of an eventual end product.
- Write out the details of anything relevant that you use; always use the format and style required by your institution for your final list of references and/or bibliography.
- If you start to formulate an idea, immediately jot it down and copy to the file for the most relevant chapter or section of your report. Integrate it into the chapter later, or remove if not used.
- For reports, the Methods sections tend to be relatively straightforward to write, so are useful starting points.
- It is also relatively useful to write short initial drafts of paragraphs, or parts of paragraphs, that will form part of your literature review.

Interim synopses

Although it is can be challenging, write an early synopsis of the research, outlining the key points as you conceptualise them at that time.

- Return to this regularly – every few weeks for longer assignments.
- Browse it and see how it strikes you.
- Does it sound convincing? Is it a good reflection of the way your research is taking shape?
- Update, fine-tune or add to the synopsis so that it evolves with your research.

As you read

Decide as you go

In the section on literature searches, you are encouraged to make decisions early on about how much of any source you will use and in what way. In doing so, you will have a relatively clear view of what it is that you want to say about the source. This is an ideal time to jot down, at least in draft, the point that you will make using that source.

Keep it brief

Make your points about source materials as brief as possible. For most sources, you will only be able to write a passing reference within a sentence. Develop the discipline of summarising the relevance of what you have read into a single sentence. This will mean that the first draft of your literature review will be much easier to assemble.

For supervisor requests

If your supervisor asks to see a section or chapter, use this as an opportunity to get started on writing up the report. Your supervisor will be aware that failure to get started on the writing is a major reason for students not completing their dissertation.

Assume you will forget

In the earlier stages of research, it is tempting not to write things down, assuming that the most important facets will still be memorable in a few months' time. This tends to lead to frustration later, and many forgotten details.

As you read, or at the points where you tease out a complex concept, be disciplined in making good notes as reminders. Consider writing this up straightaway in draft form while it is clear in your mind.

Capture the moment

Write each chapter, section or paragraph at the point when it is live and interesting to you: the writing up will feel easier. It is likely to come over as more interesting to the reader, too.

Writing strategy: pacing, timing and input

Keep it fresh

Writing too much at once can lead to boredom and de-motivation.

☐ Consider spreading the writing into short blocks over a longer time span, so that you are fresh each time you come to write. This helps to produce clear, sharp thinking that is reflected in your script.

Avoid rushed deadlines

Writing under pressure of a deadline means that the writing may come across as rushed, dull or inaccurate.

☐ Work backwards from deadlines, detailing how long it will take you to write, revise and fine-tune your writing.

☐ Build in additional time for each stage, to allow for unexpected delays and difficulties.

☐ Start as early as possible so that you have time to meet any emergency.

☐ Avoid telling yourself that you will work better under pressure, unless you have managed, successfully, a piece of writing of this length and complexity already.

☐ Assume that the final tasks, such as writing the abstract and fine-tuning your drafts, will take at least 10% of your project time, and possibly longer.

By section

Most reports and dissertations fall naturally into chapters and/or sections. If yours doesn't, then plan out the anticipated contents into coherent sections.

☐ Write at least a rough outline of each section or chapter at the point that you complete the research or work involved. It is likely that you will want to make changes later, so getting the core details down on paper, along with your thoughts and analysis, is more important than aiming at a perfect early draft.

Ask for input

☐ Find a friend or peer who is also undertaking a long assignment. Make sure they are covering a completely different topic, so that there is no chance of accidental copying of each other's work. Arrange to share a chapter or section of your work – and be open to constructive criticism.

The most important aspect is using the opportunity to get something down on paper as that then gives you something to work with, or improve upon.

Leave fine-tuning until later

☐ Your decisions about what to include, in what ways, and to what level or depth will change over the course of the project, as you read new things and as your own work unfolds. This means that, whilst it is good to draft sections as you go, it isn't worth fine-tuning the work too early in the process.

A 10,000 word limit? Pah! Make it 100,000 and give me a real challenge!

LIBRARY

The other students complained that Olly had an unfair advantage when it came to writing up

Take the plunge

☐ The longer you leave writing the first sections, the harder it can be to write at all. You will find it easier to remain motivated writing later chapters or sections if you have the satisfaction of knowing that you have already drafted some of your work ahead of schedule.

Organising your material for writing

Use the formal organisational features

One essential consideration is to know the required formal structure for your finished assignment. This is a key issue so is covered separately in Chapter 23.

Decide the theme of each chapter

For chapter-based dissertations and similar kinds of long assignment, it can be challenging to decide which material fits best into each chapter of the main body of the report. Often, there are several legitimate ways in which material might be divided up into themes for chapters. Decide which themes or strands of your argument fit best together and then stick to that. Avoid jumping ahead, or back, to material covered in other chapters, even if that means that some interesting yet more minor connections between aspects of the material need to be omitted.

Organise each chapter

As for other assignments, bear in mind the basics of good structuring.

Themes Decide on the main theme for the chapter.

Argument Decide the main argument(s) that you will be developing in that chapter. Use that argument as a thread to hold the rest of your material together and to guide the reader through.

Sort your material Sort your material so that everything that relates to that chapter has been brought together and is to hand in one place before you start to write it. Consider drawing up a checklist of what you intend to include and in what detail. Clarify in your own mind:

- what you plan to cover
- how each piece of information relates to the next
- how you will move from one set of information to the next as you write
- what you will be able to include and what you will need to leave out.

Sequence Decide the best order for presenting all of the material that you intend to use for that chapter. Much of it should follow from the logical development of your main argument for that chapter. Plan to introduce material in such a way that there appears to be a natural, logical flow from one section to the next.

Opening and closing Provide an Introduction and Conclusion to each chapter. Summarise within both of these the main themes and arguments of the chapter, even if this feels rather repetitious.

Clustering As you write, keep checking that material related to the same point is located together. Readers should not feel they are hopping back and forward between points.

Paragraphing

Check that each paragraph is well-organised in its own right. Each should focus on a definable topic, which, typically, would be introduced in the first sentence.

Paragraphs should be logically ordered. It may be necessary to provide bridging sentences to help the reader to move from one set of paragraphs to the next if there is not an obvious link between these.

For research reports

For research reports, the required structure helps a great deal with the decision-making. You write the methods in the methods section, the results in the results section and so on.

Once you allocate the right material to each section, ensure that it is well organised within that section too. It is useful to draw upon the general principles outlined above. For example, the material needs be logically organised within each section and well-paragraphed. For reports, use of sub-headings can help to signpost transitions from one theme to another (see page 185).

Working from examples

Use previous examples of similar assignments, usually available via your library, in order to gain a good sense of how material is organised within your subject and how to make best use of the words available to you, in a style consistent with your subject discipline. (If examples of assignments are not available, look back at the section on journal articles for some steer. See Chapter 9.)

Aspect   Check off ☑ each aspect once you have considered it fully.

☐ **Abstract**
- How does the author manage to sum up the whole of their research in so few words? What do they include?
- Look at the rest of the work to consider the choices that the author made about what material to include and exclude from the main body and the way that they paraphrased their lengthier sections within the abstract.

☐ **Formal structure**
- Are you expected to use chapters or sections or some other format to organise your material?
- How many words are allocated to each section or chapter?

☐ **Introduction**
- What is the range of information contained within the Introduction?
- How is this material organised?
- How is each theme introduced?

☐ **Methods**
- How are methods described? What level of detail is included? How is this section worded?
- Are any particular sub-sections typical within your subject?

☐ **Results/findings**
- In which section of the report or dissertation are you expected to provide your results?
- At what level of detail are these described?
- How are these worded? What do you notice about the writing style?
- Are tables and/or charts typical?

☐ **Conclusions/Recommendations**
- Where are these located within reports/dissertations in your subject?
- At what level of detail are these discussed?
- What kinds of conclusions or recommendations are typical?

☐ **Citations and references**
- How do authors introduce passing references to other pieces of research within their own? What kind of wording do they use to do so?
- What kinds of commentary or analysis are typical?
- How do they pick up on their citations within their references or footnotes?

☐ **Appendices**
- What kinds of material, typically, are presented in the appendices?
- How do authors make links between material in the main body of their work and in the appendices?

Chapter 23
Getting the structure right

Whilst most long assignments require you to address similar considerations and in the same order, the exact requirements on structure vary by discipline and context. The longer the assignment, the more likely it is that you will be expected to produce it as chapters rather than as continuous text (as for essays) or sections (as for research reports).

Where research is undertaken for a client, then Recommendations are typical, but these would not be typical of other kinds of student report.

Research projects

Subjects in sciences, social sciences, business and healthcare tend to require research reports to be divided into sections, with the use of plentiful clear headings and sub-headings.

Long essays

These are more common in arts and humanities subjects and tend not to favour any sub-headings within the main body of the work.

Dissertations

For sciences and social sciences, dissertations are generally divided into chapters that equate broadly to the sections of a research report. Check the requirements for your course.

For arts and humanities subjects, the literature search and methodology are integrated into the Introduction. The core chapters develop your argument, each chapter investigating an aspect of the overall topic. You design this structure for yourself, so need to outline it and its rationale as part of the Introduction.

Theses

Normally, theses are written using chapters.

Sections/Chapters

Section-based
1 Abstract
2 Title page
3 Contents
4 Introduction, including research hypothesis or proposal
5 Literature review
6 Methodology/Research design/Methods
7 Results
8 Discussion of results
9 Conclusions (if required)
10 Recommendations (if applicable)
11 Bibliography
12 References
13 Appendices

Chapter-based
1 Abstract
2 Title page
3 Contents
4 Introduction, including literature review and methods
5 Chapters: discussion and analysis of the material
6 Conclusions
7 Bibliography
8 References
9 Appendices (if relevant)

More details are provided on pages 186–95, below.

Structure: what is the purpose ...?

The following pages (186–95) outline some of the key purposes of different aspects of research reports or articles when produced by academics or professional researchers. Depending on the subject, these might be arranged differently by section/chapter, but the purpose would be similar, nonetheless. These are not identical to those for student assignments, but inform the thinking of examiners when marking your research. The different nuances that examiners might bring are outlined alongside these.

Aspect	Purpose of this for professional researchers	Examiners are looking to see that you ...
Overall project	• To advance understanding of a specific issue, building on what has gone before, and laying groundwork for future enquiry.	• understand how knowledge is constructed in your subject • draw on what you have learnt already on your programme and integrate a broad range of skills • manage complexity, making sensible decisions in an independent way, with a good feel for when to ask for help or advice • can follow a brief, as set by the tutor, yourself, a workplace or client • have aptitude for a research career in higher education, government, business or industry or other fields (if the examiners were asked to write a reference to that effect)
Abstract	• To summarise the key points of the research project so that others can decide quickly whether it is worth reading in full. • To help others to search and browse for relevant research.	• can think clearly and precisely – and can present that thought in writing • can construct an abstract in the style typical for your academic discipline
Title page	• To provide the title, author details, date, details of who commissioned or funded the research (if applicable).	• can set out your research in a professional way, following instructions
Contents	• To help the reader find each chapter, section, appendix or table quickly and easily.	• can organise information clearly and accurately, taking your reader into account

Aspect	Purpose of this for professional researchers	Examiners are looking to see that you ...
Research hypothesis or proposal	• For the researcher: to set boundaries to their work, helping to provide a clear focus. • To clarify to the research world and funding bodies exactly what is covered by that piece of research – and the assumptions being made.	• combine originality with common sense: you can put together a sensible proposal/hypothesis that meets the brief • formulate a precise, finely worded, well thought out proposal or hypothesis
Introduction	• To provide contextual background such as why the research was commissioned or undertaken, what it aims to achieve, and a rationale for the focus or angle taken. • For some disciplines, the Introduction is a larger section that provides the research background, literature and methods (see sections below).	• provide evidence of a broad background understanding to your topic and write about this in a way that avoids waffle or irrelevant details • make sensible judgements about what other relatively academic readers, who are not expert in your topic, would need to know as a starting place for making sense of your research • present a reasoned case for undertaking the research: that it has some purpose or significance or addresses a relevant issue • set the scene for the reader about what you did, and why, without going into too much detail that would be covered in the rest of the report
Literature review	• For the researcher to be as informed as possible about their specialism or area of expertise. • To ensure that the research is well grounded in the theory, methodology and knowledge base of the subject. • To ensure that their work is original and hasn't been covered by someone else. • To make clear to their readers how their research has made use of existing sources of information – how these have been interpreted for the purposes of this research.	• have researched widely into the background of the subject • select the right material and convey to others its relevance to your research • present previous research in a structured way that shows the development of understanding of this issue

Aspect	Purpose of this for professional researchers	Examiners are looking to see that you ...
Methodology/ Research design	• Ensure ethical codes are adhered to, in spirit as well as letter. • To inform the reader of the methodological principles that inform the research. • To help the reader to grasp the thinking behind the research, so that they can form their own conclusions about whether the design was fit for purpose or contained some flaws.	• understand the methodological assumptions and philosophies relevant to your subject discipline • understand the ethical considerations – and take these on board fully • have thought through each aspect of your research carefully to see that it is fit for purpose • have designed your project to be internally consistent: the purpose, philosophy, methods and conclusions are mutually supporting • explain your methods fully, but briefly, with a clear rationale for why you chose them. Don't account for why you haven't chosen methods that clearly would not be suitable for your discipline/topic.
*Methods *Usually presented as part of the section above.	• To provide a clear outline of exactly how the research was conducted, with a rationale for why particular methods were chosen. • To enable others to make sense of the findings (in terms of the methods used). • Where applicable, to enable others to test out the results through replicating the research methods.	• select or design appropriate methods for meeting your proposal or testing your hypothesis exactly as written • follow through on these in a systematic way, exactly as you outlined • understand the terminology as relevant to your subject, and use it appropriately, such as in identifying variables and conditions (page 139).
*Participants *As above.	• To clarify how they chose their sample, and specify which variables were controlled for.	• clarify how you chose the sample, and which variables were controlled for • followed ethical guidelines
*Materials *As above.	• To provide further details of the research methods, such as guidance notes given to participants.	• clarify precisely the materials, data or sources that you used for the research • designed materials that were fit for purpose and audience

Aspect	Purpose of this for professional researchers	Examiners are looking to see that you ...
Results	• To inform the reader of the outcome of the research (mainly for research presenting quantitative data). These should be accurate and true.	• present data and findings clearly and accurately, using the best graphics • identify the key findings rather than presenting everything • demonstrate integrity in presenting true results rather than correcting the figures to prove a particular point
Discussion	• To draw out the significance of the findings and what this means for understanding the issue in the context of the field and/or the brief. • To evaluate the extent to which the results can be used as the basis for generalisations. • To evaluate the methodology (if relevant). • To draw out lessons about the potential relevance of the research and where future research might take the issue further.	• describe your findings briefly, precisely and with integrity • interpret your own findings correctly • evaluate appropriately the significance or relevance of your findings and make that clear to your reader • evaluate your methods with a critical eye, demonstrating that you understand what worked or did not work as expected, why this occurred, and what is likely to work better (if relevant) • identify how future research could build on your methods or findings, or take them in new directions For arts and humanities subjects, most of your chapters will consist of discussion. Each will focus on a distinct part of your analysis of the materials and your argument.
Conclusions	• To draw together and summarise thoughts about the research findings and methods, and their significance.	• understand which aspects are the most significant to include, and summarise these succinctly • present these logically and coherently, drawing on material you have previously presented

Aspect	Purpose of this for professional researchers	Examiners are looking to see that you ...
Recommendations	• Where these are applicable to the brief: To draw out suggestions for action, based upon the findings.	• make recommendations that follow logically from the brief and from your findings • focus your recommendations closely on the needs of the client • present numbered recommendations clearly, following the order in which the issues were presented in the body of the report • make recommendations that are sensible and feasible, given the context • ensure that priorities are identified • continue to adhere to ethical principles • have drawn out the risks, costs or other barriers to the implementation of the recommendations
Bibliography	• To provide details of the material used as background for the project, whether cited in the text or not.	• have read broadly around the subject, and that your reading indicates a good background knowledge of the field • demonstrate through the rest of your report that your breadth of knowledge and understanding is consistent with the bibliography
References	• To provide details of the sources cited in the text.	• based your own research on previous work in your field • are able to draw appropriately on the work of others • can cite and reference sources correctly • attribute work to others appropriately • apply the correct conventions for referencing sources, as directed by your course
Appendices	• To provide supporting details and materials which, if included in the main body of the report, would interrupt its flow for the reader.	• conducted the research yourself, as the appendices are likely to reveal copied data and material more easily • collated and interpreted data correctly • produced materials that met ethical and other guidelines and were fit for purpose.

Writing it up: opening sections

Introduction

Chapter-based dissertations

Use your introduction to provide a succinct summary of your research. Provide your rationale for the research, making the case briefly for its significance, interest or relevance. Give the background, indicating key research on the topic, and incorporating your literature review.

Research reports

Provide a succinct summary of your research. State your research thesis or hypotheses briefly: what are you setting out to test or demonstrate? Summarise what you did, the number and type of research conditions, brief details of your sample, the results, and whether these were significant or not, and at what level of significance. Aim to fit in as much key information as you can in as few words as possible.

Commissioned reports

If your report is undertaken for a client, such as a business or agency, provide background about:

- who commissioned the report and why
- the scope of the report: what it will cover
- definitions of any terms
- the methods used
- a summary of findings and recommendations.

Literature review

For some subjects, this forms part of the introduction; for others, it is a separate section. Either way, avoid describing the content of previous literature. Instead, focus on what each item contributes to the debate. More details about how to approach the writing of the literature review are provided in Chapter 9.

Methods

Use this section to provide clear details about how you gained your data and analysed it. Readers can then decide whether your results and conclusions are valid. State briefly but clearly, and in full, how your research was conducted. Depending on your subject, this might include a discussion of how you found, selected and analysed source materials;

the number and types of research conditions; what exactly these were; the dependent and independent variables for each; and any statistical methods you used. Mention if you are replicating a previous research study or deliberately taking a different approach to working with material used in previous research.

The writing style of the methods section is descriptive. Give precise details in the correct sequence, such as:

A third of solution X was heated to Y degrees. Then, 40 mg of solution Z was added.

Participants If working with participants or samples, state how you chose these and the research methodology employed. Provide relevant details about the number and characteristics of your sample; how many groups there were and features of each, including the control group(s).

Materials Describe accurately the types and/or amounts of any materials you used within experiments or in the field, and any special features of these. If relevant, provide brief details of any specific instructions or materials that were given to participants. Provide a copy of these as an appendix.

Results or summary of findings

Before interpreting your results, summarise your findings succinctly. Do not enter into analysis of the result – just state what they are.

For arts, humanities and other discursive research, an analysis of your findings is integral to most chapters.

For science-based, experimental and number-based subjects this means providing a summary of the research data and outcomes. Use headings and tables to set these out clearly within the body of the report and/or in appendices. Typically, you would present results both as a brief paragraph, and in tables or charts which summarise the data. State whether these support the research hypotheses and, if so, at what levels of significance.

Writing it up: discussion and conclusions

Discussion

This is usually the longest part and may form several chapters of a dissertation. Here is where you undertake a critical analysis of your findings.

For arts and humanities subjects, divide this material into logical chapters (see above, page 189). If relevant, piece together the findings emerging from the research and your interpretations of the material.

What do your findings tell you?

- What do your data or findings mean?
- What trends or patterns do they indicate? Or what new light do they throw on an event or situation?

Are findings consistent with expectations?

- Were they what you had expected at the start of the research, given its focus?
- Are they consistent with previous theory and research? If not, why might that have been the case?
- Is there anything unusual about your findings? If so, what would explain that?

What is significant about your findings?

- What is important or relevant about your findings?
- How does your research add to what was known about the topic before?
- Does it support previous research?
- Does it offer insights into how previous research or theory does, or does not, apply, in particular instances?
- Does it open up new questions or avenues for further research?
- Does it indicate practical ways forward for professional practice?

Critique your research

- In retrospect, had you framed the issues correctly?
- Had you focused on the right issues?
- Could the research design be improved upon?
- How might any short-comings or limitations in your methods or sample have impacted on the outcomes?
- Do your findings suggest that it would have been useful to have manipulated the variables differently or used a different kind of control condition?
- If the research hypothesis was not supported, consider why that might have been the case.

Conclusions

Conclusions sum up your research, setting out its significance and your findings. These are summarised into your Abstract (page 193) and indicated in your Introduction. For some subjects, the conclusions are subsumed into the Discussion section.

If a separate conclusion is required, draw together, in summary, your key findings, observations or judgements. Don't introduce new material or references at this stage.

Recommendations

The function of recommendations is to suggest ways forward by proposing specific action. These are not typical for all student assignments, and are found mainly where there would be real-life applications, such as for employment- and client-related projects.

- Recommendations should be relevant to the brief and feasible to carry out.
- It should be evident to the reader that the recommendations are based on the evidence, not plucked from thin air as good things to do.
- List recommendations in a logical order.
- Number recommendations.
- Cross-reference each recommendation to the relevant section or page numbers within the report such that it is clear to the reader how the recommendation relates to the research findings.

Writing it up: abstract and final matter

Abstracts

Although the abstract is inserted at the front of the report, before the contents page, it is usually easiest and most practical to write this last. The abstract is often the part that is used most by readers, and signals to readers not just what your research is about but whether it is worth reading. It showcases your work and sets the tone for the examiners in what to expect from the rest of the assignment.

It is typical for this to take many drafts. You need to make every word count. That may take many attempts at selecting what to include, what to leave out, and how to phrase the content.

What to include

Summarise your research, in brief. State, in clear and straightforward terms, the rationale for researching the topic, its scope, an indication of your sources, the research methods, and your conclusions. For experimental reports, include the research hypotheses, the methods used to test these, the results, whether the results supported the hypotheses and at what level of significance.

Summaries

For some courses, and especially for commissioned reports, you may be asked to provide a summary rather than an abstract. This may be a little longer than an abstract but the same basic principles and content apply. For commissioned reports, include your conclusions and the main recommendations.

Final matter

The following sections can be developed as you go and/or finalised after the main parts of the assignment are completed.

Contents

List all the chapters and sections, including appendices and references. Provide page numbers.

List of tables and illustrations

List any illustrations, charts, graphs, maps etc., with the page number for each.

References

List the sources you cited in your assignment, using the system required by your course. See page 28.

Bibliography

If required, list relevant further reading.

Appendices

Provide such items as are essential for enabling the reader to follow your methods or make sense of your analyses. Include instructions or materials given to participants, datasets, tables and graphs. Only include items referred to in your report. Number them exactly as you did in the report.

Charts, graphs and tables

For each of these, as relevant, provide:

- a heading that defines precisely what it is designed to show
- the type and scale of measurements used
- the source of the data (with dates)
- precisely labelled axes
- a key, if that would help the reader.

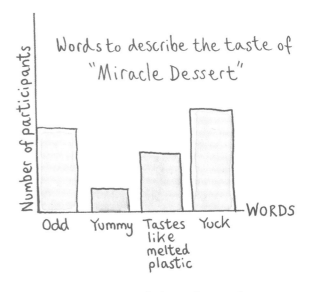

Jeevan's first recommendation to her employer was to abandon the launch of *Miracle Dessert*

What students say: structuring my work

My supervisor said that my dissertation was like reading 12 separate essays. I had put loads of work into each chapter but hadn't given any thought to how it read as a whole. My advice to others would be to invest time in making good links between chapters.

I was so excited about my discussion section that I raced through all the earlier sections just to get to it. My discussion *was* good, but my examiners said that they couldn't see how I got to this from my earlier material, and this had lost me marks. In retrospect, I should have used earlier chapters to create solid foundations to build my argument on.

For me, everything seemed interconnected, so I found it hard to decide how to break my material up into chapters. My first draft had only a few very long, complicated chapters, which even I found hard to read. I kept repeating material from one chapter or paragraph to another in order to honour the connections I could see. My supervisor said that I made a lot of interesting links but advised me to let them go. She pointed out that they were weakening the overall structure, making it hard for the reader to follow my argument.

I was more used to writing reports than essays, and I think this made it hard for me to adapt to writing a dissertation structured into chapters. For my reports, it was fairly obvious what I needed to include under each section. When it was just up to me to decide what should go into chapters, and even how many chapters to have, I wasn't sure what to do. I didn't appreciate how long it would take me to sort this out, and hadn't factored it into my scheduling. I wish I had read more dissertations of that kind before I began writing, to see what writing in chapters was like.

Writing is something I love and I took great pride in making my dissertation flow beautifully as a well-written piece. Unfortunately, I put far too much effort into this, and not nearly enough into the research and thinking about my material. It didn't take my supervisor long to start picking holes in my thinking, even though he did acknowledge that the writing was very good. I gradually learnt that having strong lines of argument and credible data were just as important in 'telling a good story' – which was the bit I really enjoyed.

The appendices didn't seem important to me – they seemed the place to dump bits and pieces that didn't fit anywhere else or to show off how much data I had. I didn't bring much critical awareness to what I was including, and why, or how I was organising it. It was only in my viva that I realised this hadn't been a good idea.

Reflection: Structuring your work

- What insights about structuring your work can you learn from these students' experiences?
- How will you plan your project in order to take those insights on board?

Structure – which sections are required?

PLANNING TOOL

For research reports written in sections (rather than chapters), find out which sections you are required to include for your assignment. Decide how many words to allocate to each section, following custom in your subject. Check that this matches the required word length.

Section	Need to include?	Words allocated	Details
Abstract/summary	Yes/No		As instructed on your course.
Acknowledgements	Yes/No		Typically just a few lines.
Contents page	Yes/No		
List of tables and diagrams	Yes/No		
Introduction	Yes/No		Usually about 5–15%. Summarise the research. Include the research hypotheses as applicable.
Literature review	Yes/No		Typically around 15% of total words, depending on the subject.
Methodology and methods	Yes/No		Generally around 15%, including research design and numbers of research conditions.
● Materials	Yes/No		Include as part of methods. Rarely more than 1–2%. Include examples in appendices.
● Participants	Yes/No		Include as part of methods. Identify characteristics of the sample. Rarely more than 1–2%.
Results/findings	Yes/No		Usually short – around 5% for numerical findings or 10–15% for qualitative findings.
Discussion	Yes/No		Usually about 35–45%.
Conclusions	Yes/No		If required, usually about 5–10%.
Recommendations	Yes/No		If included, usually no more than 5%, and reduce words allocated elsewhere.
References	Yes/No		Not usually included in the word count.
Bibliography	Yes/No		Not usually included in the word count.
Appendices	Yes/No		Custom varies on whether to include in the word count.
Index	Yes/No		Not usually required.
Charts/tables	Yes/No		Custom varies on whether to include in the word count.
Total word count	–		

Structure – which chapters?

For assignments that are to be written in chapters (rather than sections), decide how many chapters to include for the main body of your work. Decide how many words to allocate to each, and check that the overall total matches the required word length. Update this as your research progresses.

Section	Need to include?	Words allocated	Details, including names of your chapters
Abstract/summary	Yes/No		As instructed on your course.
Acknowledgements	Yes/No		Typically just a few lines.
Contents page	Yes/No		
List of tables/diagrams	Yes/No		Include if relevant.
Chapter 1 Introduction	Yes/No		Provides the background to your research. Usually about 10–15%; including literature review, overview of the research, and methods used.
Chapter 2	Yes/No		
Chapter 3	Yes/No		
Chapter 4	Yes/No		
Chapter 5	Yes/No		
Chapter 6	Yes/No		
Chapter 7	Yes/No		
Chapter 8	Yes/No		
Conclusions	Yes/No		Typically about 10–15%.
References	Yes/No		Not usually included in the word count.
Bibliography	Yes/No		Not usually included in the word count.
Appendices	Yes/No		Custom varies on whether to include in the word count.
Index	Yes/No		Not usually required.
Total word count	–		
Does the word limit include those in charts and tables	Yes/No		

Chapter 24
Fine-tuning your writing

It is likely that you will have written some or all of most sections as you went along. Some parts may be complete. Nonetheless, typically, there will be many small glitches to iron out through further redrafting.

Redrafting and editing

There is no set number of times to draft and redraft a piece of work. Keep going until you are happy enough with the final version – or you are at a point where there is no time to do more. As you find aspects that need attention, correct them or mark them up clearly for you to amend later.

Read it through

An often overlooked, yet essential, aspect of writing is the need for repeated rereading of successive drafts. This entails:

- reading drafts to check that you have used the word limit to best effect – that your writing is succinct and every word counts
- reading for style
- reading for clarity, precision and accuracy
- reading for meaning and coherence
- reading for consistency.

It is likely that, if you do this systematically, you will make many small changes each time. You will also find that changes to one aspect create the need for further amendments: adding a paragraph to improve the sense, flow or coherence may create an imbalance in the material covered, or put you over the word limit. Amend until you arrive at the best achievable balance within the time limits and word allowance.

Nearly perfect ... !! Just the occasional repetition, omission and mistake, some things to chase up, clumsy phrasing, inconsistencies, things I had forgotten I had included – I wonder why I did – and some bits that I have no idea what I meant when I wrote them ...

Such fine-tuning represents a considerable time commitment but repays the effort taken. It requires high levels of concentration, which can be tiring. So, for long assignments, take regular breaks so that you are looking at the work with a fresh eye. As part of your project planning, plan in sufficient time to do justice to your work through such redrafting.

Fine-tuning and final checks

For a piece of work of this magnitude, it is assumed that you will be assiduous in checking the basics of grammar, spelling, typographical errors, accidental cuts in the text, missing sections, and for any unexpected and incorrect amendments made by the word-processing software – such as substituting homophones (there/their) or bizarre alternatives to the word you thought you had typed.

If you spot these as you go, correct them. This helps to ensure that you don't miss them later. However, it isn't worth spending time checking for these until you have decided the content and phrasing of your penultimate draft.

Make every word count

When the word limit is set for the assignment, it is assumed that you will need to make full use of the word allowance. As a result, you may well find it difficult to make the word limit stretch to cover the material that you want to include. That is typical.

Part of the art of writing a long assignment is to find ways of saying as much as possible within as few words as possible.

Plan for the word allowance

Manage the frustration: Be prepared to be baffled by the word allowance – it usually starts to seem 'unreasonably' low. Managing your expectations can help make it less frustrating.

Prepare for the word challenge: It is in your interest to indicate broad reading as well as detailed analysis of your findings. Finding ways of doing this within the word limit can be challenging. Plan time to do this.

Balance 'start' and 'end' wordiness

At the start of your research, as the word requirement may be much higher than for any previous assignments, it might seem that you could never write so much on one relatively small topic.

Typically, this results in:

- excessive wordiness in the first parts you write
- much time spent later cutting out words, in order to fit in other material, *and/or*
- risky decisions to omit important material rather than redraft large sections.

When you complete a draft, check it for wordier sections. Aim to provide a balanced level of detail …

- for sections written both earlier and later
- across the length of sections or chapters
- across the whole assignment.

Manage the word limit

Avoid tangents and anecdotes

Almost every researcher grapples with a natural desire to include material that they find interesting and 'essential', but which would, in practice, make their work unwieldy or too lengthy. Be a ruthless editor: if something isn't really relevant, don't include it.

Cut

Write succinctly. Summarise and edit as you go – so that you can slot in new points and references later as these arise.

Cluster research references

You cannot refer in the same detail to all the related research material. Use 'passing references' briefly, in lists where appropriate, to give weight to your argument and show breadth of reading, as in the example below.

> This was also supported by research into the visual responses of apes (Suarez, 2011; Lim, 2012), monkeys (Williams, 2008) and chimpanzees (Ghotti, 2006; Patel, 2009 and Urban, 2013).

Summarise

Be ready to redraft sentences, paragraphs or whole chapters so as to fit in material as necessary, and to use the word limit effectively.

- Be prepared to do this more than once.
- Plan space for this into your schedule – it can be a time-consuming activity.

Writing style

Writing style

The writing style should be:

1 *formal* – remove slang and abbreviations

2 *academic* – follow academic conventions such as citing and referencing others' work correctly

3 *subject-specific* – follow the style appropriate to your subject.

Formal style

Typically, academic writing is written in the third person and in a passive voice. However, in some subjects, especially those that take an interpretative approach, the first person and active voice are used.

Person and voice

Find out and check off ☑ person and voice as preferred in your subject.

Person

☐ the first person: I/we

☐ the second person: you

☐ the third person: he/she/it/they/one

Passive or active voice

☐ active: I carried out a survey in June.

☐ passive: The survey was carried out in June.

Continuous prose or sections

This varies depending on your subject and, to some extent, your research design and methods.

- Science and social science reports tend to be written in sections, each of which is subdivided into numbered and headed sub-sections. It is usually acceptable to write parts of some paragraphs using bullet points, providing these are introduced by the preceding sentence.
- For arts and humanities subjects, and for long essays, dissertations and theses generally, the argument is usually produced as continuous prose (or text). It is less typical to include headed sub-sections or bullet point.

Headings for sections

Provide a heading for each main section of reports. Use section headings to break up your report and to introduce different kinds of subject matter. Use consistent headings and numbering throughout.

Example: using clear numbered headings

4	**Methodology and methods**
4.1	*Methodology*
4.1.1	The overall approach taken by the research …
4.2	*Research design*
4.2.1	There were three conditions, using …
4.3	*Methods*
4.3.1	In condition A, participants were asked to …
4.3.2	In condition B, participants were asked to …
4.4	*Materials*
4.4.1	Instructions. Each participant was given …

Presenting the text

Present your text so that it is easy for the reader to navigate and read.

- Include only essential diagrams in the body of the work. Place others as appendices at the end.
- Number each page, including all appendices; provide page numbers on your contents page.
- Use fonts that are easy to read.
- Leave clear margins at each side.

Grammar and punctuation

Spend time checking and rechecking for typos and any errors in grammar and punctuation. Browse a style book such as Strunk and White (2008) to gain a feel for areas where you might have weaknesses in formal style, then use it for reference.

Precision and accuracy

A key task at the writing stage is to ensure that your message comes across clearly and as intended. Slight changes to the grammar, spelling or word order can alter the meaning of a sentence. In everyday speech this can be overlooked, but a research paper should express everything with exactitude.

Authors may know, in their own minds, what they mean to say, and to whom or to what they are referring at any given time. However, they need to ensure that this is conveyed precisely in what they write. The reader shouldn't be left to guess what is meant, even if they could make a reasonable guess.

Specialist terminology

Although it is important to develop a good understanding of the specialist terminology within your field, it is just as important to use this correctly and when needed, and not just to sound clever. It is easy to ruin a good piece of research through the over-use or misuse of specialist terms or jargon. The effect can be that the thinking process comes across to the reader as confused or pompous. Readers may not be able to grasp the point being made.

Define your terms

Where a term might be open to more than one interpretation, state precisely and briefly the ways in which it will be used within the context of your work. This often arises when a word or term has an everyday meaning and a more precise meaning within the field.

Precise use of pronouns and possessives

Pronouns: e.g. 'they', 'it', 'he', 'she', 'them'
Possessives: e.g. 'her', 'its', 'his', 'their'.

Lack of precision in these words can leave writing sounding vague and confused. Check specifically that it is absolutely clear, from your word order, exactly what or whom is referred to when using these words. Look for potential alternative interpretations, as in:

The shark tried to bite the boat but its thick metal hull prevented it from succeeding.

The subject of the verb

Check whether it is evident to the reader who or what is the subject of the verb (the 'doing word'). Aim to keep the subject of your verb close to that verb. If your sentence contains several clauses or use of pronouns, it may not be evident which 'he' or 'they' is meant. Don't leave it to the reader to guess. Aim to keep the subject of your verb close to that verb. For example,

Julie reported that she has a dog named Fifi. She likes to be taken for a walk twice a day, to chew bones and to have her tummy rubbed.

Avoid separating the subject of the verb by a clause that refers to something else. If you do this, the reader is likely to assume that the verb applies to the last item immediately before the verb. For example,

The beaker containing the ball, which was round and made of glass, was placed on the bench.

Here, it isn't clear whether it is the beaker or the ball that is round and made of glass; both could be true.

Double meanings

When writing, we tend to see only the meaning that is in our own minds. When proof-reading, check whether anything could be interpreted in more than one way, as in:

I'm having a friend for lunch.

Long and complex sentences or passages

It is sometimes necessary to use long, complex sentences with many clauses. However, these can make it harder for the reader to follow the argument, even when written correctly. Use sparingly.

Coherence, consistency and clarity

For long assignments written over many sittings, the writing style and even some core arguments can tend to change over time. If so, and if this is not then picked up and amended, these inconsistencies can render the end product rather disjointed and confusing. Use the checklist below to address each of the following points. Check off ✓ once completed.

Coherence and focus

Read the whole assignment through, looking specifically to ensure that:

- [ ] each section refers back specifically to your research proposal and/or the questions or hypotheses contained within it

- [ ] everything in the report is focused on your research proposal – and that you haven't wandered off topic into interesting tangents

- [ ] similar information is grouped together

- [ ] everything is in the most appropriate section or chapter

- [ ] your line of reasoning flows in a logical and coherent way

- [ ] the messages in each section of your report are mutually self-supporting

- [ ] assertions made in one section are not contradicted by those elsewhere in the report nor by the data provided

- [ ] the conclusion refers back to your research question or hypotheses

- [ ] if your perspectives on the issue changed over time, this is explained or made coherent in terms of your final position on the issue

- [ ] it is clear where you stand on the research questions: what the answers were and/or whether the research hypotheses were supported.

Consistent voice

Once you have completed all sections and redrafted them for content, coherence and focus, re-read them for consistency in style. Check for:

- [ ] 'one work': the work reads as a single whole

- [ ] 'one author': the work reads as if written by a single person

- [ ] wordiness: do you change between wordier and more concise styles between sections?

- [ ] active/passive: are some sections written in the active voice ('they did this …') and others in the passive voice ('this was done by them …')?

- [ ] paragraph lengths: do some chapters or sections consist only of short snappy paragraphs of a few sentences whilst others consist only of much longer paragraphs and more winding arguments?

Clarity

- [ ] *Expertise*: I have developed a sound understanding of specialist terminology, and use it appropriately as needed.

- [ ] *Specialist terms*: I have explained any specialist terminology I used.

- [ ] *Jargon*: I have avoided or edited out unnecessary use of specialist jargon.

- [ ] *Lengthy sentences*: I have avoided or rewritten excessively long sentences and paragraphs.

- [ ] *A fresh eye*: I left at least a few hours between when I wrote a section and when I checked it. (This makes it more likely that you will read it from the perspective of a new reader, and will notice omitted words or poorly phrased material.)

- [ ] *Precision*: I have ordered words in the correct sequence to express precisely what I intend to say.

- [ ] *Double meanings*: I have checked whether anything I have written could be interpreted in ways I hadn't intended. If in doubt, I rephrased it.

Final draft: dissertation or report

Use the checklist before completing your final draft. Check off items once you are satisfied these are completed correctly and comprehensively. **Done** ☑

Meets set requirements

1. ☐ It meets the assignment brief.
2. ☐ It is true to the agreed proposal (if relevant).
3. ☐ It is within 5% of the required word limit.
4. ☐ It is on target to meet the submission date.

Communication, accuracy, precision

5. ☐ Overall, it is clear and easy to read.
6. ☐ It has been checked for coherence, consistency and clarity (page 201).
7. ☐ Its rationale comes across clearly.
8. ☐ The title is precisely worded and makes clear what the dissertation or report is about.
9. ☐ The abstract is comprehensive and succinct.
10. ☐ The thesis, position statement or hypotheses are precisely worded.
11. ☐ My main messages are easily apparent to the reader throughout the work.
12. ☐ A clear line of reasoning, or argument, runs through the work and gives it coherence.
13. ☐ Results/findings are presented accurately.
14. ☐ It states whether the results support the hypotheses and at what level of significance.
15. ☐ The literature review shows the breadth, depth and relevance of previous research.

16. ☐ The research method is accurately written, with full details written precisely and succinctly.
17. ☐ The report analyses, critically, my results, findings and methods in the light of previous research, theory and/or professional practice.
18. ☐ My conclusions are stated clearly.

Contents, structure and style

19. ☐ All required sections are included: pages 195–6.
20. ☐ All material included is relevant.
21. ☐ All material is presented in the appropriate section or chapter.
22. ☐ Material is well organised and sequenced.
23. ☐ The amount of material in each section/chapter is appropriate.
24. ☐ The overall work is balanced in the way that words have been allocated to different chapters, themes and arguments.

Proof-reading and presentation

25. ☐ It has been checked for style (page 199).
26. ☐ Every sentence, paragraph and section has been checked to see that each makes sense.
27. ☐ All chapters, sections, appendices, charts and tables are clearly headed and numbered.
28. ☐ Citations within the text are all included in the list of references.
29. ☐ References are provided in the required format and each checked carefully for accuracy.
30. ☐ It has been checked for spelling.
31. ☐ It has been checked for grammar.
32. ☐ It has been checked for punctuation.
33. ☐ It has been checked for 'typos'.
34. ☐ Appendices and diagrams are numbered consistently throughout.
35. ☐ Pages are numbered.
36. ☐ The list of contents is accurate, complete, and includes page numbers.
37. ☐ It is bound, if required.
38. ☐ Any necessary cover sheets and integrity statements, are completed and attached.

Chapter 25
Viva exams

What is a viva?

A viva or viva voce exam is the term used for an oral examination based upon your research.

At Masters and undergraduate levels

At these levels, universities vary in whether they require everyone to attend an oral examination or whether they select only certain individuals.

If this is on a selective basis, there are several reasons why any particular individual would be called for the viva. It is not likely that they will be told why they have been called for a viva. If you are selected, it is likely to be for one of the following reasons.

- *Your work is outstanding and/or amongst the best of the cohort*. They may wish to check, through close questioning, that you really did complete the work yourself and do know what you are talking about. They may wish to congratulate you on your work. It may be that the external examiners see the best students to help them to check your university's assessment processes.

- *Your work is on the border between grades*, such as between merit and distinction, or pass and fail. In such cases, good responses in the viva will enable you to gain the higher grade.

- *Lack of clarity*. Some aspects of your work may have been confused or unclear. In this case, you are being invited to talk it through.

Lily was determined to defend her thesis no matter what!

At doctoral level

For doctoral theses, there would normally be a viva examination.

For doctoral theses, the viva is regarded as an integral part of the overall assignment. You can expect this to last for around two hours or more. Be prepared to experience in-depth questioning on any aspect of your work, from a philosophical understanding of your work right through to apparently small details such as incorrect punctuation or capitalisation of particular words, or errors in your references.

Traditionally, this viva is referred to in terms of you 'defending' your thesis. The close questioning can feel very intense and formal. Examiners can appear to be unusually serious and even as if they are trying to trip you up. Don't assume that this form of questioning means that your work is weak, that you have failed – unless they tell you that explicitly – or that the examiners just do not like you.

Focus on what you know and on getting across what your research adds to the field. Avoid trying to second guess what the examiners are thinking or what a line of questioning might mean. Especially at this level, you are the expert so it is very likely that if you have managed each stage in an appropriate way, and have interpreted your results sensibly, you will manage to produce acceptable responses.

Preparing for a viva

Take it seriously

You may feel, if you have been working on your research for many months, or even years, that you should be able to answer questions about your work with ease. That is a good approach to take, and basically true, as long as you are not complacent and do prepare for it.

Know your own work

Do read through your work more than once before the viva. Think about what you have said.

- Where might you be challenged?
- What kinds of questions would you ask if you were the examiner?
- What are the weak aspects – how would you defend them?
- How have you made good use of previous research in the field?

What will I be asked?

It isn't possible to predict the questions you will be asked – nor is it always easy to tell, in the exam, why you have been asked a particular question.

> I must find out more to see if that could work for a project I am taking on.

> Oh no! They asked me about my method – I must have got it all wrong!

It might be, for example, that the examiners:

- find a point interesting and want to know more
- know someone undertaking related research, and are interested in potential similarities
- want to gain a better sense of whether your work has broader applicability
- consider a point you made is open to different interpretations and want to clarify your intention
- want to understand the difficulties you encountered and how you dealt with them
- cannot understand a point and are providing an opportunity for you to explain
- want to check that you recognise the relative importance of points you have made
- want to confirm that you did conduct all the research yourself
- are asking routine questions.

Typical questions that are asked, and for which you can prepare, are listed on pages 205–6.

Clarity of message

Jot down a list of potential questions and summary answers.

- For each, consider how you would express the answer so that it comes across clearly.
- Ask a friend or relative to test you on your answers. Do they find your answers clear? Do they understand what you are saying?
- Don't worry about stumbling, stuttering, restarting sentences or sounding anxious – your examiner will be used to that. Focus on clarity in your reasoning and in providing answers that are accurate and sensible.

Potential viva questions

Remembering the material

Consider whether you will recall your answers to potential questions best if written as short paragraphs, series of bullet points, a recording of yourself repeating the answers, or from strong visual images.

- Organise your material so that it plays to your memory preferences.
- For more about memory preferences, see Cottrell (2013).
- Jot down the answers you prepare to questions that you think the examiners might ask. Read over these several times.

Generic overview

Examiners generally start the viva examination with some more general points. Consider how you would answer such questions such as:

- What is your research about?
- Tell us what you were setting out to do?
- Why did you choose this subject?
- Why this topic?
- What inspired your research?
- Why did you define the topic in this way?

As you know so much about the subject, it can be easy to drift into too much detail, especially if you are distracted by nerves. It is good to sound enthusiastic about your research, but do also save some material for future questions.

Do

- Prepare a brief, well-planned mental overview to draw upon to answer opening questions.
- Be clear, in advance, of the main messages you want to convey. (How many points are there? What do you want to get across about each?)
- Be aware of the other questions that you are likely to be asked, and leave space for the examiners to ask you about those.
- Let your enthusiasm for, and interest in, your subject shine through.
- Provide hooks: if you think that there are particular aspects of your research that are especially interesting, allude to these. The examiners can then decide whether to pick up on these aspects further.

Avoid

- Overloading examiners with early detail.
- Telling the blow by blow history of how you approached the research, from child interest to the finished article.
- Being too succinct: let your expertise show.

Your understanding of the field

Your examiners will be looking to see that you have produced the work yourself. Some ways of checking this in the viva are as follows.

- Asking about material that you have mentioned in your literature review.
- Checking whether you recognise who are the experts in your field.
- Listening out for your comments about how you drew upon the ideas or methods of other researchers, such as published research or other doctoral theses.
- Noting whether you relate your way of working or your findings to that of experts in the field.
- Noting whether you are aware of how your work fits into the range of work already published in your field.
- Checking whether you understand the methodological approaches used in your field and have reasons for applying, or deviating from, these in your work.
- Asking specific questions about these.

Do

- Check back over your literature review.
- Browse key works and consider, again, their relevance to your work.
- Sum up, for yourself, how your work adds to the field.

Potential viva questions

Questions about methods and results

You may be asked to justify your methods or to provide further details about them. Be prepared for variations on the following questions.

- Why did you choose to collect your material in this way?
- You selected to use X methodology. Tell us why you chose that approach.
- How did you come up with your research design?
- How did you go about collecting your material?
- How did you decide on your sample?
- Why did you do X rather than Y?
- Did you consider doing X?
- Do you think your sample was really big enough/representative?
- Was it difficult working with the material in that way? How did you resolve those difficulties?
- Were you satisfied with the materials you were able to find/the number or type of participants that took part?

Interpretations and conclusions

Your interpretation of your material and the conclusions you draw are likely to be of particular interest to the examiners. Reread those sections of your work especially closely and be prepared to justify your conclusions and/or any recommendations that you made. Argue your case from what you found; be prepared for questions that might sound rather combative, as follows:

- You argue X, but do you feel that you have enough evidence to demonstrate that?
- I was very interested that you found X to be the case. The leading research in the field presents a rather different picture. Tell us why you think your results are so different?
- It wasn't quite clear to me how you arrived at that conclusion from your material/results? Can you take me through your thinking?
- You argue that X should be done, but could there be any risks?
- I liked that you argued XYZ. However, I did have a question about X.

Potential errors and omissions

The examiners would normally raise any mistakes and omissions. Be ready for the more obvious aspects.

- Read through your submitted work with a critical eye, looking for potential errors.
- Make a list of any aspects of your research that might have been worrying you even before you handed it in – or anything that struck you once you had submitted it.
- For each issue you identify, consider how you can justify why you did it and/or be clear about what you would do differently now.

Oh no! Why on earth did I write that!

Significance and direction

- What do you think were the most important things that you discovered?
- Do you think we know much more about X than we did before?
- You have paid a lot of attention to X. Why did you choose to focus on that aspect?
- There has been a lot of work undertaken on X recently. How does your work add to that debate?
- It wasn't quite clear how you arrived at that conclusion from your material/results?
- This is very interesting. Where do you think it could be taken next?

Managing the viva exam

Be organised

As for any other exam, prepare for the practicalities.

- Wear a functioning watch.
- Sort out in advance any everyday distractions.
- Ask friends, family and colleagues not to phone and distract you before the exam.
- Plan your time carefully so as to arrive at the venue early, allowing for transport problems.
- Once there, avoid other people. Stay focused.

What to take with you

Check the regulations for what you can take into the room: it may be different than for written exams.

- Take a copy of your work, in an identical format to the submitted copy. If the examiner asks you to look at a certain page or diagram, you must be able to turn straightaway to the same place.
- Take anything that helps you to manage the environment: water, layered clothing so you can adjust to the temperature, tissues, etc.

Starting the viva

Examiners vary in how skilled they are at putting students at ease; some are warm and welcoming and tell you exactly what to expect. Others are less adept or can be anxious themselves. Don't read anything into their body language or tone of voice.

- Be as natural as you can (even if it feels forced). Be polite and interested. Smile. Say hello.
- Give your name. Check you are in the right room.
- Listen to the examiners' names.
- Take your cue from the examiners. If they are formal, be formal. Aim to match their tone. If they take the lead, listen. If they want you to take the lead at times, be prepared to do so.

Defending against challenges

It is the examiners' role to challenge your ideas, check that the work is your own, draw attention to mistakes and omissions, and check how far you can take your answers. Don't take this personally or imagine the worst if they seem to challenge everything you have written.

- Don't let the content or tone of the challenges throw you off course. Return to what you did, what you found out, your interpretations, your own rationale. Ground your answers in your own expertise as far as possible.
- Argue your case with reason and examples.
- Draw attention to points made in your work: show that you are on top of your material.
- Don't assume that you must know the answers to every question or have read everything published, even if the questions suggest this.
- If the examiners propose a different approach or interpretation, consider that calmly. You may prefer it. However, don't assume that a feasible alternative means your way is necessarily wrong. Defend your position if it is tenable.
- If you find yourself waffling, stop. Look for a more concrete angle grounded in your work.
- If you realise you are repeating yourself, just say so and stop.
- Be prepared for the examiners to raise many points that might seem petty, such as typos.

Outcome of viva

- If the written work was strong and clearly your own, you are likely to pass even if your viva performance wasn't sparkling.
- The most likely outcome is that you pass, possibly with a distinction, subject to correcting all errors, grammar and punctuation.
- If the work and the viva are both weak, you might fail. Often, students are asked to rewrite some or all of the work for resubmission. This gives you a second chance to pass.

Preparing for a viva

Use the checklist before completing your final draft. Check off items once you are satisfied these are completed correctly. **Done** ☑

Advance preparation

1 ☐ Read through my work thoroughly.
2 ☐ Identify areas of potential challenge.
3 ☐ Consider responses to such challenges.

Prepare for the likely questions

4 ☐ Consider the list of potential questions on pages 205–6 so that these do not come as a surprise.
5 ☐ Make a list of additional questions that I would ask about my work if I were the examiner.
6 ☐ identify those questions that I feel are most likely.
7 ☐ Identify questions I would want least to be asked.
8 ☐ Jot down points that I would want to make if asked questions identified for (6) and (7).
9 ☐ Consider whose research I want to refer to, and how, during the viva.
10 ☐ Rehearse answers to the questions that I would feel least comfortable answering.

Clarity of message and recall

11 ☐ Prepare a general mental overview of my research to draw upon.
12 ☐ Jot down a brief summary of what my research adds to the field (in terms of method and/or theory, knowledge, interpretation, application, etc.).
13 ☐ Rehearse my summary so that it comes across clearly and precisely.
14 ☐ List the key messages I want to convey. Number these.
15 ☐ Ask a friend or relative to test me on my answers. Ask for feedback on clarity.

16 ☐ Practise the answers that I consider to be complicated. Identify the key points. List and number these so that they stand out clearly. Give each point a name or label, so it is easier to remember.
17 ☐ Organise my material so that I have a feel for which material to use for different kinds of question.
18 ☐ Organise my material so that it plays to my memory preferences.

Prepare the opening minutes

19 ☐ Learn the examiners' names, if available.
20 ☐ Google the examiners. Look for a photo so that I can put faces to their names.
21 ☐ From their publications, or the internet, what appear to be the examiners' interests?
22 ☐ Visit the exam location if possible, so I know the route and the environment.
23 ☐ Rehearse my calm entrance so I feel in control of the start of the viva.
24 ☐ Read through my work thoroughly.

Practicalities

25 ☐ Bring working watch (or equivalent).
26 ☐ Sort out any potential distractions.
27 ☐ Ask others to allow me to focus on the day.
28 ☐ Put together all my creature comforts, ready to take with me.
29 ☐ Prepare my journey carefully.
30 ☐ Take a copy of my work.

Final considerations

Once it is all over …

It is likely that your project has taken up a considerable amount of your time, thoughts and emotional energy for some time. Especially in the final stages, you have been very focused on completing and fine-tuning your report or dissertation to make it as good as it could possibly be. You may even have found yourself dreaming about it.

If so, you can expect that once it is all over, you may experience a sense of having a gap of some kind in your life. It may even seem as if your life has entered the doldrums and that things feel rather 'flat' or that you are bored. This won't last for ever but it can take students by surprise. If you have been looking forward to having your weekends back, it may feel disappointing if time now seems to lie heavily on your hands.

Prepare for the end of your dissertation by planning specific things to do. Don't assume you will only want to rest and sleep. Arrange to meet people you haven't seen for a while. Timetable activities that will require you to use up some of your spare energy. Line up some books to read or games that you haven't had time to enjoy – including some that will continue to stretch your mind.

Include activities that you would consider a reward for you and for others who have helped you whilst you were studying. Cook them a meal or plan a meal out as a treat.

Making the most of the experience

Before you began the assignment, you were encouraged to consider an audit of the skills and qualities that you were bringing to the project, and those that you were likely to need in order to complete it.

If you planned and organised your project as suggested in the previous chapters, you will have developed a number of skills that are transferable to other contexts. Many of these will be the kinds of skills that employers look for in graduates and for executive jobs – such as working closely to a brief, taking the initiative, resolving problems with your own solutions, taking full responsibility for the outcome, forward planning, and project management.

Take another look at pages 14–15. Give some thought to how far you have developed your skills over the course of the project. Whilst these are still fresh in your mind:

- jot down what you have learnt from the experience
- consider where else these skills and qualities could be applied – and how you might adapt them to new contexts
- consider how you would describe these skills and qualities to an employer both in a job application and at interview.

Would you want to do it again?

Consider, too, whether you enjoyed the experience. If so, there may be opportunities to undertake further research. This could be as a research student or in your current employment if you have a job. There are also many careers where research is an important component of the role. The careers service at your college or university can tell you about these.

Congratulations …

Your work is finished.

References

Allen, G. (2011). *Intertextuality (New Critical Idiom)*. London: Routledge.

Atkinson, P. (1995). 'Some perils of paradigms'. *Qualitative Health Research* **5**(10), 117–24.

Bell, J. (2005). *Doing your Research Project: A Guide for First-Time Researchers in Education, Health and Social Science*, 4th edn. Maidenhead: Open University Press.

Burgess, R. G. (1984). *In the Field: An Introduction to Field Research*. London: Routledge.

Cottrell, S. M. (2011). *Critical Thinking Skills: Developing Effective Analysis and Argument*, 2nd edn. Basingstoke: Palgrave Macmillan.

Cottrell, S. M. (2013). *The Study Skills Handbook*, 4th edn. Basingstoke: Palgrave Macmillan.

Cottrell, S. M. and Morris, N. (2012). *Study Skills Connected: Using Technology to Support Your Studies*. Basingstoke: Palgrave Macmillan.

Culler, J. (1981). *The Pursuit of Signs, Semiotics, Literature and Deconstruction*. London and Henley: Routledge & Kegan Paul.

Dawson, C. (2012). *Introduction to Research Methods: A Practical Guide for Anyone Undertaking a Research Project*, 4th edn. Oxford: How to Books.

Denscombe, M. (2007). *The Good Research Guide for Small-scale Social Research Projects*, 3rd edn. New York: McGraw Hill/Open University Press.

Gadamer, H. G. (1990). *Truth and Method*, 2nd rev. edn. New York: Crossroad.

Glaser, B. (ed.) (1995). *Grounded Theory, 1984–1994*. Mill Valley, CA: Sociology Press.

Glaser, B. and Strauss, A. (1967). *The Discovery of Grounded Theory*. Chicago, IL: Aldine.

Greer, G. (2006). *The Female Eunuch*. London: Harper Perennial. First published 1970.

Hammersley, M. and Atkinson, P. (1983). *Ethnography: Principles and Practice*. London: Tavistock.

Hart, E. and Bond, M. (1995). *Action Research for Health and Social Care – A Guide to Practice*. Buckingham: Open University Press.

Husserl, E. (1962). *Ideas: General Introduction to Pure Phenomenology*. New York: Collier.

Jakobson, R. (1980). *The Framework of Language*. Oxford: Oxon Publishing.

Kahneman, D. (2011). *Thinking, Fast and Slow*. London: Penguin.

Kristeva, J. (1980). *Desire in Language: A Semiotic Approach to Literature and Art*. New York: Columbia University Press.

Kuhn, P. (1970). *The Structure of Scientific Revolutions*, 2nd edn. Chicago, IL: University of Chicago Press.

Kvale, S. (ed.) (1992). *Psychology and Postmodernism*. London: SAGE.

Leitch, V. B. (1983). *Deconstructive Criticism: An Advanced Introduction*. New York: Columbia University Press.

Levin, P. (2005). *Excellent Dissertations*. Maidenhead: Open University Press.

Lévi-Strauss, C. (1964). *The Raw and the Cooked*. Paris: Plon.

Lewin, K. (1946). 'Action research and minority problems', *Journal of Social Issues* **2**(4), 34–46.

Lovitts, B. E. and Wert, E. L. (2008). *Developing Quality Dissertations in the Humanities: A Graduate Student's Guide to Achieving Exellence* [*sic*]. Sterling, VA: Stylus Publishing. Student edition.

Malinowski, B. (1922). *Argonauts of the Western Pacific*. London: Routledge & Kegan Paul.

Malinowski, B. (1935). *Coral Gardens and Their Magic: A Study of the Methods of Tilling the Soil and of Agricultural Rites in the Trobriand Islands.* London: Routledge.

Mead, M. (1928). *Coming of Age in Samoa: A Psychological Study of Primitive Youth for Western Civilisation.* New York: William Morrow.

Minsky, R. (1998). *Psychoanalysis and Culture: Contemporary States of Mind.* Cambridge: Polity Press.

Moi, T. J. (1985). *Sextual/Textual Politics: Feminist Literary Theory.* London: Methuen.

National Research Ethics Society (NRES) at: www.nres.npsa.nhs.uk.

O'Dochartaigh, N. (2012). *Internet Research Skills,* 3rd edn. London: SAGE.

Orna, E. and Stevens, G. (1995). *Managing Information for Research.* Buckingham: Open University Press.

Pears, R. and Shields, G. (2013). *Cite Them Right: The Essential Referencing Guide,* 9th edn. Basingstoke: Palgrave Macmillan.

Pring, R. (2000). *Philosophy of Educational Research.* London: Continuum.

Saussure, F. de (1998). *Course in General Linguistics,* translated and annotated by R. Harris. Chicago: Open Court.

Spradley, J. P. (1980). *Participant Observation.* New York: Holt, Rinehart & Winston.

Strauss, A. and Corbin, J. (1990). *Basics of Qualitative Research: Grounded Theory. Procedures and Techniques.* Thousand Oaks, CA: SAGE.

Strunk, W. Jr and White, E. B. (2008). *The Elements of Style,* 50th Anniversary edn. Needham Heights, MA: Pearson Education.

Swetnam, D. and Swetnam, R. (2010). *Writing your Dissertation,* 3rd edn. Oxford: How to Books.

Thomas, G. (2009). *How to Do Your Research Project.* London: SAGE.

Thorne, R. (2013). 'Smart Ideas for Effective Studying', *The Independent,* 17 January 2013, pages 2–3.

Walters, M. (2005). *Feminism: A Very Short Introduction.* New York: Oxford University Press.

Woods, P. (2006). *Successful Writing for Qualitative Researchers,* 2nd edn. London: Routledge.

Index

abstract 35, 180, 186, 193
academic discipline, knowing your ...
  23, 26
academic integrity 20, 28, 39, 40, 41,
  90, 95, 107, 109, 112, 170
academic skills 6, 15, 16, 23
action research 102
ambassadorial role 130
analysis 148, 149, 150, 166, 167,
  168, 170, 171
anthropology 104
anxieties 1, 2, 47; see confidence
appendices 35, 90, 193
argument 35, 175, 201
articles see journal articles
arts, research in arts and humanities
  101, 103, 105, 123–4, 141, 171,
  185, 199
  see constructivism; critical theory;
    historical method;
    phenomenology
assessment criteria 39, 63, 64, 65
assignment brief 26, 27, 31, 34, 39,
  63–6, 113, 115, 186, 202
attributing sources see referencing
audit of skills 16, 17–18

basics 9, 10, 13
benefits of your research 45
bibliography 190, 193
boredom, managing 45, 46, 49, 182;
  see challenges; inspiration;
  motivation; peer support
boundaries 131, 159
brief see assignment brief
Bristol online survey 155

case studies 163–8
catastrophic thinking 55
categorising 172, 174
causation 100, 101, 137, 138
challenge, level of 39, 40, 41, 46, 68
challenges 1, 3, 4, 23, 24
  setting yourself challenges 55
checklists 14, 15, 17–18, 23, 29, 30,
  36, 37, 38, 39–41, 45, 46, 47,
  48, 49, 50, 51, 53, 54, 55, 56,
  58, 59, 60, 64, 65, 66, 76, 82–3,
  85, 88, 92, 93, 96, 106, 112,
  115, 116, 118, 124, 128, 132,
  136, 142, 143, 147, 150, 152,
  153, 154, 156, 160, 161, 162,
  168, 176, 184, 195–6, 199, 201,
  202, 208

using checklists 5, 33, 113
children see participants
citations see referencing
commissioned research 163, 164,
  166, 168, 190, 191, 193
complaints process 111
conclusion, writing the 35, 56, 189,
  192, 201
conducting research 119–76
confidence 47
confidentiality 108, 112, 132, 133,
  136, 165
conflicts of interest 109, 112
consents 108, 134–5; 136, 141; see
  also permissions
constructivism 99, 105
contextualising findings 166, 167,
  174, 175, 176
controlled conditions 94, 95, 96, 98,
  100, 139–40
  use of controls 95, 139, 140
  see empiricism; experiments;
    variables
controversial issues 46
course requirements 52
criminal records checks 37, 38
criteria see assessment criteria
critical theory 105
criticality 117
  critique of methods 96
  see journal articles
CV 45

data and datum 122
  data collection 65, 119–76
  data presentation 173
  rich data 103, 143, 157, 163
  permission to use 136; see
    permissions
deadlines, managing deadlines 39,
  40, 56, 65, 181
declaration of interests 109
Deferral and Barring Service (DBS
  checks) 37, 38, 134
defining terms 98, 105, 145
determinism 100
diary, and planning 52
discipline see academic discipline,
  knowing your
discourse analysis 105
discussion 189, 192
dissertations 191, 202
  analysing dissertations 29
  what is a dissertation? 21

structure 185
double-blind experiments 140
drafts 35, 41, 56, 166, 197

ecological validity 94, 104, 137
editing 35, 197, 198
elaborating the task 32, 34–5
empiricism 100, 101, 137
employability 23
employer projects 69, 91, 135, 165;
  see work-based projects
environmental protection 111, 112;
  see ethical considerations; work-
  based projects
essays (long essays) 1, 6, 21, 185,
  199
ethical considerations 66, 96, 97,
  107–12, 129, 131, 143, 144,
  150; see consents; permissions;
  participants, working with
Ethics Committee 107
ethics and online research 141
ethics panel 87, 90
ethnography 104, 144
evidence
  the evidence base 20, 26, 85–6,
    121–8
  poor use of evidence 27
  see sources
experiments 95, 137–42; see
  empiricism

Facebook surveys 155
feasibility 68, 145; see also
  parameters, setting; risk
  assessment and risk anagement
feminism 105
field-based 141
finance 37, 38, 68
finishing 56, 197–202
flexibility 33

generalisations 99, 101, 102, 137,
  143, 157, 158
Google tools 141
grounded theory 103

historical method 101
humanities see arts, research in arts
  and humanities
hypothesis 66, 170, 187
  what is a ...? 116
  formulating a hypothesis 116, 142
  testing a hypothesis 100, 170, 176

using the hypothesis 86

ideology 98, 105
immersion 99, 104
inclusion 110
independent study 2, 3, 7, 21, 23, 24, 41, 43, 44
individuality 98
inspiration 47, 48, 49, 55, 69, 70, 169
developing an idea 72
integrity *see* academic integrity
intellectual curiosity 46, 47
intellectual property 109, 112; *see* academic integrity
interpreting your findings 119, 147, 148, 149, 150, 157, 168–76, 196
interpretivism 99
intertextuality 99, 105
interviews 157–62
introduction 167, 187, 191
isolation 8, 41, 43, 49, 50

journal articles 79, 80, 82, 90
analysing articles 96

knowledge
contributing to 21, 69, 73–4, 86, 175, 192
knowing your field 82-3, 174–6, 205
the nature of 98, 99
see significance

laboratory-based 141, 143, 144
life history approach 104
literature review 77–8, 187
as a staged process 77–8
principles to inform the review 84
purpose 77,187
writing up 78, 87, 167, 191
literature search 34, 77–8, 79–84
log, project log 6, 95
lng assignments 1, 6, 199

management *see* project management; self-management; time management
marking criteria *see* assessment criteria
Masters level 203
materials 188, 190; *see* participants
methodology 66, 91, 96, 97–106, 153, 165, 188
analysis of methodology 96
methodological issues 90
methods 66, 83, 96, 121, 137–68, 188, 191; *see* data and datum, data collection; evidence, the evidence base; raw data
mindset, developing the right mindset 45, 55; *see* catastrophic thinking; motivation; inspiration; challenges

motivation 3, 24, 41, 43, 44, 45, 46, 48, 50, 55, 68
to write up 179, 180

narrative 101, 168
note-making 55, 79, 80, 142, 146–8, 170

objectivity 20, 92, 98, 101, 147; *see* empiricism; experiments
observations 143–50, 166
online *see* web-based research
opportunities 1
organisational skills 5; *see also* track, keeping track; 'To do' lists; checklists
organising your material 84, 86, 88, 171–3, 178, 183
originality 22, 25, 47, 68, 69, 70
overview, maintaining an overview 5, 32
of process 10, 11, 12,
for experiments 142
of the task 53

pacing 24, 182
paradigm *see* research
parameters, setting 75, 76, 143, 165, 168
participants 95
communicating with 131, 132, 133, 136, 152–3, 155, 156
selecting 143, 157, 162, 190
working with 110–11, 120, 129–36, 153, 157–61
children and vulnerable people 111, 112, 131, 134, 136
ethics 108, 110
materials for 132, 133, 152, 152–5
vulnerable groups 107, 111, 112, 131, 134, 136
see boundaries; consents; controlled conditions; ethical considerations; inclusion; interviews; observations; work-based projects
passing references *see* references
peer support 34, 41
learning from others 5, 49, 55
social networks 49
people skills 15, 16
permissions 37, 124, 134–5; *see also* consents
phenomenology 103, 163, 164
pilot 114, 117, 118, 120, 121, 138, 142, 143, 155
planning 7, 11, 12, 33, 40
for what might go wrong 47
podcasts 46
position, research 20, 46, 115
positivism 98
post-modernism 105
precision 90, 95, 98, 115, 138, 152, 191, 200, 202; *see* defining terms; experimentspreparation 7, 11, 12

presentation, of written assignment 66, 199
primary sources 101, 123
principles, of good research 89–96
probability 126
process 32, 34–5, 142, 145, 147, 150, 162
procrastination 55–6
project log 6, 29
project management 4, 31–42
projects, choosing *see* topic, choosing the right topic
proofreading 35
proposal 11, 12, 34, 40
developing your proposal 61–2
writing up your proposal 113–18
psychoanalytic 105

qualitative 93, 144, 151, 169; *see* data and datum, rich data
quantitative methods 93, 98, 151, 169; *see* experiments
questionnaires *see* surveys

raw data 96, 101, 121
reading, breadth of 26, 77, 78, 79, 80, 115, 164
keeping reading manageable 80
using your reading 172, 181
recommendations, making 167, 168, 190, 192
record keeping 95, 142, 143, 145–8, 154, 155, 161; *see* precision
reference tools 28, 79
referencing 66, 79, 109, 181, 184, 190
keeping records for 79, 95
making passing references 84, 198
reflection 3, 5
reliability 94, 152
replication 69, 94, 151, 191; *see* scientific approach
reports 183, 185, 202
research *see* methods; methodology; position, research; proposal)
basics 4–5, 9, 10, 13
design 90, 91, 92, 137, 164–6, 170
flawed design 170
gathering information 119–76
good research 20, 25, 26, 89–96
models of research 29
paradigms 97, 98–9
projects 19, 22
purpose 23, 70, 85, 164, 186
what is it? 20
researcher
behaviours 140, 144, 148, 149, 150, 153, 156, 157, 159, 160
ethical behaviours as 107, 109, 110
impact 99, 102, 103, 151
presenting yourself as a researcher 130, 136, 153, 156, 158, 159
the role of 97, 102, 103
see declaration of interests; ethical considerations; methodology

resource management 37, 39
results 35, 189, 191; *see* interpreting your findings
risk assessment and risk management 39–42, 111, 131
routine, developing a routine 54, 180

safeguarding 111
safety 111, 112, 131, 133
samples, selecting 125–8, 145
Sample Size Calculator 122
scale 4, 22, 122
scheduling 10, 36, 53, 54, 59
schools of thought 82
scientific approach 98; *see* controlled conditions; empiricism; experiments; generalisations; objectivity; precision; replication; validity; variables
security 111
selecting materials 80, 81, 82–3, 84, 85, 86, 87, 88, 91, 165, 173, 176, 178
    see samples, selecting
self-management 3, 5, 8, 10, 15, 41, 44
    developing the right mindset 45, 198
semiotics 105
significance *see* knowledge, contributing to
    'so what?' 13, 20, 35, 147, 163, 169, 175, 189, 192, 206
    statistical 126, 142, 145
skills
    academic 6, 14–16
    for research-based assignments 17–18, 23
    in writing 177
Skype 161
social life 49, 55
sources 96, 165; *see* primary sources
    secondary sources 123
    specialist sources 81, 82, 84
    using source materials 172–6, 181
stages, working in stages 10
starting, getting started on the project 9, 51, 53, 70
    settling down to study 53
    sticking with it 55
structuralism 105
structure 27, 29, 66

students' experiences 1, 8, 13, 24, 44, 62, 74, 120, 178, 194
study/life balance 55
subjectivity 92, 99, 101, 103, 143, 157
submitting your work 35
    submitting the proposal 63, 64, 113, 118
summaries 193, 198
supervisor 8, 57–60
    supervision checklist 60
    expectations 58
    making use of 39, 40, 41, 59, 109, 178
    what supervisors look for 25
    working relationship with 57
support 49, 50
    asking for help 28, 59
    in the workplace 50
Survey Monkey 155
surveys 151–6
synthesis 26, 86, 174, 176

task management skills 15, 16; *see* project management; time mangement
terminology 6, 9, 200; *see* defining terms; precision
theory
    testing theory 98, 143
    theoretical perspectives 97
    drawing on theory 90, 105, 147, 163, 175
    see literature review
theses, doctoral 126, 185, 203
thesis statements 114, 115
thinking, clear thinking 8, 169, 178; *see* defining terms; precision
time management 50, 51–6, 180
    allocating time to tasks 52
    and pacing your work 24, 45, 51, 54
    see scheduling; routine, developing a routine
title 34, 65, 75–6
'To do' lists 6, 33
topic 65
    good topics 68
    choosing the right topic 26, 27, 34, 35, 46, 67–74, 76, 145, 164–5
    evaluating topic options 71, 73, 76

choosing in the context of your field 82–3
    see inspiration
track, keeping track 3, 5
triangulation 101, 166

validity 94, 152
    see ecological validity
variables 94, 95, 98, 100, 139, 141, 143; *see* controlled conditions; experiments
    dependent and independent variables 139–40
verification 95
viva exams 66, 203–8

web-based research 141, 155, 160, 161
word limit 13, 24, 63, 65, 178, 198
work-based projects 102, 144, 163, 164, 166, 168; *see* employer projects
workplace and study 50, 102, 135
writing *see* abstract; conclusion, writing the; drafts; introduction; literature review; proposal; structure
writing strategy 179, 180–4
    accuracy 200; *see* defining terms; precision; writing style, use of language
    writing up your research 56, 87, 166, 177–216
    writing up sections and chapters 185–96
    fine-tuning 182, 197–202
    getting started 11, 12, 72, 181, 182
    from models and examples 184
    the process of writing 177
    structure and organisation 167, 183, 184, 185–95, 202
    synopses 181
    for your supervisor 181
    thinking through writing 72, 170
writing style, 197, 199, 201, 202
    use of language 26, 27, 66, 87, 88, 96, 117, 167, 200–1

Notes

Notes

Notes

Notes